Prai
BARGAINING W

"Analyzes some of history's most tumultuous conflicts while offering invaluable guidance on everything from business disputes to messy divorces . . . Focusing on unfair, even evil, actions—such as blackmail, labor disputes, extortion, theft—and the adversaries behind them, Mnookin dissects the trappings that interfere with rational thinking and reveals pragmatic approaches to elicit resolution and results."

—*The Harvard Gazette*

"Bob Mnookin has produced a seminal book that is remarkably timely and should help inform our U.S. government officials as they address international conflicts from Iran to North Korea. I only wish the book had been written when I was heading a variety of international negotiations during the Clinton Administration."

—Ambassador Stuart E. Eizenstat, author of *Imperfect Justice*

"Are you angry at the evil done to you in your personal life, in your business dealings, or in your nation's affairs? Mnookin's masterly analysis of real cases can help you decide whether to fight the devil, negotiate with the devil, or question whether the other side really *is* the devil."

—Professor Robert Axelrod, author of *The Evolution of Cooperation*

"*Bargaining with the Devil* should be required reading for anyone who faces a profound conflict—whether as a manager, lawyer, or concerned citizen. Through riveting tales recounted with crisp elegance, Mnookin shows how to approach life's most difficult disputes with dignity and purpose."

—Ben W. Heineman, Jr., senior fellow, Harvard University schools of law and government

"Business executives and managers, no less than diplomats, often face adversaries they don't like or trust. Through wonderful stories, Mnookin shows that sometimes we should resist, but that we should negotiate far more often than our intuitive or emotional self would suggest. *Bargaining with the Devil* explains how to approach life's difficult conflicts and make wise decisions."

—Max H. Bazerman, Straus Professor of Business Administration, Harvard Business School, coauthor of *Negotiation Genius*

"This important new book fills a void and should be required reading whether you are a professional negotiator, a public official, or a private citizen."

—Ken Feinberg, mediator and special master; author of *What Is Life Worth?*

ALSO BY ROBERT MNOOKIN

Beyond Winning: Negotiating to Create Value in Deals and Disputes (with Scott Peppet and Andrew Tulumello)

Negotiating on Behalf of Others (co-edited with Lawrence Susskind)

Barriers to Conflict Resolution (co-edited with Kenneth J. Arrow, Lee Ross, Amos Tversky, and Robert Wilson)

Dividing the Child: Social and Legal Dilemmas of Custody (with Eleanor Maccoby)

BARGAINING WITH THE DEVIL

When to NEGOTIATE, When to FIGHT

ROBERT MNOOKIN

SIMON & SCHUSTER PAPERBACKS

NEW YORK LONDON TORONTO SYDNEY

Simon & Schuster Paperbacks
A Division of Simon & Schuster, Inc.
1230 Avenue of the Americas
New York, NY 10020

First Simon & Schuster trade paperback edition April 2011

SIMON & SCHUSTER PAPERBACKS and colophon are registered
trademarks of Simon & Schuster, Inc.

For information about special discounts for bulk purchases,
please contact Simon & Schuster Special Sales at
1-866-506-1949 or business@simonandschuster.com.

The Simon & Schuster Speakers Bureau can bring authors
to your live event. For more information or to book an event,
contact the Simon & Schuster Speakers Bureau at
1-866-248-3049 or visit our website at www.simonspeakers.com.

Design by Level C

Manufactured in the United States of America

10   9   8   7   6   5

The Library of Congress has cataloged the hardcover edition as follows:

Mnookin, Robert
    Bargaining with the devil : when to negotiate, when to fight / Robert Mnookin.
        p.   cm.
    1. Negotiation.   2. Conflict management.   3. Negotiation in business.
I. Title.
    BF637.N4M58   2010
    302.3—dc22   2009048661
ISBN 978-1-4165-8332-5
ISBN 978-1-4165-8333-2 (pbk)
ISBN 978-1-4165-8364-6 (ebook)

For my four little devils—Eli, Hailey, Isaac, and Sophia

Contents

BARGAINING
WITH
THE DEVIL

Introduction

Should you bargain with the Devil?

In an age of terror, our national leaders face this sort of question every day. Should we negotiate with the Taliban? Iran? North Korea? What about terrorist groups holding hostages?

In private disputes, you may face devils of your own. A business partner has betrayed you and now wants to negotiate a better deal. A marriage is ending and a divorcing spouse is making extortionist demands. A competitor has stolen your intellectual property. You are furious. Your gut tells you to fight it out in court. To negotiate with this person would give him something he *wants*. It would reward him for his bad behavior. You want your rights vindicated, and the thought of negotiating with your adversary seems wrong.

This book is about these kinds of conflicts, which pose some of the most challenging questions in negotiation. A disputant must decide: Should I bargain with the Devil, or resist? By "bargain" I mean attempt to make a deal—try to resolve the conflict through negotiation—rather than fighting it out. By "Devil," I mean an enemy who has intentionally harmed you in the past or appears willing to harm you in the future. Someone you don't trust. An adversary whose behavior you may even see as evil.

These days it is not fashionable to talk about evil, particularly among professionals concerned with dispute resolution. It smacks of smug moralism and religious fundamentalism. It has religious overtones connected with notions of sin. Moreover, many dispute resolution professionals would argue that it has no stable definition or inherent meaning. Many believe that the concept is entirely subjective: an individual who is involved in a conflict will often perceive the adversary as evil, but it is *only* a perception; a detached observer might disagree. Others would add that the notion of what is evil can vary greatly depending on time and place. This is not simply an academic debate about definitions. In my field, an air of taboo hangs around the word *evil*. It is considered a slippery and explosive term, much overused, loosely deployed, and too often exploited by religious and political leaders to malign their enemies and lead their followers into battle.

While I agree that these dangers exist and demonization can get in the way of clear thinking, I do not believe that the concept of evil is incoherent or meaningless. In my view, intentionally inflicting grievous harm on human beings without a compelling justification is evil. The Nazis' persecution of the Jews, the Hutus' slaughter of the Tutsi, and the Taliban's penchant for throwing acid in the face of girls who dare to go to school—all of these are evil acts. So were the attacks of September 11, 2001, when suicidal terrorists intentionally and without justification killed nearly three thousand innocent civilians.

My question, and this book, have their roots in September 11. In the fall of 2001, less than a month after the attacks, Harvard Law School's Program on Negotiation sponsored a public debate at Harvard on whether President Bush should be prepared to negotiate with the Taliban. This debate led me to begin thinking about a more general question: In any particular conflict, how should you decide whether or not it makes sense to negotiate?

At the time of our debate, events were moving quickly. Bush had just issued an ultimatum to the Taliban government in Afghanistan: Shut down al-Qaeda's training camps and turn over Osama bin Laden and his lieutenants, or we will invade.

The Taliban, surprisingly, had responded by inviting President Bush to negotiate. In addressing a council of clerics on September 19, the Taliban leader Mullah Mohammed Omar said, "If the American government has some problems with the Islamic Emirate of Afghanistan, *they should be solved through negotiations*" (emphasis added).[1]

My colleague Roger Fisher and I were invited to discuss how Bush should respond to this offer. Roger Fisher is probably the best-known negotiation guru in the world. He is the leading proponent of what is called interest-based or "win-win" negotiation. His seminal book, *Getting to Yes*, has sold over three million copies. I am his successor as chair of Harvard's Program on Negotiation.

Roger and I share common views on many important issues. But not in this case.

Roger took the position—as I knew he would—that President Bush was wrong to issue an ultimatum and that the United States should accept the Taliban's invitation to negotiate. His argument was consistent with his view, expressed in many of his books, that one should always try to resolve conflict through a problem-solving approach to negotiation based on the interests of the parties.

Essentially, Roger supports the categorical notion—prevalent in the field of dispute resolution—that you should *always* be willing to negotiate.

The core argument behind this notion is straightforward and appealing. Before you resort to coercive measures—such as warfare or litigation—you should try to resolve the problem. To negotiate doesn't mean you must give up all that is important to you. It only requires that you be willing to sit down with your adversary and see whether you can make a deal that serves your interests better than your best alternative does. People and regimes are capable of change. You can't hope to make peace with your enemies unless you are willing to negotiate.

You've also heard the categorical answer on the other side. The Faustian parable suggests you must *never* negotiate with the Devil. He's clever and unscrupulous. He will tempt you by promising something that you desperately want. But no matter how seductive the possible benefits, negotiating with evil is simply wrong; it would violate your integrity and pollute your soul.

I must confess a natural aversion to categorical claims of "always" or "never." There are usually examples that can puncture such arguments. In my debate with Roger, I explained that my two greatest political heroes of the twentieth century are Winston Churchill and Nelson Mandela. Each had to decide whether to negotiate with an oppressive and evil enemy. In May 1940, Churchill refused to negotiate with Adolf Hitler, even though Nazi forces had overrun Europe and were about to attack a weakened Britain. In 1985, on the other hand, Nelson Mandela chose to *initiate* negotiations with a white government that had erected and enforced a racist regime.

If there is no easy, categorical answer—if sometimes you should bargain with the Devil and other times you should refuse—how in particular circumstances should you decide? How should you think about the problem? What are the considerations? The challenge is making wise decisions. This book addresses that challenge.

We will explore eight real, concrete cases in which a disputant had to decide whether to negotiate or resist. These are hard cases that cover a broad range of situations. Some are international conflicts involving evil regimes. Others involve business and family conflicts.

In all of them, the stakes are high and at least one party is enraged by the other side's behavior. Demonization is rampant. Primal emotions, such as the desire for revenge, may be hard to distinguish from moral impulses: a deep aversion to the idea of "legitimating" the enemy or rewarding bad behavior; a strong desire for vindication and justice. How do you make a wise decision in the face of such strong feelings?

We won't look at these decisions in hindsight and ask, Did it turn out well? That would be too easy, and unfair to the protagonists of these stories. We will go back in time, follow the action as it unfolds, and evaluate the decision based on what the decision-maker knew at the time.

The stories of Churchill and Mandela have each become an archetype, a stock narrative that people tend to use as a convenient rationale for a decision they have already made. When they don't want to negotiate, they tell the story of Churchill and the failure of appeasement. When they want to negotiate, they tell the Mandela story.

With the benefit of hindsight, both of these decisions look obviously right. But what if you go back to the time when the decisions were made? Do they still seem wise?

These were much harder decisions than they might at first appear, and I devote a chapter to each. In Churchill's case, the war was going so badly that the American ambassador thought Britain would soon be overrun. Although Churchill always proudly maintained that his government never even considered negotiating with "that man," the truth is very different. He and his War Cabinet ministers secretly debated— for three days—whether to pursue peace negotiations with Hitler. Powerful arguments were made in favor of negotiation. Mandela, too, made an enormously difficult and risky decision. In order to initiate negotiations with the apartheid regime, he had to figure out a way to keep the talks secret from his own colleagues.

We also explore the stories of two individuals caught in evil regimes.

Both faced decisions in which lives were at stake. One refused to negotiate with the KGB and lived to be celebrated. The other chose to negotiate with the Nazi Adolf Eichmann and saved hundreds of lives—only to be later condemned as a Nazi collaborator. Each in his own way was heroic.

The four business and family cases are all based on real disputes that I observed firsthand. They involve two giant computer companies fighting over software rights, a symphony orchestra torn by labor conflict, a bitterly divorcing couple, and three siblings in combat over an inherited vacation home.

There are, of course, some big differences among these cases. The most important distinction has to do with what I mean by "evil." I don't believe in the Devil in a religious sense, but I do believe that Hitler and Eichmann were evil, as were the KGB and the apartheid regime. By contrast, none of the antagonists in our private disputes was evil, in my view, although they were demonized and in some cases *perceived* as evil by their adversaries.

Another distinction relates to what was at stake. The chapters concerning international devils involve matters of life and death. The business and family cases, by contrast, involve money and relationships—very significant relationships that had completely broken down. The alternatives to negotiation are different as well. In business and family disputes, there is typically an enforceable legal remedy: the disputants can go to court if necessary. This was not true in our international cases.

Given these differences, why consider these cases together? First, because this is a "how to think" book designed to show you how to "think outside the box." In my many years of teaching I've learned that it's often easiest to get students to embrace a new set of ideas by thinking about them in an unfamiliar context, and then applying them to contexts they are more familiar with. Second, because all eight cases involve demonization and its by-product: distorted thinking. Through these stories, I will examine *how* people in intense conflict decide whether to negotiate. What role do emotions play? What is the relationship between analysis and intuition? Are there common traps that interfere with wise decision-making? And is there an approach that can improve the likelihood of making wise decisions?

I think there is. In this book I will offer a framework—a disciplined way of thinking—that you can apply to any situation. As part of that framework, I will delineate two opposing sets of traps that can stand in the way of a wise decision. The "negative" traps, particularly demonization, stoke our anger and tempt us to refuse to negotiate when we probably should. The "positive" traps, although far less common in disputes like these, may tempt us to negotiate when perhaps we shouldn't. My framework will help you avoid both sets of traps.

We are going to face some moral quandaries as well. What if, emotions aside, your own moral compass suggests that doing business with this Devil is simply wrong, even though it might provide some pragmatic benefits? Suppose you could foresee a deal that would serve your own interests but would harm others?[2]

In each chapter, you will see a protagonist struggling with the decision of whether to bargain or resist, and the influence of the traps. You will see how they made their decision and why. I will tell you whether I think they made a wise decision. I will also give you enough information to draw your own conclusion. You may not agree with me, but you will know where I stand.

Now let me return to the Taliban in 2001 and my debate with Roger Fisher.

We all know what happened soon thereafter. President Bush refused to negotiate. The Taliban refused to turn over bin Laden, citing Islamic law, and did not agree to shut down the training camps. After receiving both congressional and U.N. authorization, Bush launched war in Afghanistan and toppled the Taliban government.

But on the facts known *at the time,* was President Bush's decision wise?[3] In the debate, I contended that it was.

My argument went as follows:

What were the interests at stake? For the United States, our most important interest was to protect American lives and deter future terrorist attacks. The Taliban's primary interest was to stay in power and maintain the rule of Islamic law.

What were the alternatives to negotiation? For the United States, the best alternative was to use military force. Although the outcome of a war is always uncertain, it appeared we had the capacity to topple the Taliban regime, shut down the training camps, and perhaps capture many of the culprits. The Taliban's alternative was much worse. If the United States attacked, they would probably lose control of the government; their best alternative would be to go into hiding and wage guerrilla warfare.

Were there likely potential negotiated outcomes that would meet the interests of both parties? Was there a reasonable prospect that such an agreement would be carried out? Slim to none. The Clinton administration had made similar demands with respect to bin Laden, al-Qaeda, and the training camps, and the Taliban had been entirely unresponsive. They had done nothing. The Taliban didn't seem to have the capacity, let alone the will, to shut down the camps or turn over bin Laden. In fact, some observers believed that bin Laden had more power and influence over the Taliban regime, partly due to family ties, than they had over him.

What were the costs to the United States of choosing to negotiate? Substantial. The Taliban regime was not an innocent bystander. It had harbored bin Laden and thousands of Islamic terrorists from around the world. The Clinton administration had clearly warned the Taliban, more than a year earlier, that it would hold them responsible for any terrorist attacks by bin Laden.[4] To negotiate now would severely undermine our credibility, not simply with terrorist groups around the world but with the Taliban and other governments that harbored terrorists. In this sense, negotiation would have established a dangerous precedent. It would have also undermined President Bush's ability to assemble and lead an international coalition to fight terrorism.[5]

Finally, was our alternative—use of military force—legitimate and morally justifiable? In my view, yes. Bin Laden had publicly declared war on the United States several years earlier,[6] and the September 11 attacks were undeniably acts of war. Under domestic and international law, American use of force was permissible.

On the basis of this cost-benefit analysis, I concluded that Bush would be wise *not* to negotiate with the Taliban.

Like most Americans, I saw the September 11 attacks as evil: grievous harm had been intentionally inflicted on innocent victims without adequate justification. I thought the guilty parties should be punished and that further attacks should be deterred. Fortunately for me, my pragmatic analysis led to the same conclusion that my moral intuition did. Both said, "No negotiation," albeit for different reasons. So my decision about the Taliban was a relatively easy one. The fact that the Taliban regime had condoned an evil act was relevant to me, but not dispositive.

The harder case is when pragmatic and moral demands conflict. What if your analysis says, "Negotiate," and your principles suggest it would be wrong? What do you do? How should you go about thinking it through?

Consider, for example, a business dispute based on real events that could happen to any one of us.[7]

You are the founder of a small, privately owned research and development company in Silicon Valley. You recently learned that your joint venture partner, the giant Bikuta Corporation of Japan, has secretly developed a competing product which it is now selling under its own name in the Chinese market. This "new" product is essentially a knock-off of the design you licensed to Bikuta (along with essential know-how) two years ago. There is no doubt in your mind that Bikuta has violated your contract, which provides that Bikuta will manufacture and distribute *only* your product "worldwide" for five years—and pay you a license fee of 15 percent of sales.

When you confront Bikuta's president, he is unremorseful. He says your original design does not "fit" the Chinese market and that Bikuta owes you nothing for Chinese sales. He also wants to renegotiate your 15 percent royalty rate, which he suddenly claims is too high.

You feel stunned and betrayed. Bikuta thinks nothing of stealing your know-how, ignoring its contractual obligations, and trying to bully you into accepting less than you are due. You are also angry with yourself for being so trusting.

Any businessperson can identify with this case. The gut says "Do battle!" and "It would be unworthy to negotiate." But what's the wise thing to do—financially, morally, rationally? In the face of a bully, do you fight or negotiate?

The tension between conflicting moral and pragmatic demands is central to each one of the real-life dilemmas I present in this book. By the time you finish reading it, I hope my framework will give you a new and useful way to think not only about Bikuta, but about all those situations in which you will have to decide whether to bargain with the Devil.

PART I

Understanding the Challenge

ONE

Avoiding Common Traps

The news about Bikuta is alarming. You have sacrificed the last five years of your life as CEO of ResearchCo., the start-up that you founded. The company is now profitable, but just barely. And you are in a terrible bind. You have licensed your design and know-how for the "FreeFlow," an implantable arterial stent, to the Bikuta Corporation of Japan. The deal gives that company exclusive rights to manufacture and sell the FreeFlow everywhere in Asia—except China. In exchange, Bikuta was to pay you a license fee of 15 percent of sales. Now you've discovered that your so-called partner has essentially cloned your product, renamed it the "EasyFlow" (hardly even changing the name, you note with disgust), and started selling it in China. When you challenged Mr. Bikuta—the founder and CEO—he denied using your intellectual property in making the EasyFlow. You don't believe it for a moment, and you're worried about the future of your company. Bikuta Corporation is your most important joint venture partner. What should you do?

You call the Kramers, your sister and brother-in-law. Evelyn and Fred have a stake: they were the first investors in ResearchCo. and the sixty thousand dollars they put in, combined with your own savings, launched the company and kept it going while you developed a business plan and secured the first rounds of venture financing. Without their help, you'd still be an engineer at Johnson & Johnson. You trust them; they are energetic, loyal, and blunt. And they are a study in contrasts.

Your older sister Evelyn is warm, optimistic, and savvy about people. After college, she volunteered for the Peace Corps in Guatemala, later earned a Ph.D. in Spanish literature, and now chairs the Spanish department at San Jose State. She is comfortable in her own skin, and a calming presence. She practices yoga and meditates every day. Women find her looks attractive but nonthreatening, and men find her appealing. People are naturally drawn to Evelyn—perhaps because she tends to see the best in them.

Most people are drawn to Fred, too, but for different reasons. Adventurous and enthusiastic, Fred is a take-charge kind of guy who enjoys being a partisan and relishes competition. A former Marine, he charged through business school and rose through the ranks at Oracle, a large Silicon Valley software company, to become a vice president of sales. He is also a fitness fanatic. He runs daily, tracking his mileage and times as precisely as he tracks the software sales of his team. His passion is rugby—an English form of football, played without pads. Fifteen years ago he started the Silicon Valley Rugby League. Every Saturday morning during the season, with the drive of a Marine drill sergeant leading his men on a twenty-mile run through a swamp, Fred takes his Oracle team into battle, apparently oblivious to the fact that he is now about twenty years older than everyone else on the field. Evelyn thinks he's crazy—he comes home stiff, sore, and bruised. In their marriage and in his life, he lives by the Corps' code: *Semper Fi.* Their marriage works.

"Bikuta is ripping us off," you tell Fred and Evelyn as they arrive at your office. "They're using our technology to manufacture and sell stents in China. When I confronted Mr. Bikuta, he gave me a load of B.S. He claimed that our design wouldn't work in the Chinese market and that they had developed their product independently, with their own R&D. But we got hold of one of their stents. It's not identical to the FreeFlow, but our engineers confirmed that it's based on our knowhow. Did they think I wouldn't find out? That I wouldn't mind? What kind of sucker does Bikuta think I am?"

You stand up and begin pacing around the room. "Mr. Bikuta wouldn't disclose their sales figures in China, and he flatly refused to discuss paying royalties on those sales. Then the bastard had the gall to invite me to come to Japan to negotiate a lower royalty rate on sales of FreeFlow in the rest of Asia! He actually threatened me, saying that if we don't lower the licensing fee, they will simply sell their 'own' product worldwide!"

Fred's response is immediate. "I hate to say I told you so," he exclaims, "but this is exactly what I was afraid of. Once the Japanese have mastered your technology, they steal it or invent around it and toss you aside."

"I know, I know," you grimly acknowledge. "You warned me. I'm angry with myself." You recall the hundreds of hours you spent courting this company. The long, saki-soaked dinners. The rounds of golf developing a relationship with Bikuta-san. For three years the joint venture seemed to work so well. Bikuta's quality control and manufacturing efficiency are superb. Their distribution was fantastic. For eleven straight quarters, sales of the FreeFlow went up. Bikuta fully accounted for the sales and paid you your fee the day it was due. Maybe you got lulled into dropping your guard. In fact, during the past year you and Bikuta started discussions about expanding your agreement to include sales in China. Now it seems this was all part of the con.

"While he and I were cordially negotiating, he was already stabbing me in the back," you say.

"Oh yeah, they do that—use negotiations as a cover for a sneak attack," observes Fred, who fancies himself something of a history buff. "It's the story of Pearl Harbor."

"Fred, I can't stand it when you talk like this," Evelyn interrupts. "You sound like even more of a bigot than you actually are. People are people. Any businessman wants to make money for his company. Remember you, too, were impressed with Bikuta and liked him. Remember the weekend you hosted him to a round of golf at Pebble Beach? You told me afterward that, unlike some of your American golfing buddies, Bikuta was scrupulously honest about keeping his score—that he had actually counted every one of his strokes. *You're* the one who always says, 'Character is revealed on the golf course.' "

Fred ignores this rebuke. "I've done many deals with the Japanese. They don't think the way we do. They nod and say 'yes,' and half the time it means no. And they can be bullies. The whole culture runs on status and hierarchy—those on top exploit those below."[1] Fred turns to you. "You've got no choice. To negotiate now would be to reward bad behavior. Tell them that if they don't stop selling in China, you'll terminate the joint venture and sue their ass off."

Fred doesn't need to convince you; this is exactly what you want to do. You feel humiliated and you want revenge.

You say, "I doubt we will get far filing a lawsuit in China or Japan."

"No, obviously the Chinese and Japanese courts are worthless," says

Fred. "Sue them here in California. Take your case to an American jury. Teach Bikuta a lesson."

You frown and think to yourself: If only it were that easy.

Evelyn, showing increasing signs of exasperation, finally cannot contain herself. "What macho nonsense!" she exclaims. "Let's not get carried away. Suing Bikuta will destroy what's been a profitable relationship so far. It will make your lawyers rich and distract you from the business. Go to Japan. Sit down with Bikuta. See what he has to say. What do you have to lose? And besides, have you considered Bikuta's perspective?"

You give Evelyn an incredulous look.

"Bikuta *asked* you to include China in the license agreement originally," she reminds you. "And you refused. Because you wanted to preserve your options. And haven't you been talking lately with some Chinese firm about making stents for the Chinese market? You know how seriously the Japanese take their business relationships. Maybe Bikuta heard about this and thought you were going to cut them out."

"But that was our right! We can enter the Chinese market with anyone we want. We have no obligation to Bikuta," you scoff.

"Don't listen to Evelyn," Fred interjects. "Bikuta was represented by international counsel. I'm sure his lawyer explained to him what the corporation's obligations were. Evelyn is such a bleeding heart. Every time some seventeen-year-old assaults an old lady and grabs her purse, she talks about what a difficult home life the kid's had."

Evelyn ignores this comment. "Of course you have the *legal* right to find a new partner for the Chinese market," she tells you. "I'm not saying that Bikuta isn't at fault. I'm just saying, give Mr. Bikuta a chance to do the right thing. Maybe you can negotiate a lower fee but extend the contract to the Chinese sales."

Fred explodes. "Evelyn, whose side are you on? There's a principle at stake here. You cannot do business with people who intentionally violate their agreements. Once they've screwed you, you can't just go back to business as usual. It sends the wrong message—not just to Bikuta, but to anyone else you might do business with. You might as well put a big sign on your head saying, 'Please, exploit me and I'll come back to the table! I'll accept any kind of behavior, right or wrong!' Is that how we want to be perceived? No! Besides, from a purely financial standpoint, Bikuta has no incentive to give us a dollar more than they absolutely have to. Every dollar they pay in royalties to us is a dollar less profit for them. And vice versa. *That's* the reality."

Evelyn rolls her eyes. "Fred loves to rant about the harsh 'realities' of business, but frankly I'm the one who's being realistic. Bikuta's a lot bigger than we are. They can afford the costs of litigation a lot more than we can. If we sue, they will probably stop selling our product entirely. If we negotiate—extend the joint venture to China—and if total sales go up, we could make more money even with a lower royalty rate."

The dilemma described above is quite realistic. The question is: Should you negotiate with the enemy or not? Fred and Evelyn are both making some sense. Each offers a point of view that has emotional and intellectual appeal. But you also see flaws in both arguments, and you are pretty riled up yourself. You want to make a wise decision, not one based solely on emotion. How do you sort through these arguments? Where do you begin?

After helping to resolve many business and family disputes over the years, I have come to believe that for most of us, confronting an enemy poses exceptional negotiation challenges. When I say "enemy," I do not mean just an ordinary competitor; I mean someone who has deeply wronged us and poses a serious threat to our well-being—someone we may even see as evil.

In the introduction, without elaboration, I proposed a definition: *An act is evil when it involves the intentional infliction of grievous harm on another human being in circumstances where there is no adequate justification.*[2] This definition has three essential elements. First, for an act to be evil, the perpetrator must intend to inflict harm. Carelessness is not enough. Second, the harm must be very serious. I use the word *grievous* to connote harms that are severe. Third, the infliction of harm must lack an adequate justification or excuse. Of course, the judgment about whether a justification is adequate may in some cases be reasonably debatable, and may depend on one's moral perspective.

Does every person who commits an evil act by definition become an evil person? I think not. Instead, I would call someone an evil person only if by disposition he or she repeatedly commits evil acts. This distinction is important. Too often we may condemn someone on the basis of a single action. Psychologists have shown that otherwise decent people may, because of obedience to authority or peer pressure, commit evil acts in particular contexts.[3] A centrally important finding of social psychology is that in evaluating the behavior of others, we tend to exaggerate the importance of a person's dispositions or traits and underestimate the influence of context. This tendency is well documented; social psychologists call it the "fundamental attribution error."[4] But when it comes to justifying our own behavior, our tendency is the exact opposite—we are quick to use contextual pressures to excuse behavior of which we are not proud.[5] "I did something bad," we may tell ourselves, "not because I am a bad person, but because the situation put me under so much pressure."

Bikuta's actions were certainly intentional. They might cause your company serious economic injury. And from your perspective they seem utterly unjustifiable, although Bikuta might see things differently. If Bikuta has violated the contract by using your intellectual property, that would be wrong, but I doubt the economic injury to your company represents harm that is substantial enough to justify the characterization of this act as evil. I think it would be even more of a stretch to conclude that Bikuta is an evil person, or that his corporation is evil.

But that doesn't lessen or invalidate how any of us might feel in such a situation: betrayed, humiliated, disrespected, dishonored. To the question, Should I bargain with this Devil? we *feel* the answer should be a resounding no. (Sometimes expressed as "That'll be a cold day in hell" or "Over my dead body!")

In helping clients work through such conflicts, I have found that wise decision-making poses three different challenges. The first is to avoid emotional traps that can lead to hasty and knee-jerk decisions. This chapter identifies and explores these traps. The second challenge is to analyze the costs and benefits of alternative courses of action. That is the focus of the next chapter. The third challenge is to address the ethical and moral issues that often arise when one is trying to decide whether to negotiate with an enemy. That will be our focus in chapter 3 and the case studies that follow.

But first let's focus on why these situations are so challenging. Psychologists and neuroscientists have discovered that people perceive reality and make judgments in two fundamentally different ways.[6] One, which I'll call *intuitive reasoning,* is automatic, effortless, and affective (related to emotions and feelings). It triggers instant responses and influences the meaning we attach to facts by linking the current situation to past experiences and stories we know. It will often motivate our behavior.[7] The other mode, which I'll call *analytical reasoning,* is conscious, deliberative, systematic, and logical: what we usually call "rational."

All human beings apprehend reality using both the intuitive and analytical modes, and our evolutionary survival depended on both kinds of reasoning. This "dual processing" system also guides our decision-making. Not surprisingly, both cognitive modes have advantages and drawbacks. The intuitive system picks up nonverbal cues and makes rapid appraisals.[8] But it's quirky and selective about the data it receives, which can lead to mistaken conclusions and poor decision-making. The analytical system, on the other hand, is disciplined and more systematic. It explicitly evaluates information in making a decision. But it may not always yield a clear answer. Finally, it may miss the forest for the trees.

Individuals vary to the extent that one or other mode of reasoning is dominant.[9] Each mode, alone, is incomplete, and there is, as we will discuss later, often an interaction between the two.

Another difference between the two modes—particularly relevant when we're locked in conflict with an enemy—is their operating speed. The intuitive system responds instantly, while the analytical system, which requires real effort and is ponderous and time consuming, plods far behind.[10] Indeed, the intuitive system may have evolved to protect us from imminent physical threats. However, it is not very discriminating when it comes to threats. It works pretty much the same whether the threat is to our physical safety or to something more conceptual: a relationship, a business, a self-image, anything that's important to us. It floods us with adrenaline so we can fight or flee. This is terrific when we're dealing with a saber-toothed tiger, but not so useful when we're sitting in our office with Fred and Evelyn dealing with questions like, Should I negotiate with Bikuta? Once our emotional alarms and "hot cognition" buttons are triggered, it may take time—minutes, hours, or even days—before we are truly capable of thinking logically. And even then, intuition may continue to run the show.

WHAT ARE THE TRAPS?

The conversation with Fred and Evelyn illustrates why intuitive judgments are not always wise. Fred's perspective reflects a number of traps, or cognitive distortions, that commonly lead us to refuse to negotiate when we probably should. These "negative" traps are in the left-hand column below, and they are by far the more common response when we are in conflict with an enemy. But a second set of traps, listed in the right-hand column, can have the opposite effect, causing us to negotiate when maybe we shouldn't. Evelyn's perspective reflects some of these "positive" traps.

Negative Traps Promoting Refusal	Positive Traps Promoting Negotiation
Tribalism	Universalism
Demonization	Contextual rationalization and forgiveness
Dehumanization	Rehabilitation and redemption
Moralism/Self-righteousness	Shared fault and responsibility
Zero-sum fallacy	Win-win
Fight/Flight	Appeasement
Call to battle	Call for peace/Pacifism

a) *Tribalism* involves an appeal to a group identity, where you see your own side—the in-group—as familiar and reliable, while the other side is an out-group that should be distrusted and disfavored. The group identity rests on shared characteristics such as family or kinship structures, language, religion, race, ethnicity, or a common history. In our example, Fred perceives Bikuta as a member of a foreign tribe—the Japanese—who are different, don't think the way "we" Americans do, and who are not to be trusted. At the opposite extreme is the trap of *universalism*. This presumes that people are all essentially the same and underestimates the importance of differences created by culture, history, and group identity. In Evelyn's words,

"People are people. Any businessman wants to make money for his company."

b) *Demonization* is the tendency to view the other side as "evil": not just guilty of bad acts, but fundamentally bad to the core. Fred sees Bikuta's actions—secretly opening a factory in China, manufacturing a competing stent, and asking for a reduction in the license fee—as revealing his underlying character. Evelyn's perspective reflects the opposite extreme: *contextual rationalization.* She suggests that Bikuta's behavior is best understood as the product of external pressures and thus can be easily forgiven.

c) *Dehumanization* involves seeing the enemy as being outside the moral order, less than human. Said to be a central process in prejudice, racism, and discrimination, this trap justifies treating the "other" as an "object." Fred's characterizations of the Japanese lean in this direction. More extreme examples can easily be found. In 2008, Imam Yousif al-Zahar of Hamas characterized Jews as "the brothers of apes and pigs" before calling them a people "who cannot be trusted" and "have been traitors to all agreements."[11] The opposite trap might involve a belief that all people are capable of change and deserve an opportunity for *rehabilitation* and *redemption.* In Evelyn's words, "Give Mr. Bikuta a chance to do the right thing."

d) *Moralism* and *self-righteousness* create a tendency to see the other side as entirely at fault while you are innocent and worthy. Fred feels Bikuta is completely to blame, has purposely and flagrantly violated the joint venture agreement, and deserves moral condemnation. The opposite trap is the tendency to assume that in every conflict there is *fault on all sides* and that the burden of responsibility should be shared. Evelyn suggests that while Bikuta may be at fault, you are partially responsible as well for not being more attentive to Bikuta's desire to enter the Chinese market.

e) The *zero-sum* trap involves seeing the world in terms of a competition: what one side wins, the other side must lose. Conflict is seen as purely distributive: anything that benefits your enemy is necessarily bad for you. Reducing the license fee, according to Fred, can only help Bikuta and hurt you. One sees this trap everywhere. In divorce disputes, for example, spouses often argue over the allocation of money, or time spent with the children, as if more for one spouse can't possibly be good for the other. The opposite trap is the naïve assumption that **win-win** is *always* possible, that the pie can always be expanded so that both sides are better off. Evelyn suggests that if joint venture sales will be expanded by reason of lower license fees, both you and Bikuta could be better off economically. She may (or may not) be right.

f) The *fight/flight* trap involves seemingly opposite behaviors, but both are automatic reactions and relate to "hot cognition." In the face of intense conflict, you may: (1) unthinkingly charge into battle or, (2) at the other extreme, flee, conceding what is important to you in the hope of avoiding a fight. Fred obviously wants to fight. Evelyn wants neither to fight nor to flee, but she is perhaps inclined toward *appeasement*. Better to negotiate with Bikuta and make concessions, she argues, than fight a possibly losing legal battle.

g) The final trap, the *call to battle,* involves a political figure, business executive, or family member mobilizing his or her "troops" for a fight in a righteous mission against evil. This call uses the language of war and will often rhetorically draw upon demonization, tribalism, dehumanization, and moralism. While the leader inevitably claims his motivation is only to do what is best for the group as a whole, the call to battle often serves the leader's own political interests as well. Far less common is the opposite extreme, a *call for peace,* based on the premise that almost any conflict can be avoided or ended through sensible peace-seeking initiatives. The call for peace may invoke notions of universalism, forgiveness, redemption, and shared responsibility.

What is critical to understand is that *each column represents a cluster of reinforcing prisms that can distort judgments.* The negative traps are most prevalent when we see our adversary as an evil enemy. Even in business cases like Bikuta, where the adversary clearly isn't evil, we can easily fall prey to these negative traps and *perceive* our opponent as evil, which causes us to speak and behave as though the opponent *is* evil. This is equally true in the international and personal realms. The negative traps encourage us to exaggerate the costs of negotiation and underestimate the benefits; the positive traps do just the opposite. Both are common default modes for dealing with conflict, and many of us have a decided preference for one or the other. Which way we lean is largely a function of basic personality style, but it is also influenced by past experiences, stories that have been handed down to us, and the personal narratives from which we draw our deepest sources of identity. Fred, for example, sees himself as a warrior, a champion against injustice. His worldview: "The world is a harsh place; people will exploit you if they can." He is quick to see evidence that confirms this story. Evelyn is an optimist, a peacemaker whose instincts tell her that going to battle is unproductive. Her worldview: "There is good in everyone; all you have to do is tap into it." She focuses selectively on evidence that confirms *her* story.

In sum, it is not that Fred and Evelyn are completely ignoring the need for analysis and relying solely on intuition. Rather, I believe that they each started with a gut reaction to your news about Bikuta, jumped to a conclusion, and then hired the analytical system as a lawyer to argue the case. It's as if the intuitive part of their brains has taken charge of the analytical investigation. That's why neither seems at all open to the other's perspective. Indeed, knowing them as well as you do, you could have almost predicted their advice before the meeting.

How can you avoid these traps? A critical first step is to recognize and acknowledge them. Be aware of your strong emotions. There is no way to avoid them, especially when you are in conflict with a devil. Another step is to expose yourself to different perspectives, as you've done by calling Fred and Evelyn to your office. They are not persuading each other, but if you feel pulled in both directions, that can slow you down and prevent you from making a hasty decision.

Now you are going to shift gears and consciously open yourself to careful analysis. For that, you may need expert help.

TWO

Bargaining and Its Alternatives: Costs, Benefits, and Beyond

It's a relief when Fred and Evelyn finally leave your office. You feel upset and confused. Fred inflamed your anger toward Bikuta and made you want to fight. But Evelyn made you feel ashamed and a little guilty. She's such a good person, with such generous instincts. Maybe you *are* partly responsible. Perhaps you should give Bikuta another chance?

Fortunately, you have a trusted advisor named Mr. Spock, the secret weapon of many entrepreneurs in Silicon Valley. He is a clear thinker and a brilliant strategist. But he's not warm and fuzzy. He is emotionally detached, humorless, someone your wife describes as a "cold fish." That's fine with you—you're not looking for a drinking buddy. Actually, you're quite fond of the guy. He is very direct, totally reliable. And he is available on reasonably short notice.

In fact, Spock has already arrived at your office. Never one to engage in pleasantries, he drops into a chair and says, "I got your email describing the dispute with Bikuta. What's your thinking?"

"I'm furious. I'm so upset I'm not sleeping at night."

"Okay, let's keep the emotions out of it," Spock intones. Many of his conversations begin like this.

"Easy for you to say!" you protest. "I've been working my ass off to build this company. I'm lying in bed at night wondering if the company is going to survive. My brother-in-law warned me about doing business with a big Japanese company. He said they would eventually screw me, and he was right. Now I have to put up with his obnoxious gloating."

"Let's stick to the facts," Spock responds. "Stay with me here. How important is Bikuta's business to your company?"

"It accounts for forty percent of our revenues and an even higher percentage of profits. That's why we've grown so fast. I've got ten new employees because of the deal with Bikuta. And now he decides it's okay to stab me in the back? He can't get away with this! I've spent five years of my life building this business." Your voice is rising. "I will not tolerate being made a fool of!" you shout.

"Look, you've got to calm down if you want my help," Spock says coolly.

Spock can be infuriating.[1] Like his *Star Trek* namesake, his abnormal insistence on logic and emotional self-control makes him seem like an alien. But that's why you called him. You say, "Where do we start?"

"To begin with, give me a copy of the contract with Bikuta, all the correspondence, and any relevant financial records showing the history of the relationship. What does your lawyer say?"

You hand Spock sixteen cartons of bulging files and a legal memorandum prepared by Ron Star, your outside lawyer. Spock asks for a quiet corner and goes off to read this ton of verbiage. An hour later, he has mastered every page and is back in your office.

"*Now,*" you say, "you have a better sense of my predicament."

"I do," he says. Spock looks at you with a glimmer of what might be compassion. But you know it isn't. "As I understand it, Bikuta has proposed that you renegotiate the contract. You are trying to decide whether to accept this invitation. Negotiation is an option. But is it the best option? That's what we have to think through."

"Negotiating is the last thing I feel like doing," you retort.

"What you *feel* like doing is not the issue. You must rationally decide on the best course of action," says Spock. "Let's start by talking about what you might do away from the table if you decide not to negotiate."

"I want to sue them! I want to expose them publicly. If there's any justice in the world, Bikuta should be forced to stop using our technology and to pay us damages. But you've read Star's memo. My prospects in court aren't good."

Indeed, Star's memorandum makes for depressing reading. Although there is ample evidence that Bikuta has used your trade secrets in making its Chinese product, Star says, the problem lies in enforcing your joint venture agreement. In theory, you could sue Bikuta in three different jurisdictions: China (where the knockoffs are being sold), Japan (where Bikuta's headquarters are located), or California (where your company is based). But your odds of success are grim.

Suing in China would be hopeless, Star says—a waste of money. In China, the theft of intellectual property is rampant. Relationships count for more than formal contracts; Bikuta is already doing business in China and your company is unknown there.[2] The Chinese government is taking steps to repair its reputation, at least with respect to patents and copyright, but it has a long way to go.[3] The likelihood that a Chinese court would protect your intellectual property is near zero.

Your prospects in Japan are not much better. While Japanese courts are not known to be corrupt, Bikuta would still have a home-court advantage. More to the point, Japanese law offers little protection for trade secrets, and a Japanese court would never try to enjoin Bikuta's activity in China.[4] Finally, it would take two or three years to get a court ruling and it would cost a fortune; Japanese litigation is notoriously expensive.[5]

Suing in California is the only hope, and even this is problematic. Because Bikuta makes no products or sales in the United States, a court might well throw out your claim for lack of jurisdiction. But if you could get past this hurdle, according to Star's memo, you'd have a good chance of winning on the merits.

Spock says, "Obviously, if you decide to sue, the best place to bring suit is in California. But I agree with Star's analysis. All in all, because of the jurisdictional problems, you'd have only about a fifteen to twenty-five percent chance of an ultimate victory in a California court. Meanwhile, your legal costs would be huge and the lawsuit would distract you from building your business."

Spock then asks a tough question: "Suppose you get everything you say you want: you sue Bikuta and *win*. Assume that the court can enforce the judgment and stop Bikuta from selling this product in China. What happens next?"

You don't know what he's getting at. "We throw a big party?" you venture.

"No—I mean, going forward, who will sell your product in Japan and the rest of Asia? Your contract with Bikuta expires next year. Would you want to renew that contract, even on renegotiated terms? Would you want Bikuta to continue to manufacture and distribute for you?"

"Are you kidding?" you say. "How can I trust them?"

"Okay, let's put Bikuta aside for the moment. Who would you work with in Asia? Do you have some other joint venture partner lined up and ready to go?"

You squirm. You don't have anyone. There are some prospects, you tell Spock, but it would take at least a year to check them out, negotiate a deal, transfer the technology, and get manufacturing up and running. In the meantime, your position in the market would erode. And the new partner might not agree to a 15 percent royalty rate, either.

"Okay, let me summarize what we've got so far," Spock says. "If you don't negotiate with Bikuta, you have litigation as an alternative. We've just examined the costs and benefits of going that route. I think we've established that even in the California courts the odds are you won't ever get to the merits of the case because of the jurisdictional problem. In all events litigation will cost you plenty and be a big distraction. We also looked at your business alternatives. You don't have to use Bikuta as your manufacturer and distributor—you can find someone else who might be a more trustworthy partner. But you'd lose a lot of time and maybe some market share."

You stare at him dully. You need a cup of coffee.

"Now, what about Bikuta's alternatives if he can't make a deal with you? Are there other firms that can provide the technology?" Spock asks.

"None," you reply. "Unless he can use our technology, he really can't have a competitive product—at least for several years. If we sue him and stop him from using our know-how, he's out of this market."

This last thought starts to cheer you up.

———

This conversation illustrates how the consummate "rational actor"—a Mr. Spock–like character—might begin to analyze your problem. Mr. Spock, of course, is the well-known character from the *Star Trek* television series: the pointy-eared science officer of the U.S.S. *Enterprise* and executive officer under Captain Kirk. Spock is half Vulcan and half human, and his behavior reflects the Vulcan ideals of logic and strict emotional mastery. His trademark is his weird mix of nerdy brilliance and deadpan humor, and I use him advisedly here.[6] In this book, Spock has a method and we can follow it. (In a sense, we can cultivate our inner Spock.)

Let's step back and think about what Spock is doing. He has just identified your alternatives if you don't negotiate with Bikuta: your choices away from the table. He has begun to consider Bikuta's alternatives as well. We'll see why in a moment.

"Now, what's really important to you here? From what you've said . . ."

Spock then proceeds to list what he sees as your interests:

- Maximizing your revenues from the FreeFlow.
- Building up sales in Asia.
- Entering the Chinese market.
- Protecting your intellectual property.
- Maintaining your reputation as a dependable joint venture partner.
- Resolving this conflict as quickly and cheaply as possible.

You nod your agreement. That about sums it up.

"Now, what about Bikuta? What's important to them?" Spock asks.

You say they are a terrific manufacturing firm with outstanding distribution channels throughout Asia. But they have little R&D capacity, so they need to enter into joint venture deals or licensing agreements with other firms. Their core long-term interests, like yours, are growth and profitability.

Spock looks up: "Who are these other joint venture partners? Any in California or elsewhere in the United States?"

You smile. "Not yet . . . but I recently heard that they are hoping to make a deal soon with Pressure-Measure Company, another venture-financed Silicon Valley start-up that's bigger than we are. My friend Tom Zimring, a venture capitalist, is on their board."

Spock shows no emotion but you can tell he is pleased. "Obviously, Bikuta Corporation should care about its reputation as a reliable joint venture partner. That's another interest. A well-publicized lawsuit here might affect its chances of making a deal with Pressure-Measure—and with others in the future. If I were in their shoes, I'd much prefer renegotiating the deal with you than facing litigation in Silicon Valley, even if I thought I had a good chance of winning on some jurisdictional technicality."[7]

"Does this mean we should sue?" you ask.

"Not so fast," Spock replies. "It means that you want to make them aware that, unless you are able to work out a reasonable fee with respect to the China sales, you will sue them here in California with as much publicity as possible. You could also make them aware of your friendship with Zimring. You could acknowledge, however, that such litigation is not an attractive alternative for either of you and that there might be a variety of deals that would better serve the interests of both companies."

You then ask the obvious. "Suppose we were to make a new joint venture deal, one that covered China sales and perhaps had a new formula for license fees. Maybe a sliding scale that depended on total sales. How could I be sure they'd keep their word going forward? I don't trust them. I'm not about to get screwed a second time!"

Spock replies, "You *can't* be sure. You have to worry about enforcement. That's where your lawyer comes in. The new contract has to have some teeth. You will want to make sure that a California court has jurisdiction, that there are strict representations and warranties, and that the loser of any future enforcement action must pay the winner's legal fees."

You are beginning to feel less desperate. It seems you have more options than you thought.

What has Spock done here? In assessing the Bikuta case, he has asked five basic questions that are useful for ordinary conflicts of all sorts. Because our focus in this book is on negotiating with an adversary—indeed, someone whom you see as an *enemy*—I will frame the questions in those terms.

1) *Interests*: What are my interests? What are my adversary's interests?

2) *Alternatives*: What are my alternatives to negotiation? What are my adversary's alternatives?

3) *Potential negotiated outcomes*: Is there a potential deal (or deals) that could satisfy both parties' interests better than our alternatives to negotiation?

4) *Costs*: What will it cost me to negotiate? What do I expect to lose in terms of tangible resources: money and time? Will my reputation suffer? Will negotiating set a bad precedent?

5) *Implementation*: If we do reach a deal, is there a reasonable prospect that it will be carried out?

We will now consider this method in more detail, with examples from other contexts.

Interests: *What are my interests? What are my adversary's interests?*

When individuals are in conflict, they often think in terms of "positions"—what they want or demand. For example, Bikuta insists that it should pay no royalty on Chinese sales, while you demand "fifteen percent or else!" These are positions, not interests. Interests are the fundamental needs and concerns that lie *underneath* those positions. There is only one way to meet a position, but often many ways to serve an interest. In this case, as we've seen, your company and Bikuta Corp. each have a financial interest in long-term profitability. Because there may be many options that might serve these core interests, framing the conflict in terms of core concerns (rather than positions) will give you more flexibility when you get to the later steps.

Ironically, people in conflict often find it difficult to articulate their interests. This is usually because they haven't thought about them, or are not used to thinking about goals on this level. They know *what* they want—or what they say they want—but not *why* they want it. For anyone embroiled in a dispute, the analysis begins with the following questions:

What are my basic goals in this situation? What am I trying to achieve—and why? In the big scheme of things, what's important to me?

Some of your interests may be tangible, for example, money, goods, resources, and physical property. Other important interests may be intangible, such as maintaining the morale of your employees, upholding your reputation, and being treated with self-respect. There may also be "trade-offs" between interests. Prioritize them—some may be very crucial, others less important but "nice to have."

Next, given the available information, what do you know about your adversary's interests? What do they value—and why? This will help you evaluate any potential deal from their perspective. This can be particularly challenging at the organizational and international levels, where identifying the interests at stake requires an extra set of questions: Whom do you talk to? Who defines the interests? Is the "adversary" in fact comprised of subgroups that have competing interests?

Note that you probably won't *feel* like pondering the enemy's interests. Force yourself. I explain why below.

Alternatives: What are my alternatives to negotiation? What are my adversary's?

This question highlights your choices away from the negotiating table. If you decide *not* to negotiate, what actions can you take unilaterally—without the cooperation of the other side? And how well do those actions serve your interests?

One alternative might be to do nothing: walk away from the deal and ignore the conflict. Another alternative might be to find another partner. There is also the use of coercive force. Every bigger child who snatches a toy from a smaller one understands the attractions of a self-help strategy. However, legitimacy is an important consideration, especially when using force, so one must be ready to justify any coercive tactics. Where legal rights are involved, a lawsuit is a coercive alternative. In a labor-management conflict, strikes or lockouts are, for the most part, alternatives used to coerce concessions in bargaining. In the international arena, a naval blockade or an air strike may be an alternative to diplomatic negotiations.

Next, for each alternative, consider the full range of possible outcomes. With regard to litigation, for example, it's not enough to consider only the best possible outcome. What happens if you lose the case?

What are the odds of winning or losing? Even if you win, are there any negative consequences?[8]

Once you have evaluated your alternatives, identify the best of the lot. This is your Best Alternative to a Negotiated Agreement, or "BATNA." If you later decide to negotiate, this will be an important reference point for evaluating any deal that is on the table. You should *never be willing to accept a negotiated deal that doesn't serve your interests better than your BATNA.*

Finally, try to assess your enemy's alternatives and how they could affect you. You may not know exactly what their alternatives are, but sometimes you'll have a good idea. In this case, you know that Bikuta won't be able to license a similar product from any other R&D company. You also know that if you do bring suit, Bikuta's BATNA is to defend against it in court (or risk a court-imposed injunction and damages).

The better your BATNA—that is, the better your alternatives away from the table—the more bargaining power you have at the table. The same is true for your adversary. Therefore, before you decide whether to negotiate, you should work hard to create the best possible alternatives for yourself and to diminish, if possible, your opponent's perception of his own BATNA.

Negotiated outcomes: Are there potential negotiated outcomes that can satisfy both sides' interests better than our respective alternatives to negotiation?

This step requires some creativity and several steps. First you must imagine a range of potential deals. Then you must evaluate them in light of each party's interests: What are the benefits and risks to each side? Finally, you must compare those deals with each party's BATNA and ask, Which is better?

This, too, involves some guesswork, but the goal is pragmatic. If a potential deal doesn't meet your adversary's interests better than its BATNA, why should they agree to it? Indeed, if either side's BATNA is clearly superior to any deal you can envision, it makes no sense for that party to negotiate.[9] But if you can envision negotiated deals that could be better than both sides' BATNAs, you should proceed to the next steps.

Costs: What are the expected costs of negotiation?

The negotiation process itself imposes costs, which you will incur regardless of whether you reach a deal. These must be taken into account.

> *Transaction Costs:* The negotiation process involves costs in terms of *time, money, manpower,* and *other resources.*[10] For example, most department stores, restaurants, and museums do not negotiate on price. Why won't Macy's negotiate over the price of a suit? Because the store in Herald Square alone receives about thirty thousand visitors a day and negotiating with that many people would be inefficient.[11] Consider the expense involved in training salespeople to negotiate with customers, the cost of devising complicated compensation schemes with incentives for "good negotiators," the time that might be wasted on haggling, and the possible damage to reputation and branding. These costs outweigh the benefit of any extra sales that might be made with selective price adjustments.
>
> The negotiation process may also impose costs arising from the *disclosure of information.* Parties usually have to disclose information in order to reach a deal. Certain disclosures are riskier than others, particularly if one is negotiating with an adversary capable of exploiting this information in the future. For a business, disclosing intelligence-gathering capabilities or trade secrets may be unacceptably risky. For an individual, disclosing personal desires or preferences may weaken her bargaining power in the future.
>
> *Spillover Costs:* Negotiating with one party may adversely affect you in future dealings with other parties. One such cost may involve *reputation.* For example, a physician may prefer not to settle a malpractice claim, even if settlement would be cheaper than litigation, in order to avoid any implication that she was in any way at fault.
>
> A related spillover cost concerns *precedent.* Although settling a frivolous lawsuit for a token amount might make sense in light of immediate cost savings, a defendant might

worry that his willingness to negotiate at all might invite a flood of similar claims. Similarly, an employer might refuse to negotiate with unlawfully striking workers for fear of encouraging future strikes.[12]

Implementation: If a deal is struck, will it be implemented?

This question is strategic and practical. Even if a deal is made, there is a risk that it may not be honored. This is particularly true when you are dealing with an unreliable adversary.

One dimension to this problem involves the relationship between agents and principals. Your adversary may simply lack the authority— or the institutional or political power—to bind his constituents to the deal. Or the other side may be a diverse set of stakeholders who can't agree. For example, suppose you need the agreement of all the adjacent homeowners to put up a new fence, and there is no clear representative with whom to negotiate.

Another dimension is time. Even if you believe that your adversary has the capacity to implement a deal, you must consider safeguards. Many deals involve implementation over time. Even if your enemy abides by the agreement now, he might have an incentive to defect later. Commercial lawyers who participate in deal-making often put a great deal of effort into preventing such defections by building penalties into the deal. Many commercial contracts include provisions for third-party enforcement—litigation in a particular jurisdiction, or arbitration—if the counterpart proves unreliable.

But in some cases there is no effective formal enforcement mechanism. What then? Where there is a good relationship, personal trust may be sufficient. But with an adversary who has violated agreements in the past, the lack of any enforcement mechanism may be a deal killer. This factor is particularly common in the international sphere, where there is often no effective third-party enforcement. Instead, decision-makers must rely on a complicated system of monitoring, deterrence, and "soft-enforcement."

————————————

These five questions provide a framework for analyzing the benefits and costs, opportunities and risks. It won't provide a bright-line test or crank-the-handle algorithm. But you shouldn't be looking for that here anyway.

Risk assessment is not an exact science. The future is uncertain, especially when dealing with an adversary. After the fact, some of your predictions may prove to be wrong. Some of the five questions you will be able to answer with confidence, such as identifying your own interests and priorities. Others, such as what your adversary really wants and how he views his own alternatives to negotiation, may be much harder for you to pin down. You won't know precisely how your adversary will behave in response to your own actions. Disputes are dynamic, not static. Your moves affect the other side's moves, and vice versa. If you were to draw a decision tree, it would be extremely complicated. Economists call this "strategic interdependence."

In fact, in many disputes, two reasonable people could analyze the same situation and reach different conclusions, based on different predictions and different assessments of the costs and benefits. Moreover, differences in their values and priorities would also influence their evaluations. There may be trade-offs among interests.

That said, however, this framework can guide your analysis and may lead to a reasonably clear conclusion about whether you should negotiate or resist—a "yes" or "no." If so, and if you are comfortable with that decision, your inquiry might stop here.

But bargaining with a devil may raise issues that go beyond simply comparing costs and benefits.

THREE

Recognition, Legitimacy, and Morality

Suppose you've heard Spock out. You understand his analysis. But his recommendation doesn't sit well with you. What if you feel that continuing to do business with Bikuta is simply wrong—against your personal values? It's not that you disagree with Spock's pragmatic assessment of benefits and costs, but rather that you find his kind of analysis incomplete.

You say to Spock, "I appreciate your evaluation, and I understand why you think I should negotiate. But I think it would be wrong."

When dealing with a "devil" it's difficult to avoid a sixth question: What issues of recognition and legitimacy are implicated in my decision?

You may be troubled by what you see as issues of principle. You may be asking yourself: What happened to the idea of justice? You may think that Bikuta deserves to be punished for what his company did in the past. Spock's approach tends to be forward-looking, and any negotiated deal would have to serve Bikuta's interests as well as yours—why else would he agree? But the idea of simply "moving on" may be downright offensive, especially if issues of honor, personal integrity, and identity are involved.

Spock is puzzled. "You mean it would be a mistake to negotiate? Are you worried about the impact on your reputation with others? Or about setting a bad precedent? We've taken those factors into account as costs of negotiating."

To the extent your concerns can be expressed in terms of future consequences, Spock's approach can encompass them. For example, you might feel that by negotiating with Bikuta, you would be condoning his past behavior and thereby encouraging more wrongful acts in the future. You might fear that negotiating with Bikuta would signal to others that you think his claims are legitimate, which could only help him. Or you might worry that choosing to negotiate may harm your reputation. With all of these concerns, so long as you identify the pragmatic consequences that might flow from them, Spock can include them in his analysis.

But what about concerns that don't comfortably fit into Spock's framework? Suppose you say, "You're missing my point, Spock. This isn't about costs and benefits. This goes way beyond license fees and sales in China. It's about my reputation with *myself.* To negotiate with Bikuta would compromise something very personal to me. It would make me complicit in his behavior and that's a line I'm not willing to cross."

This is an important challenge. What is the proper role of moral judgments like these in decisions of this sort?[1] Are they simply another trap?

Let's look at the "dual processing" model again. Neuroscientists and psychologists are now studying how human beings make moral judgments.[2] Some psychologists think that moral judgments are primarily like aesthetic judgments: "They are gut feelings or intuitions that happen to us quickly, automatically, and convincingly. We see an event, or we hear a story told as gossip, and we know immediately that the act in question was right or wrong."[3]

This suggests that the intuitive system encompasses not just survival instincts but subjective impressions of all kinds: likes and dislikes, value judgments, and affinities that give our lives passion and meaning. I believe that moral judgments, too, arise from the intuitive side of the brain; they are gut feelings that are instinctively reached and deeply felt.

Are they traps? Maybe. It depends on how you handle them. They certainly look like some of the traps that I discussed earlier, and they can be traps if you use them as an excuse for not going through Spock's five questions.

Should you ignore a moral principle that is critically important to you? Definitely not. My own preference is for a process that recognizes that moral judgments both do and should involve an interaction between intuition and analysis. When fully explored by the analytic part of the brain—that is, when the analytic side is acting as a dispassionate judge weighing *all* the arguments, not a lawyer defending a foregone conclusion—I believe that moral values should, and in some cases must, be factored into decision-making.

So here's the crux of the matter: You have fully analyzed the Bikuta situation and now it's time to make a decision. The dispassionate judge in you sees a strong argument in favor of negotiation; but your moral intuition is rebelling. What should you do?

This Faustian tension between pragmatism and principle is the heart of this book. To explore this tension further, let's raise the stakes and consider a real-life case where the adversary really *was* evil.

———————

Anatoli (Natan) Sharansky was twenty-nine years old when he was seized by the Russian secret police, the KGB, taken to Lefortovo prison, stripped naked and searched, and told that he was being charged with treason, a capital offense. He was accused of passing state secrets to the CIA. The charges were bogus. His real offense was that he had become a public spokesman for the Soviet Zionist movement. He had regularly provided the major American and European television and newspaper correspondents in the Soviet Union with interviews and information about "refuseniks"—Soviet Jews who had been refused permission to emigrate to Israel.

The KGB wanted to make a deal with Sharansky, and they used a combination of carrots and sticks in their efforts to induce his cooperation. In exchange for a confession and a condemnation of the refusenik movement, they offered Sharansky a short prison sentence, after which he would be free to leave the Soviet Union and join his wife in Israel. Implicit in the deal was the understanding that once Sharansky had left the Soviet Union, he could repudiate his confession as coerced. The stick included subjecting Sharansky to a merciless campaign of psychological torture, social isolation, continuing threats of extreme punishment, and harsh conditions.

Instead of cooperating, Sharansky adopted a stance of absolute refusal to make any deal with the KGB. He faced down a succession of high-level KGB interrogators, refusing to confess to anything or to provide any information that would implicate his friends and colleagues.

He pleaded not guilty to the criminal charges, dismissed the state-assigned lawyer (who was a Communist Party member), and insisted on the right to defend himself during the trial. He then used the trial as a forum to denounce the charges as a sham and vilify the Soviet regime. He was convicted on the bogus espionage charge and condemned to a thirteen-year sentence: three years in prison, with the remainder in a forced labor camp.

For the next nine years, Sharansky endured harsh physical conditions in Soviet prisons and labor camps. "During the long months of interrogation and isolation before my trial, and for all the years that followed, my captors were determined to break me, to make me confess to crimes I had never committed," he later wrote in his memoir.[4] He steadfastly refused all forms of cooperation, and even went on a nearly fatal hunger strike as a protest against the authorities.

Finally, in 1986, the Soviets released Sharansky in a prisoner exchange with the United States. Sharansky was released in Berlin and the United States released a captured Soviet spy.

To the very end, Sharansky refused to bargain with the Devil. On February 10, 1986, Sharansky was flown to East Berlin, accompanied by a KGB agent. A car was waiting to take him to the border. As they stepped off the plane, the KGB agent instructed Sharansky, "You see that car . . . Go straight to it and don't make any turns. Is it agreed?" Sharansky replied, "Since when have I started making agreements with the KGB? You know that I never agree with the KGB about anything. If you tell me to go straight, I'll go crooked." He then defiantly zigzagged his way to the car. The next day he walked across the Glienicke Bridge to his freedom.

Sharansky's decision provides a rich context for exploring the issues raised earlier in this chapter. Sharansky himself has provided a wealth of information in his memoir and subsequent interviews.[5] How did he make this decision—and continue to uphold it during the long years of his imprisonment? Was it based on analysis or intuition? Was it a pragmatic decision or a moral one? Above all, was it wise?

BACKGROUND

Sharansky was born in 1948 in Stalino, a city in the Ukraine. While ethnically Jewish, his family, like most Jews during the Soviet period, was not religiously observant. From an early age, Sharansky was taught that Jews were often persecuted and that expressing any form of dissent was dangerous. He was five years old when Stalin died in 1953, and he remembers the day vividly. His father told him that Stalin had been a "terrible butcher" who had killed "many innocent people," that shortly before his death Stalin had again begun persecuting Jews,[6] and that another pogrom might soon be in the offing. Moreover, "Papa warned us not to repeat these comments to anyone. This is when I first learned that in order to survive in Soviet society you had to function on two levels at once: what you really thought and what you allowed yourself to tell other people. I lived with this dual reality until 1973."

Sharansky grew up "unaware of the religion, language, culture and history of my people." As a youth he had little interest in a religion that could only be practiced in secret. "Because Jews of my generation had no desire to live a double life, or to be handicapped by a Jewish affiliation that meant little to us, we constantly looked for a means of escape." Sharansky's means were his brains—he was a chess prodigy who excelled at math and had a passion for learning English.

Because of his mathematical gifts, and despite being a Jew, Sharansky was accepted to the Moscow Institute of Physics and Technology, a prestigious, highly competitive school that liked to compare itself to the Massachusetts Institute of Technology (MIT). While a student there, inspired by Andrei Sakharov and his Committee for Human Rights, Sharansky became interested both in human rights and the Soviet Zionist movement, a dissident group that sought to pressure the Soviet regime to grant Jews the right to leave the USSR for Israel and thus "make *aliyah*." Through this movement he developed a strong Jewish identity and the courage to speak out: "[F]or the first time in my life, I was no longer afraid to say what I really believed—about my fellow citizens, the country I lived in, and the values I adhered to. At the age of twenty-five I finally learned what a joy it was to be free."

In October 1973, through his work with the Soviet Zionist movement, Sharansky met Natasha (later Avital) Stieglitz, who quickly became the love of his life. They soon moved in together. Later that year,

Sharansky followed Natasha's example and applied for permission to leave the Soviet Union for Israel. In doing so, he knew it was only a matter of time before he was fired from his job as a computer specialist at the Institute for Oil and Gas.

Natasha's exit visa came through in mid-1974. The couple struggled with the question of whether she should leave without him, and if so, whether they should marry before her departure. They decided they should marry and that she should not put her exit visa at risk through a delay. They married on July 4, 1974, in a Jewish ceremony. The next day she left the Soviet Union for Israel, where she took the name Avital. Sharansky, hoping that his own exit visa would come through quickly, assured her that he'd be there within six months at the latest. In fact, they were not to be reunited for twelve years.

Sharansky increasingly devoted his energy and time to the Soviet Zionist movement, especially after he lost his job in 1975. Because of his excellent English, he became an important spokesman for the Jewish dissidents with the Western press. He developed close relationships with the Moscow correspondents of the major media from America and Europe, and frequently granted interviews and provided information about the plight of Soviet Jews in general and refuseniks in particular.

After several years, the Soviet authorities decided to crack down on the movement. On March 4, 1977, the newspaper *Izvestia* published a full-page article denouncing Sharansky and several other Jewish activists, accusing them of passing state secrets to the CIA. Soon thereafter, Sharansky was arrested.

After his arrest, Sharansky ended up spending nine years in prison and labor camps, including more than four hundred days in unheated, damp, four-by-six-foot "punishment cells," with half rations. He also spent about two hundred days on hunger strikes.

He chose this course instead of joining his wife in Israel. Based on what he knew at the time, was this a rational decision?

It certainly looked as though he was analyzing the situation rationally. He was a chess master. He had studied game theory and was well grounded in mathematics. He saw himself as locked in a strategic contest with the KGB, and he relished formulating and refining his tactics.

Even before his arrest, he had been interrogated by the KGB on several occasions and had framed these dealings as akin to a chess game. He took comfort in thinking through in advance what the KGB's moves might be, and how he might respond and defend.

> I had trained myself not to pay attention to the threats of the KGB interrogators I occasionally met with. Instead of answering their questions, I told them only what I wanted them to hear. In their presence I felt like a chess player facing a much weaker opponent. They did exactly what they were supposed to, and I knew all their moves in advance: their threats and warnings, their attempts at blackmail, their flattery and their promises.

During the key period between his arrest and trial, he had sixteen months to refine his game. He also drew upon the memory of a computer program he had written as part of his graduate thesis, titled "Simulating the Decision-Making Process in Conflict Situations Based on the Chess Endgame." He remembered that "an important element in my program was a hierarchical list, a 'tree' of goals and conditions for attaining them. And now, as I stared at the chessboard in my cell, it occurred to me that I could take a similar approach in the game that I was about to play against the KGB."

Now let's pay close attention to Sharansky's description of his thought process.

> What are the goals of *this* game? I asked myself. Clearly it was *impossible to establish a goal of "minimizing the possible punishment,"* for that would mean submitting to the will of the KGB. After some thought, I decided upon three goals, and I sketched them out on a scrap of toilet paper, part of the daily ration of rough tissue paper the guard had given me at breakfast: Obstruct → Study → Expose. (Emphasis added.)

Upon further thought, he changed the first goal slightly. "Unfortunately, it wasn't in my power to obstruct, so I neatly crossed out that word and replaced it with a more modest goal: 'Not to cooperate.'" Next he had to decide what it meant "not to cooperate"—what he would disclose, what he would not disclose. He spent a considerable amount of time diagramming the ends and means with each goal, dividing each into "more elementary parts" until it looked like a tree.

Analysts often construct decision trees to analyze rational decision-making under conditions of uncertainty. But on closer inspection, Sharansky's tree looks suspiciously bare—in fact, it's missing a couple of branches. If Spock had been at Sharansky's side during this harrowing period, he wouldn't have let Sharansky get away with this.

Spock would have begun by observing that Sharansky appeared to have three obvious interests. First, to minimize punishment and avoid execution. Second, to join Avital in Israel. Third, to promote the Soviet Zionist movement. On hearing a statement like the quoted passage above, Spock would immediately protest that Sharansky makes no mention of any interest in saving his own life, regaining his freedom, or joining his wife in Israel. In fact, Sharansky has already cut those branches right off the tree. He appears to have jumped ahead a few steps and presumed that it would be impossible to negotiate a deal that would serve these interests at an acceptable cost—that *any* negotiated deal that even remotely served these interests would mean "submitting to the will of the KGB."

Spock would have said, "Not so fast. This sounds rather like zero-sum thinking, with strong overtones of demonization and moralism." At the very least, Spock would have insisted that Sharansky consider *all* his alternatives and weigh the pros and cons systematically. We will come back to this issue later.

Now let's return to Sharansky's thought process. If he made no deal with the KGB, what were his alternatives? There was really only one alternative: to defy the KGB and insist that his case be tried. Sharansky was very clearheaded about the possible outcomes if he went to trial. He understood that there was *no* chance that he would be acquitted. Given the reality of the Soviet system, his conviction was preordained once he was arrested and charged. The only question was the penalty. Under the Soviet statute under which he was charged, the penalty was either death or fifteen years in prison. To most utilitarian analysts, that would qualify as a terrible BATNA.

What were the odds that Sharansky would be executed? He had no way of knowing. On the one hand, the KGB clearly intended to make an example of him. Many refusenik dissidents had been arrested before, but they had been charged with the lesser crime of participating in "anti-Soviet" activities, which ordinarily carried only a five-year sentence. Sharansky was the first refusenik to be charged with a capital crime, and the KGB never let him forget it. Indeed, the KGB tried to give him the impression that the risk of execution was very great if he didn't cooperate. Interrogators repeatedly used the word *rasstrel:* death by gunfire. However, Sharansky also knew that his captors had an incentive to exaggerate this risk in order to make him confess.

Sharansky's own perception of the risk of execution fluctuated wildly during the sixteen months of his pretrial imprisonment and interrogation. Initially, he thought a death sentence was extremely unlikely— little more than a theoretical possibility—for two reasons. First, the Soviet regime of the 1970s was imposing capital punishment far less often than in the Stalinist period, when many dissidents had been summarily executed. Second, Sharansky was well-known in the West and knew that Avital would do everything possible to ensure that his case received continuing publicity. He reasoned that the KGB could not afford to kill him or keep him completely hidden from the outside world because they would have to provide some proof to the media that he was alive. For the same reason, he believed that they would likely not kill his parents and brother, who remained in the Soviet Union.

But later Sharansky came to feel that the threat of execution was real. At a critical time shortly before the trial, when the KGB tried hardest to coerce him, they applied a variety of psychological pressures to make him believe that *rasstrel* was a substantial possibility. His cellmate, a likely KGB collaborator, continually made sardonic jokes about how the executioner would soon smear Sharansky's head with iodine (to mark the target for the bullet) if he kept up his stubborn refusal to deal with the authorities.

The KGB reinforced these "jokes" with their own comments. One of the more sophisticated interrogators, named Volodin, made statements such as:

> We tolerated you for a long time. We warned you and your friends. But even our patience has its limits. You ought to know our Soviet history. In every case where somebody was charged with crimes such as yours and did not confess and repent, he was executed. Well, not every case. There were times where there was no death penalty, and the accused received twenty-five years.

We're not threatening you. I'm merely explaining your situation, which is my duty as an investigator.

Assuming he escaped the firing squad, however, Sharansky knew he could count on a long prison sentence. This, too, carried great risk and uncertainty. Because of the harsh conditions in Soviet prisons and work camps, he might not survive. Even if he stayed alive, he might not survive psychologically; he feared that at some point in his incarceration, the KGB would finally break him and extract a confession. In his calmer moments, he thought the KGB would eventually let him go, perhaps in a prisoner swap with the West or out of sheer pressure from world opinion. But he had no idea whether this would happen in five, thirteen, or thirty years.

Did Sharansky have a realistic sense of what kind of negotiated deal might be possible? The answer is yes. For the sixteen months between his arrest and his trial, Sharansky was continuously subjected to KGB interrogation. Reasonably early in the process he got the first hint of the kind of deal the KGB might offer if he were prepared to negotiate.

[The interrogator's] tactic was to tell me about two other prisoners he had recently dealt with who had decided to cooperate with their investigators. They were both foreigners, a Dutchman and a Frenchman, and were arrested for passing out dissident literature. As I could see from the protocols of their interrogation [which the KGB shared with him], each had loudly insisted on his rights, but soon recanted. Then, after returning home, both men had repudiated their confessions, and the Dutchman had even written a book about his imprisonment. [The interrogator's] message was obvious: recant, and you, too, will be released. Then you can say whatever you like.

Later the KGB was even more explicit:

Our only goal is to defend state interests. You're young, and your wife is waiting for you in Israel. If you help us suppress the anti-government activity of the Zionists and the so-called dissidents, you'll receive a very short sentence—maybe two or three years. Perhaps you can even be freed right after the trial. We can make a deal about everything. We are not judges, of course, but we do have some influence in the courtroom.

The precise terms of a negotiated deal were not spelled out. Exactly how short a sentence would he be offered? Would his parents and his brother be allowed to emigrate as well? Would a confession and general renunciation of the Soviet Zionist movement be enough? Or would the KGB also require that Sharansky reveal information that might jeopardize specific Soviet Zionists who had been his colleagues? Sharansky believed that once he made *any* concessions, the KGB would "own him," that he would be forced down a slippery slope and would need to make further and further concessions. Obviously, the scope of Sharansky's required cooperation would rationally affect his assessment of whether to make a deal. But without entering into negotiations, there would be no way to explore the KGB's "bottom line."

Suppose an acceptable deal could be made that required Sharansky to do no more than confess and generally renounce the Soviet Zionist movement. Could the KGB be trusted to uphold its end of the bargain? Sharansky said the answer was yes. Although this may be a surprising conclusion to some, he reached it logically—by thinking about the KGB's interests. He knew his enemy well. The KGB was a "repeat player" that needed to negotiate with other refuseniks. Therefore, Sharansky reasoned, the KGB had a strong interest in maintaining its reputation within the refusenik community for honoring such deals. Sharansky reports that his assessment was based on precedent: the KGB's previous dealings with refuseniks who had cooperated.

Sharansky also considered the costs of negotiating.

Sitting in my cell, I asked myself the obvious question: why *not* recant and then repudiate it after I was released? But I already knew the answer. First, any confession I made would mean betraying my friends. When [dissidents] Yakir and Krasin decided to cooperate with the authorities, it was enormously demoralizing for the dissident community. I had no desire to undermine the movements I believed in, or to do anything that would leave my fellow refuseniks and dissidents with an even greater feeling of hopelessness, or of the KGB's own impotence.

Second, I knew that the only reason that the world paid any attention to a small group of Soviet dissidents and Jewish activists was our strong moral position. While collaborating with the KGB might be understandable, it would severely compromise that stance. The moral righteousness of our struggle was our greatest asset, perhaps our *only* asset. To cooperate with the KGB would mean letting down our growing number of supporters in the free world and undermining their continued determination to help us.

Finally, on a more practical level, I knew that every time the KGB made a political arrest, it required permission from the political leadership. If I recanted, it would only make it easier for the KGB to receive permission to initiate new repressions and another round of arrests.

If you accept that Sharansky's *only* interest was promoting the dissident movement, he did an impressive job of cost-benefit analysis. As to that interest, Sharansky found the costs of negotiating unacceptable. He believed that any sign of cooperation—even if subsequently recanted—would undermine the movement. He feared that any statement he made to the KGB might be twisted and used to implicate his compatriots in some fabricated crime. He also feared that the movement might lose Western support if its leaders were exposed as collaborators. He concluded that he would better serve the movement by resisting the KGB, and even becoming a martyr if necessary.

Spock would not quickly dismiss this conclusion as irrational. He might question some of Sharansky's predictions and assessments, and he might even caution Sharansky against grandiosity. (How could Sharansky be so sure that the movement would be better served if resistance led to his death and martyrdom?) But if we accept that Sharansky's primary interest was the Zionist movement, Spock would have to agree that noncooperation met that interest better than negotiation. Indeed, it strengthened the movement by showing the world that Jewish dissident leaders could not be corrupted by the Soviet regime.

But something remains a puzzle. Why did Sharansky so completely ignore his other interests in this calculus? Why didn't they even count enough to be mentioned? Given how much Sharansky detested the Soviet regime, surely he had *some* desire to get out of prison and join

Avital in Israel, where he could raise a family, speak freely, and further promote the movement. *Rationally, it doesn't make sense.*

And Sharansky would agree.

In April 2004, he gave an interview at the University of California, Berkeley, that shed new light on his decision-making process.[7] When asked how he decided what course of action to follow when imprisoned by the KGB, his answer had nothing to do with chess games or rational analysis.

The source of his resistance, he said, was a "*feeling* that as long as you continue saying no, you're a free person. . . . The moment you say to them 'yes,' you will go back again to that slavery of the loyal Soviet citizen." Sharansky added that this "*intuitive, automatic feeling*"—this desire "to continue being free" and "to enjoy [his] inner freedom in prison"—was "the *basis of [his] resistance*" (emphasis added). In fact, the basis of his decision was "irrational."

But reason and logic also played an important role in implementing his goal.

[I]t is very dangerous to rely only on intuition, on non-rational things. As a religious, rational person, I was relying on my instincts, but as a scientist I had to rationalize these instincts. I had to explain to myself, rationally, why I should not cooperate with them. I had to make sure that I was controlling my behavior during interrogations, in spite of the fear, which they could insert in me, threatening to sentence me to death. That's why I developed the whole system of rationalization, of what are my aims and means.

He makes a similar point about the decision tree he created in prison. In looking back at that tree now, he says in his memoir,

[It] seems like pseudo-science, a pathetic attempt to impose order on my racing and chaotic mind. But at the time it was tremendously important, as the familiar terminology from my scientific training helped me adjust to my new reality. After hours of scattered thoughts, I was finally able to organize my impulses under the rubric of a logical plan. This alone was comforting, and gave me a sense of control.

In other words, he is admitting that he rigged the analysis. His desire to survive, which favored negotiation, was so powerful that he was afraid he would sacrifice his principles. So he simply removed that "interest" from the equation.

He was very much caught in the Faustian tension I described earlier: a conflict between pragmatism and conscience. And he is telling us, with remarkable frankness, how he managed that tension. He used the intuitive, feeling part of his brain to decide what his goal should be, and then went back and manipulated the analysis so it would lead him to the "right" conclusion.[8]

The "feelings" that were so decisive here relate to self-respect, moral purpose, and identity. Spock's analysis cannot easily capture these factors, but they are very powerful motivators in human life. Indeed, a constant theme in the memoir was the importance Sharansky attached to maintaining his self-respect and not allowing the KGB or the system to humiliate him. "When I was stripped and searched, I decided it was best to treat my captors like the weather. A storm can cause you problems, and sometimes those problems can be humiliating. But the storm itself doesn't humiliate you. Once I understood this, I realized that nothing they did could humiliate me. I could only humiliate myself— by doing something I might later be ashamed of." He turned this thought into a kind of mantra: "[N]othing they do can humiliate me, I alone can humiliate myself."

As for the traps we mentioned earlier, they too played an important role. It appears that Sharansky used the *negative* traps as a survival tactic.

Take demonization, for example. Sharansky consciously repressed any impulse to empathize with his interrogators, or even to think they might in any way have any of his interests at heart. When Sharansky overheard his interrogators chitchatting among themselves about their families and children, he told himself that he must resist the natural impulse to realize that outside the prison the KGB personnel might be normal people.

What worried me most about my isolation was that if it continued I would inevitably, perhaps even unconsciously, start adapting myself to the world of my interrogators. And once that process began, helped along by my fear of being killed and by [his cellmate's] constant chatter about the possibility of reaching an agreement with the KGB, I would gradually abandon my own world and my own values. The next step was all too clear: I would begin to "understand" my captors, and would try to reach an accord with them. Unless I stopped this process, it was only a matter of time before I succumbed.

To counteract that impulse, Sharansky demonized the Soviet regime in sweeping and absolute terms. He viewed the regime as evil and soulless, oppressing not only him but his community—the Soviet Jews—and more broadly, the entire Soviet population.

Sharansky also appears to have used the zero-sum trap to strengthen his resolve. He viewed every interaction with the KGB in purely competitive terms. In a chess game, there cannot be two winners. If your opponent wins, by definition you lose. And vice versa. He genuinely loved to do battle. He saw himself as supremely intelligent, and he relished the feeling that he could outsmart and defeat his captors. Sharansky did not want to see the "evil" regime win on anything, no matter how trivial. He refused to negotiate with the KGB even about receiving care packages in prison, or about receiving fewer days in a punishment cell in return for simply conversing with an interrogator.

Finally, his extreme moralism and self-righteousness, mixed with apparent narcissism, appear to have helped him fight the fear and loneliness of life in the Gulag. Sharansky told himself that when even one individual cannot be co-opted, the entire Soviet regime is undermined. He saw himself as waging a moral battle in which he alone held the key to victory. If he did not cooperate, he won and the KGB lost. It was as if he believed that if he gave up, his whole purpose in life—his struggle against the Soviets for Jewish liberation—would be shattered.

He had little use for fellow dissidents who could not maintain this standard. In the Gulag, he confronted a former colleague, another Jewish dissident, Mark Morozov, who was negotiating with the KGB. Morozov wanted desperately to get out of captivity, and he justified his cooperation with the KGB by arguing that he would be more valuable to the Zionist movement on the outside than in prison. Sharansky felt both pity and contempt for him. His encounter with Morozov reaffirmed his intuition that "without firm moral principles it was impossible to withstand the pressure of the KGB. If you're a captive of your own fear, you'll not only believe any nonsense, but you'll even invent nonsense of your own in order to justify your behavior."

After his trial, as he left the detention prison where the KGB had tormented him for sixteen months, Sharansky saw that prison as "the place where I had emerged victorious, defended my freedom, retained my spiritual independence against the kingdom of lies, and reinforced my connection with Israel and with [my wife]." On his way to serving a thirteen-year sentence, he felt joy in having exercised his freedom by speaking the truth at the trial.

In the ensuing years of imprisonment, Sharansky continued to demonstrate extraordinary discipline and courage. With the benefit of hindsight, there can be no doubt that his refusal to cooperate accomplished exactly what he hoped: to increase worldwide pressure on the Soviet regime.

Now we return to the heart of the matter. What constitutes a wise decision?

In the Sharansky case, one could quibble with whether his decision was rational or not. Cost-benefit analysis would hardly *require* him to risk his life and liberty for the Soviet Jewish cause. His choice to resist was courageous, even heroic. And in my view, it was also wise. I say this for two reasons: First, he did not simply rely on his moral intuitions. He understood the risks. Second, he alone bore the costs of resistance.[9]

Using these criteria, what can we say about the Bikuta case? You, too, have thought through the costs and benefits of negotiation. Whatever the outcome, this will not be a knee-jerk decision. But will you alone bear the risks? Hardly. You are a CEO, not a political prisoner. You are a representative acting on behalf of a corporation and its stakeholders. The costs of your decision will be borne not just by you, but by Evelyn, Fred, and the venture investors. You are not entitled to impose your personal values on them. If you can persuade your board of directors to share your moral convictions, by all means, take the high road. *That* would be a wise decision. But I believe there is reason to be deeply concerned whenever an agent or representative allows personal morality to override a rational analysis favoring negotiation—even with a devil.

I have introduced you to the tension that arises when pragmatic and moral demands conflict. I've used two examples: one that I hope you will never encounter (Sharansky) and one that may remind you of conflicts you've already faced.

This tension cannot be resolved; it can only be managed. It can be rationalized away, but I'm not going to let myself (or you) off the hook that easily. This is a real dilemma, and you will see it come up repeatedly throughout the book. In the next chapter our protagonist decided to manage the tension in a very different way.

PART II

Global Devils

FOUR

Rudolf Kasztner:
Bargaining with the Nazis

Natan Sharansky's story had a happy ending. After risking his life by refusing to negotiate with the KGB, he won his freedom and was celebrated as a hero.

Rudolf Kasztner made the opposite decision. As a Jewish leader in Nazi-occupied Hungary during World War II, he chose to bargain with Nazi devils—including SS colonel Adolf Eichmann—in an effort to save Jewish lives. Kasztner's negotiations succeeded in saving some lives, but his story is infinitely more complicated than Sharansky's and presents some of the most difficult questions in this book. Were Kasztner's decisions wise?

Rudolf (Rezsö) Kasztner[1] was born in 1906 in Kolozsvár, Transylvania, a proud, cosmopolitan city of sixty thousand. The city was part of the kingdom of Hungary and had a significant Jewish community.[2] Kasztner's parents were successful merchants. Kasztner, educated at the elite Jewish gymnasium, was a gifted student with a facility for languages.

In addition to his native Magyar (Hungarian), he learned to speak German, French, Latin, and Romanian, the last of which became essential. Before he graduated from high school, his hometown became part of Romania—a less hospitable country for Jews—and was known as Cluj.[3] The young Kasztner also showed other talents, including a knack for maneuvering himself quickly onto center stage. At the age of fifteen, he joined a Zionist youth movement. Within a year, he was the leader of his group. After finishing high school and collecting a law degree (to please his mother), he turned to his real passions: politics, journalism, and Zionism. He took a job with a Jewish newspaper in Cluj and began to write bold political commentary, which alienated some readers but brought him to the attention of Dr. Joseph Fischer, one of the city's wealthiest and most respected Jews. Indeed, Fischer stood at the very apex of Jewish society in Cluj: he was the president of the city's Jewish Community and a member of Parliament—and thus a national spokesman for Romania's seven hundred thousand Jews.[4] It did not take long for Kasztner to become Fischer's assistant, protégé, and eventually son-in-law (when Kasztner married Fischer's daughter, Elizabeth). The two men developed a strong bond.

The Kasztner of those years was already demonstrating the strengths of character that would also become his weaknesses. "Not only was Kasztner smarter and better read than others, but he also let everyone know that he was superior in wit and knowledge. . . . Kasztner often dismissed people as stupid, incompetent, or intellectually cowardly."[5] A law school friend recalled: "He had no sense of other people's sensitivities, or he didn't care whether he alienated his friends."[6] A member of his Zionist youth group recalls him as "sharp-witted and shrewd" but unreliable: "he often made promises he couldn't keep."[7]

But he was dedicated to helping Jews in trouble. His fellow citizens were often harassed by Romanian authorities, and Kasztner "was one of the few who could deal with the authorities as an equal," writes Anna Porter.[8]

> In local government, Kasztner was remembered as a "fixer," a man others trusted to solve their problems, but he was too smart to be much loved even by those he had helped. Still, he was sought out. The Jews of [Cluj] needed someone like Kasztner to help them survive the difficult years after Transylvania was ceded to the Romanians. . . . Kasztner managed to keep in touch with bureaucrats and gentile functionaries of all political stripes. He knew whom to bribe and how much to offer, whom to flatter and how.[9]

By the late 1930s, Kasztner was also helping Jewish refugees who had fled Nazi-occupied Europe and ended up in Cluj. He raised money for them, organized food and shelter, and helped them obtain safe passage to Palestine, which was then controlled by the British. Some of this work was legal—for example, obtaining exit visas from the Romanian government—but much of it was not. The British kept strict control over entry visas to Palestine, so getting Jews aboard ships often required the liberal use of bribes. This was Kasztner's forte. He worked closely with the Jewish Agency in Palestine, which encouraged illegal immigration.[10] Anna Porter provides a vivid portrait of the Kasztner of this period:

> Kasztner was outspoken, brash, unafraid. He could be seen striding toward government offices and into police headquarters, a pale, muscular, slender man, his dark hair swept back, his well-tailored black suit stark even during the summer heat, his tie loosened over his white shirt, the collar perfectly starched. He was confident, in a hurry, his briefcase casually swinging from one hand, the other ready to wave to all his acquaintances.[11]

———

In 1940, Kasztner moved to Budapest, where his skills as a fixer would soon be needed. Kasztner's hometown of Cluj had once again become part of Hungary, and Kasztner was now a Hungarian citizen. By this time Jewish refugees had begun pouring into Budapest from Nazi-occupied Poland and Slovakia, telling of Nazi atrocities. Hungary and Nazi Germany became wartime allies in that year but Hungary retained its autonomy.[12] In comparison to Nazi-occupied Europe or Germany itself, Hungary seemed like a safe haven for Jews.

The Budapest Jewish establishment was wealthy, cultured, and among the most assimilated in Europe. Its members had dominated Hungarian industry, finance, and the professions. Some socialized with Hungarian aristocracy and had political influence. Unlike Kasztner, they considered themselves Hungarians first, and Jews second. Few in the establishment would have dreamed of moving to Palestine. Indeed, you couldn't have gotten them out of Budapest with a crowbar—a fact that was soon to contribute to their downfall. Moreover, the Jewish establishment was utterly unprepared for the needy horde of terrified Jewish refugees flooding into Hungary. Where would the refugees go? They didn't even speak Hungarian.

Kasztner, however, had grown up in the harsher climate of Romania, where Jews did not dine with the local aristocracy. He knew exactly what to do—and much of it was illegal.

Kasztner and about a dozen other "Zionist mavericks"[13] got together and formed a Relief and Rescue Committee, later known by its Hebrew name, Va'ada.[14] The Relief and Rescue Committee's core mission became the hiding and transport of Jews. Between 1941 and 1944, the committee fed and clothed refugees, obtained emigration documents (both genuine and forged), smuggled people across borders, and of course, paid bribes.

This work was made possible by an outstanding network of underground contacts—not only Zionists in other cities, but diplomats, couriers, smugglers, petty criminals, and bribable officials of every stripe—who kept them informed of what was happening to Jews elsewhere. One of the best-connected Relief and Rescue Committee founders, and a key player in this story, was Joel Brand, who in many ways was Kasztner's opposite. Where Kasztner was widely seen as an intellectual snob, Brand was a drinker, a gambler, and a "playboy" who spent most of his time in cafés and nightclubs.[15] This dissolute life had allowed him to develop an extensive network of double agents and Nazi intelligence officials who would prove useful in the days ahead.

Although the Jewish establishment disdained the Zionists and their methods, the two groups would soon come to need each other.

———————

On March 19, 1944, German troops marched into Budapest and imposed a new puppet government. In the Nazi vanguard was Adolf Eichmann, who that day celebrated his thirty-eighth birthday. An SS colonel, Eichmann was under secret orders to implement Hitler's "Final Solution" in Hungary as quickly as possible—that is, to round up seven hundred thousand Jews and transport them to death camps or forced labor camps.

Why did the Nazis invade their own ally? For two reasons: they feared that Hungary was about to negotiate a separate peace with the Allies, and they believed that Hungary was being too lenient toward its own Jews.

By this time, Germany's war efforts were faltering. The Soviets had repelled the Nazi invasion and were advancing on the eastern front.

The Allies had invaded Italy. The realization that a German defeat was a real possibility, and almost within sight, created complicated cross-currents that were difficult to read accurately at the time.

Within a day of the invasion, Nazi officials demanded a meeting with the leaders of Budapest's Jewish establishment. At the meeting, the Nazis addressed the Jewish leaders with respect and promised that as long as the Jews followed orders and didn't panic, no Jew would be harmed. These assurances fell on receptive ears. Rumors about the fate of Polish Jews had circulated widely among Hungarian Jews, but many could not believe that this could happen in a "civilised country like Hungary."[16] So when the Nazis ordered that Jewish Councils be set up throughout Hungary, ostensibly to promote a measure of Jewish self-government, the Jewish leaders complied.

Soon, however, the intended role of the Jewish Councils became clear: they were to be instruments for carrying out the Nazis' orders. Through a combination of threats and false promises, the Jewish leaders were co-opted into "contribut[ing] to the smooth running of the Holocaust." Among other things, the Jewish Councils "published the newsletters announcing Eichmann's orders, . . . delivered Jewish money and valuables to the Germans" and "compiled the lists of Jews" that would later be used for roundups and deportations.[17] When Jewish leaders protested, Eichmann assured them that these orders were simply wartime necessities and that cooperative Jews would not be in danger.[18] The Nazis were, of course, lying.

According to German records, within four months of the invasion, some 437,000 Jews from the Hungarian provinces were shipped to Auschwitz.[19] By the end of the German occupation, more than 500,000 Hungarian Jews had been killed.[20]

Much of Kasztner's work, and the critical events of this story, happened during this very short period.

———————

From the beginning of the invasion, Kasztner believed the Jewish Councils were pursuing the wrong strategy. His knowledge of Nazi procedures elsewhere—the creation of Jewish Councils, which then were enlisted in the creation of ghettos that were a prelude to mass deportations—persuaded him that Hungarian Jews were in serious danger.[21] Moreover, he knew that some Nazi officials could be bribed.

In 1942, a Jewish group in Bratislava, Slovakia, had paid the Nazis some twenty thousand dollars to stop deporting Slovakian Jews. Because the deportations had halted around the same time, the Bratislava group was firmly convinced that their bribe had been the cause of the reprieve.[22] That inspired them to concoct a much bigger plan, offering the Nazis $2 million (which they didn't have) to stop deporting Jews from other occupied countries. This scheme sputtered for lack of funds,[23] but the Relief and Rescue Committee group was well aware of it.

Kasztner thought the best approach was to contact the Nazis directly and try to negotiate protection for the Jews. But he had a problem: Whom did he represent? For whom could he speak? His first challenge was to negotiate with the Budapest Jewish establishment for permission to speak on behalf of Hungary's Jews.

Three days after the invasion, he met in an elegant café with Samuel Stern, the patrician president of the Jewish Community and the head of the Budapest Jewish Council.[24] Kasztner laid out his case: that Hungarian Jews were in danger; that Nazis were bribable, and that Zionists—not the Jewish Council—should handle this effort because they were experienced hands at this game.[25] Stern was not persuaded. Confident of his contacts with the Hungarian government, the Jewish Community leader refused to believe that his constituents could possibly meet the same fate as Polish Jews. Consequently, he expressed disinterest in receiving any assistance from the Zionists.[26]

Kasztner and his cohorts were on their own.

Through Brand's Nazi contacts, however, a meeting was soon arranged with two SS officers, both members of Eichmann's "Sonderkommando" (Special Action Commando).[27] One of these men, Captain Dieter Wisliceny, was the same Nazi who had negotiated with the Bratislava group. Kasztner and Brand thought this was a good sign.[28]

In preparing for the meeting, Kasztner and Brand focused on two goals. One was to establish the Relief and Rescue Committee as a credible negotiating partner. They couldn't claim to speak for the Jews of Hungary, so they came up with an even grander idea: they would claim to represent all of "World Jewry." They knew that many Nazis genuinely believed in a vast international conspiracy of Jews who were immensely rich and controlled the Allies and the Soviets. Kasztner and Brand decided to take full advantage of that myth—and for good measure, to claim linkage to the Bratislava group.

Their second goal was equally ambitious: to reach a deal that would protect all the Jews in Hungary. They decided to offer the Nazis $2 million—which, like the Bratislava group, they did not have—in exchange for a series of conditions.[29]

———

Before we get to the substance of this meeting, let's step back and analyze Kasztner's decision in favor of negotiation.

How did he analyze the benefits and risks? We can assume that, like Sharansky, he had a strong interest in physical survival. The best way to save his own skin would be to avoid the Nazis entirely and go into hiding or flee. But Kasztner seems to have ignored that interest. The only goal he seems to have recognized was to save as many Jewish lives as possible. No doubt because of his experience as a "fixer," he thought he could achieve that through negotiation.

He had no moral qualms about negotiating with devils. He was far too cynical for that. In fact, I think he believed that negotiating with the Nazis was justified on both pragmatic *and* moral grounds, because lives might be saved.

Did he experience any conflict between pragmatism and principle? Only to the extent that the personally safe choice—to head for the hills—would have meant *not* engaging in this negotiation. But there is no evidence he even considered that option. In fact, there is no evidence that he really did a cost-benefit analysis at all, at least one that Spock would recognize. Kasztner was a fixer, not a hider. He had been negotiating with devils all his life. That was his public identity. All his skills called for negotiation, and so did his temperament. His decision to negotiate may well have been based largely on such intuitive judgments.

So let's look more closely at his decision to negotiate with the Nazis as an occupying power. Did it make any sense? What would Spock say? We must take care to base the analysis on what was known at the time and not on how things turned out.

The sweeping deal Kasztner and Brand envisioned, if implemented, would clearly serve the interests of the entire Jewish community in Hungary. So if Spock were to advise the Relief and Rescue Committee negotiators, he would focus on implementation. He would remind Kasztner and Brand of the risks of bluffing. They had no money. They were not authorized to speak for a single Hungarian Jew, much less the

Jewish Agency in Palestine or the representatives of the American Jewish community in Switzerland. "What makes you think you can pull this off?" Spock would ask. "How confident are you of raising the money? What might be the consequences if you can't deliver?"

Kasztner would probably respond that the chances were reasonably good that money could be raised; Stern would likely help raise funds within Hungary and the balance might be secured from Jewish sources abroad—and paid over time. Playing for time was valuable.[30] In the meantime, Germany might lose the war.

Spock would then turn to the Nazi side of the bargain. Why should the Nazis agree to such a deal? Why would it be in their interests? Even if they did make a deal, there was a significant risk they wouldn't honor it. Spock would also want to know whether Wisliceny had authority to make promises on behalf of the Nazis, especially about deportation. Wisliceny might simply be taking the money for himself.

Kasztner would probably respond that, in his experience, not all Nazis were committed to exterminating Jews. Some cared little for Nazi ideology and were willing to bend the rules in exchange for cash.[31] The Bratislava episode appeared to be a prime example of this—and was presumably approved at high levels. The Nazi war machine needed money, and the Reich was under increasing international pressure to stop killing Jews. It wasn't entirely out of the question that the Reich would trade Jews for cash.

Kasztner would surely admit, however, that the whole plan was tenuous; the Relief and Rescue Committee held a very weak hand. It had no way of enforcing a deal with the Nazis, so there was substantial risk of paying a bribe and getting nothing in return.

But—and this was the key question—what were the alternatives? To Kasztner, who understood the Nazis' intentions, there were only three real alternatives to negotiation:[32] fight, flee, or hide. None was feasible on an *organized*, massive scale. Armed resistance was hopeless: Hungarian Jews had hardly any weapons, most of the young men had already been sent to work camps, and the Jewish leadership opposed open resistance as too risky. Flight en masse was impossible. Much of nearby Yugoslavia was occupied by the Nazis and the border was heavily patrolled. Individuals might be able to escape to nearby Romania, but it was hard to imagine spiriting Jews en masse across that border. The final possibility was to go into hiding. But outside of Budapest, there was nowhere to hide large numbers of Jews. Certainly not in open fields, or small towns where everyone knew each other.

So what would Spock say? Having weighed all of these factors, I believe he would conclude that it was reasonable for the Relief and Rescue Committee to see whether it could negotiate a deal with the Nazis. The prospects of success weren't great, and Nazi promises were hardly worth banking on, but it was a desperate situation. Why not try? I suspect, however, that Spock would have urged Kasztner to have a backup plan, a "Plan B." The alternatives to negotiation were terrible, but the best of the lot would involve spreading the alarm and warning Jews to avoid the ghettos and Nazi transports at all costs; better to go underground or flee.

The Relief and Rescue Committee's first meeting with the Nazis took place on April 5, 1944. Two Nazis were present: Captain Dieter Wisliceny and another SS officer. Brand and Kasztner, introducing themselves as agents of World Jewry, immediately put an offer on the table by referring to the negotiations in Bratislava. They offered $2 million, with an immediate down payment of $200,000, subject to "four stipulations": (1) no ghettos or concentration camps in Hungary; (2) no mass executions or pogroms; (3) no deportations from Hungary; and (4) permission for all Jews who held valid entry certificates to emigrate to Palestine.[33]

Wisliceny's response was a masterful blend of promises and quasi-promises. He appeared to accept at least one of the conditions, explicitly stating, "We can guarantee that there will be no deportations out of Hungary." His response to the other terms was ambiguous. For $2 million, he said, it might be possible to prevent ghettoization and to allow some Jews to emigrate. But over time, $2 million would not be enough. There would have to be more payments later. Furthermore, to demonstrate goodwill, the Relief and Rescue Committee would have to deliver the $200,000 down payment within a week.[34] "Your people will not be harmed," he promised, "so long as our negotiations are going on."[35]

Brand and Kasztner agreed to raise the money but added another condition: in order to coordinate the fund-raising effort, they and their colleagues would need to move freely around the city. The SS officers agreed and gave the Relief and Rescue Committee officers special "immunity passes" that exempted them from the restrictions that applied to other Jews. (Thus, for the rest of the war, Kasztner would not be required to wear a yellow star. He would also be allowed to use cars and phones and to largely ignore curfews and travel restrictions.[36])

Kasztner also demanded a good-faith gesture from the Nazis. "World Jewry," he explained, would want proof that its money was actually helping Jews; it would "want to see results."[37] To this end, Kasztner proposed that one hundred Jews be allowed to leave Hungary for Romania, where the Jewish Agency had chartered a ship that would take them to Turkey and then to Palestine. Such a gesture from the Nazis, Kasztner asserted confidently, "would mean that we could ask for much more money from our people in Constantinople and Jerusalem."[38]

Wisliceny made no promises but agreed to consider the matter. "Meanwhile," he suggested, "you can prepare a list of the people you want to send."[39] Thus, almost as an afterthought, a seed was planted that would later blossom into what became known as the "Kasztner Train."[40]

As Kasztner had hoped, Samuel Stern, the leader of the Budapest Jewish establishment, made a complete about-face and agreed to raise the down payment. By now, alarmed by the Nazis' anti-Jewish measures, Stern also authorized Kasztner to negotiate with the SS on behalf of all Hungarian Jews.[41]

But over the next few weeks, even as the Relief and Rescue Committee was delivering the down payment in installments, Kasztner began receiving terrible news. Through sources in German counterintelligence he learned that, despite all public claims to the contrary, the Nazis planned to ghettoize *all Jews in Hungary* and then deport them.[42]

Kasztner immediately looked for Wisliceny, who was nowhere to be found. The other SS officials were no help. Kasztner accused them of reneging on Wisliceny's promise, but they just shrugged and feigned ignorance. However, they still wanted to negotiate. For the down payment already delivered, they said, perhaps a small number of Jews could be allowed to leave Hungary.[43] A scant day later, the same officials announced to Kasztner that "as a gesture of good will," their superiors had given permission to allow six hundred Jewish families to emigrate—half from the provinces and half from Budapest.[44] Once again, they suggested that the Relief and Rescue Committee draw up a list.

Kasztner was alarmed. What had happened to the original deal? One moment they had been talking about saving the entire Jewish community; now they were down to only six hundred families. Kasztner was determined to find Wisliceny and confront him.[45] But before he could do so, he was distracted by another stunning development.

On April 25, Eichmann summoned Brand to his office and made a proposal. (Kasztner was annoyed at having been passed over. Why Brand?) Brand later described the meeting as surreal: Eichmann chain-smoked, paced around the room, and bragged about having rounded up all the Jews in Poland, Czechoslovakia, and Austria.[46] Finally getting to the point, Eichmann said that the Reich needed trucks for its war effort and was willing to trade one million Jews for ten thousand winterized trucks. (This proposal would come to be known as *blut gegen waren*—"blood for goods.") Eichmann instructed Brand to go to Istanbul, in neutral Turkey, to present this offer to "World Jewry."

"I want you to go abroad and get in direct touch with your people and with representatives of the Allied powers. Then come back to me with a concrete proposal."[47]

Brand left the meeting in shock. He thought the deal was preposterous. How could "World Jewry" produce ten thousand trucks? It would require the full cooperation of the Western Allies, who would never allow the Nazis to receive war materiel in the middle of a war. What was Eichmann up to?

In his postwar report of these events, Kasztner recalled asking himself: "What was behind these suddenly generous offers on one side, and the absurd demands on the other side? Were they lunatics or clumsy plotters, who would make such proposals?"[48] Ultimately, however, it was decided to play along and attempt to meet Eichmann's terms.

In early May, Kasztner finally got permission to travel to Cluj, where Wisliceny had been reassigned.[49] He soon discovered what Wisliceny was doing there. Local police had just begun rounding up Jews and moving them into a brickyard—a makeshift ghetto. Wisliceny himself was supervising the effort. When Kasztner confronted him about his earlier promise, Wisliceny admitted that he really had no authority to prevent deportations. "[Eichmann] gave me the dirtiest job, and I am now the one who has to transfer the Jews into Ghettos. . . . I wear a uniform, I must follow orders."[50]

"At least tell me the truth," Kasztner insisted. Was it true, as he had heard, that the Nazis planned to deport *all* the Jews in Hungary? Wisliceny waffled but promised to find out.[51] In the meantime, he said, Kasztner could prepare the list of six hundred families who would emigrate in exchange for the ransom already paid.[52]

Let's step back again and ask: What was going on? Was it time to reassess? There is no evidence that Kasztner asked himself this question, but Spock would have strongly recommended it. The original decision to negotiate with the Nazis had been made in March. It was now May and Kasztner had new information. The Nazis had lied to his face about the deportations. His original, glorious deal was dead. He had paid a substantial bribe and so far had nothing to show for it. Eichmann was pushing a bizarre proposal that would probably go nowhere (although it might allow the Jews to buy valuable time). Wisliceny and his cohorts were dangling a carrot—the prospect of emigration for a small group—but they weren't trustworthy.

Spock would say: Slow down. Think. What should be your strategy? And what should you tell your family and the Jewish leaders in Cluj?

Kasztner would probably respond that he *was* thinking, but that he couldn't exactly slow down. As he would write later, events were happening so fast that "even thoughts were too slow."[53] In that respect he was right: the ghettoization process in Cluj went so quickly that it was completed in a week.

What did Kasztner do while he was in Cluj? He met with local Jewish leaders, including his father-in-law, but it is not clear what he told them. Years later, the exact content of these discussions would become highly controversial. How much did Kasztner know about the Nazis' plans for Hungary, and how clearly did he warn his fellow Jews about the disaster that was coming? Although many Hungarian Jews had heard reports about Nazi atrocities elsewhere, and therefore had reason to understand that they, too, were in danger, others didn't know—or refused to believe—just how bad things were. Kasztner was much better informed than most. He knew from reliable sources that the Nazis planned to deport all Hungarian Jews. He also knew that

Auschwitz was an extermination camp, not simply a forced labor camp as the Nazis claimed, and that deportation to Auschwitz was a probable prelude to extermination.[54]

Kasztner later claimed that he *had* warned the Jewish leadership of Cluj, and his family and friends, of precisely this danger. Others said he had not.[55] What is undisputed is that no dire warning ever reached the rest of the community and that no Jews were advised, by Kasztner or the Cluj leadership, to flee Hungary or go into hiding.

Kasztner did, however, tell the Jewish leaders about his negotiations with the Nazis. He said he was working on a deal that might allow some Jews, including a number from Cluj, to emigrate. One can easily imagine Kasztner, the fixer, wanting to hold out hope to those closest to him. One can also imagine his tendency to believe that if anyone could pull off a miracle, he could.

Kasztner decided not to abandon the negotiation track, despite Wisliceny's broken promise. Indeed, I think he was burning to go up the chain of command. To hell with Wisliceny . . . *How could he get to Eichmann?*

With the Nazis' help, Brand left for Istanbul on May 17 to carry Eichmann's proposal to a representative of the Jewish Agency.[56] On Eichmann's orders, Brand was forced to leave his wife, Hansi, behind as a hostage. No member of the Relief and Rescue Committee had much confidence that the deal would succeed, but they hoped that by keeping the prospect of negotiations alive, they could stall for time and perhaps stop the deportations.

That hope would prove to be misplaced. Nothing ever came of the Brand mission, and Brand himself was never able to return to Hungary. In the meantime, mass deportations of Jews to Auschwitz began on May 15 and continued at horrifying speed. But for about a month, the Jewish Agency pretended to take the "Jews for trucks" deal seriously, and these sham negotiations gave Kasztner the opportunity he needed to take Brand's place in Budapest. First he began an affair with Brand's wife, Hansi. It was Hansi who served as the bridge to Eichmann. Through her own contacts, she set up Kasztner's first meeting with Eichmann and attended it with him.

Thus Kasztner was finally able to establish himself with Eichmann as the chief agent of World Jewry in Hungary. The relationship between the two men would last for the remainder of the war and test all of Kasztner's skills.

At their first meeting, Eichmann—who Kasztner knew "ruled over life and death"[57]—greeted Kasztner and Hansi with characteristic bullying, boasting that he had served as commissar of Jewish affairs in Austria and Czechoslovakia. Abruptly, however, Eichmann grew amiable and spoke of his support of Zionism, including the Jews' right to have their own state.[58] Eventually, they got down to business.

Kasztner tried to persuade Eichmann to stop the deportations while Brand carried on the negotiations in Istanbul. He was unsuccessful.

Kasztner then reminded Eichmann of the promises his subordinates had made: that six hundred Jewish families would be allowed to leave Hungary. Kasztner cannily linked this prior agreement with the Brand mission, and this connection, at least, he succeeded in making stick. World Jewry needed a showing of good faith, Kasztner argued. If Eichmann couldn't follow through on a simple promise to release six hundred families, there would be no hope of progress on the "Jews for trucks" deal.

Eichmann agreed to nothing at that first meeting, but he asked Kasztner to prepare a list of six hundred Jewish families who might be sent by train out of Hungary. On May 22, Eichmann explicitly agreed that six hundred families might be spared.[59]

In the following weeks, Kasztner and Eichmann played a game of "double-bluff,"[60] both sides playing for time, each aware that the other was unlikely to meet his commitments. Kasztner falsely claimed that Brand was making progress with the Allies in Istanbul and argued that if the deportations continued, Eichmann would have no Jews left to trade. Eichmann pretended to negotiate the "blood for goods" deal while herding ten to fifteen thousand Jews a day into boxcars for transport to Poland. Eichmann proved to be a thoroughly unreliable negotiating partner, constantly making promises and breaking them. In Hansi Brand's words, "What we had established on one day . . . the next day was found to be nothing at all."[61]

A showdown came in early June when Eichmann reneged on yet another promise—to bring several hundred provincial Jews to Budapest for inclusion on the emigration train. Kasztner decided to push back.

Instead of confronting Eichmann directly, Kasztner taunted him by making provocative statements to two of his officers. To one, Kasztner complained that Eichmann had broken his word and that Kasztner was going to inform Istanbul that all further discussions should be ended. To another, he declared that Eichmann's behavior was unworthy of an SS officer.

As expected, these comments got back to Eichmann, who summoned Kasztner to his office and threw a "fit of rage." Kasztner reports that he simply didn't respond. Eventually Eichmann calmed down and asked Kasztner, "What do you really want?"

"I must insist on our agreements being kept. Will you bring the people suggested by us from the provinces to Budapest?"

Eichmann retorted, "Once I have said no, it's no!"

"Then there's no point in continuing to negotiate," Kasztner said. He stood up and started to leave the room.

Eichmann responded with a threat: "You are a bundle of nerves, Kasztner. I will send you to Theresienstadt[62] to recover. Or do you prefer Auschwitz?"

Kasztner shot back: "It would be pointless. Nobody else would take my place."[63]

Hours of haggling followed, during which a significant shift occurred. Eichmann stopped talking about Jews from the "provinces" generally, and started talking about Jews from Cluj, Kasztner's hometown. Was this a new aspect of the devil's bargain? The record is not clear on whether Eichmann or Kasztner initiated this change in emphasis, but eventually Eichmann relented and said: "All right. The [Cluj] people are coming to Budapest."[64]

By the end of the meeting, Kasztner had negotiated the number of Cluj Jews up to about 200, but eventually the number rose to 388. (Later, Jews from other provinces would be added.)[65]

In retrospect, commentators say that Kasztner was uniquely suited to the task of dealing with Eichmann. Although Kasztner often felt nothing but despair, his smooth façade never cracked in Eichmann's presence. He got invaluable help from Hansi. Early on, Kasztner had told Hansi that he was terrified of Eichmann, who chain-smoked in Kasztner's presence and never offered Kasztner a cigarette. Hansi suggested that Kasztner bring his own cigarettes, and advised him to chain-smoke as well.[66] Kasztner took her advice and his bravado won

Eichmann's grudging admiration and respect. As Eichmann recalled in his memoir:

> This Dr. Kasztner was a young man about my age, an ice-cold lawyer and a fanatical Zionist. . . . Except perhaps for the first few sessions, Kasztner never came to me fearful of the Gestapo strongman. We negotiated entirely as equals. . . . When he was with me, Kasztner smoked cigarets, as though he were in a coffeehouse. While we talked he would smoke one aromatic cigaret after another, taking them from a silver case and lighting them with a little silver lighter. With his great polish and reserve he would have made an ideal Gestapo officer himself.[67]

For Kasztner, dealing with Eichmann's tirades and treachery was easy compared to the task of drawing up "the list." Here was another aspect of the devil's bargain, which Kasztner may not have anticipated. Which Jews should be chosen for emigration, and how should they be selected?

It was an agonizing and chaotic process. Kasztner later called it a "merciless chore."[68] Not wanting to take on the burden alone, he asked a small group of members from the Relief and Rescue Committee to direct the effort, with input from other Jewish leaders. In an effort to be fair, the committee established categories for selection, such as "deserving figures in Jewish public life" and "widows and orphans of slave labourers."[69] Not surprisingly, this process sparked intense conflict; committee members were barraged with desperate appeals and charges of favoritism. Meanwhile, Kasztner successfully haggled with Eichmann to expand the list to 1,300 people in exchange for a ransom of a thousand dollars per head. To raise the money, the committee created a new category: Jews who could pay far more than their pro rata share. In this way, 150 wealthy Jews bought their way onto the list and subsidized the others, who had no money.

The list was in constant flux, and the Relief and Rescue Committee did not have full control over it. Some people declined a spot on the train, fearing that the deal was a Nazi trap. Others on the list were deported before they could take advantage of the opportunity. Still other names were added by Nazi officials in exchange for individual bribes.

And then there was SS colonel Kurt Becher, an opportunist who was soon to play a crucial role in Kasztner's life. Becher's rank was equal to Eichmann's—both reported to Reichsführer SS Heinrich Himmler and had similar clout. But they had opposite temperaments. Whereas Eichmann was an ideologue who wanted to deport every last Jew, Becher was a pragmatist who cared only about his own career, self-enrichment, and survival after the war. Recognizing the train as a gold mine for himself, Becher maneuvered his way into the negotiation and reserved fifty places on the train, which he sold separately to Jews who bribed him directly. There is no evidence that Kasztner objected to this development. To the contrary, Kasztner recognized in Becher someone he could do business with. In the coming months, Kasztner would find Becher a more cooperative partner than Eichmann and would work increasingly closely with him.

On June 30, some 1,684 Jews finally left Budapest on the "Kasztner Train." But the passengers' ordeal continued for months more. Again Eichmann broke his word. The train's destination was not Spain or Switzerland, as promised, but a concentration camp in Bergen-Belsen, Germany, where the émigrés were held hostage as "privileged" inmates.

Kasztner was in despair. He had intended the train to be the first step in a much larger rescue. But while he had been matching wits with the wily Eichmann, the latter had succeeded in shipping off to Auschwitz nearly all of the Jews outside of Budapest.[70] Only about 250,000 Jews remained in Hungary, nearly all in Budapest. And now Kasztner's train was trapped in Bergen-Belsen.

But Kasztner did not give up. Eventually, by December 1944, nearly everyone on the train made it to safety in Switzerland.[71] Shortly thereafter, Kasztner joined his wife, Elizabeth, in Switzerland. But their reunion was temporary.

Rather than remain in safety, Kasztner returned to Nazi-occupied Europe to try to save more Jews, a mission he pursued until the war's last days. In April 1945, as the Nazis were in their final retreat, Kasztner conducted a final rescue effort with Becher. Himmler had offered to make Becher responsible for final oversight of various concentration camps. And here Kasztner made what would later prove to be another devil's bargain. He persuaded Becher to accept this duty so that together they could save Jewish lives before the now-inevitable German defeat. In exchange, Kasztner promised to help save Becher's skin by telling the Allies about his good deeds. Becher agreed. So the SS officer Becher and the Jew Kasztner (traveling with German papers) went from camp to camp, trying to prevent further wholesale deaths of inmates by asking that the camps be handed peacefully over to the Allies.[72]

In the end, what did Kasztner achieve? This question has never been definitively answered. Certainly, his negotiation efforts were indispensable in saving the nearly seventeen hundred Jews who reached Switzerland via the Kasztner train. But Kasztner also had some luck. The release of the Jews from Bergen-Belsen was very much tied to Himmler's desire, at the end of the war, to negotiate a separate peace with the Western Allies. Kasztner also claimed credit for saving tens of thousands more Jews, but these claims are harder to assess. He was very proud of a deal he negotiated with Eichmann in which, for a money bribe, Eichmann agreed to send some seventeen thousand Jews to a work camp instead of to Auschwitz. But as it turned out, Eichmann was independently under orders to send Jewish laborers to that work camp, so some commentators believe that Eichmann outsmarted Kasztner by making him pay for something that would have happened anyway.[73] As to Kasztner's negotiations with the Nazis on behalf of other Jews—including those in Budapest[74] and concentration camps—it is hard to determine with any precision what difference his intervention made. Historians differ in how much credit they give Kasztner for saving these additional lives, but most acknowledge that Kasztner played a role, and possibly a significant one.

THREE TRIBUNALS JUDGE KASZTNER

When the war ended, Kasztner had no doubts about his own conduct. In his own mind, he was a hero. He continued to work for the Jewish cause, remaining in Europe for more than two years, participating in the Nuremberg trials of German war criminals, working to recover Jewish property stolen by the Germans, and trying to track down Eichmann so he could be brought to justice. Kasztner also made good on his promise to SS officer Becher, who was arrested by the Allies shortly after the war's end. Kasztner submitted an affidavit that credited Becher with saving many Jews, and as a result Becher was soon released.

Kasztner also sought broader recognition for his accomplishments in negotiating with the Nazis. But instead, he found himself the object of ugly innuendos and even open attacks. Critics accused him of collaborating with the Nazis and enriching himself in the process. His accusers were a "mixed bunch . . . personal or ideological enemies, survivors who had lost relatives or had themselves suffered in the camps, and even some members of [the Kasztner train]." [75]

These attacks would last his entire life, and questions about his actions would prove so persistent that even today there is no consensus. During his lifetime, three different tribunals would consider charges against him and each would come to a different conclusion.

The first inquiry arose soon after the war at Kasztner's insistence. Furious about the nasty rumors swirling around him,[76] he demanded in 1946 that the World Zionist Congress in Basel, Switzerland, conduct hearings in a "court of honour." [77] A fact-finding committee was appointed and Kasztner prepared a 200-page report of his wartime activities.[78] But after two meetings, the committee was unable to reach a decision.[79] It was hardly an exoneration.

In 1947, just before Israel attained statehood, Kasztner moved to Israel with his wife and infant daughter, where the second inquiry was destined to occur. At first, things went reasonably well for him in the new state. Although anonymous rumors about his past Nazi "collaboration" continued occasionally to haunt him, he successfully established a new public life. He was welcomed by the governing Mapai (later Labor) Party and appointed to a succession of government posts.[80] But Israeli politics were deeply affected by the Holocaust and Kasztner was an open target. Within a few years he became the center of a sensational trial.

It started with Mikhail Grunwald, a bitter, right-wing crank who wrote an obscure mimeographed newsletter. In 1952, Grunwald published a tirade about Kasztner:

> Dr. Rudolph Kasztner must be liquidated! For three years I have been waiting for the moment to unmask this careerist who grew fat on Hitler's lootings and murders. Because of his criminal machinations and collaborations with the Nazis I consider him implicated in the murder of our beloved brothers.[81]

The whole thing would probably have blown over if the Mapai party had not been feeling vulnerable. Grunwald's salvo was partly an attack on the governing party, and the attorney general decided to file charges of criminal libel against Grunwald. That meant he needed Kasztner as the government's star witness. He gave Kasztner a choice: either act to clear his name or resign his government post.

Kasztner was ambivalent about the prospect of a trial in which he would be the central focus.[82] He saw the wisdom of ignoring Grunwald's insults, but he didn't want to resign his position and he wanted to fight back. Moreover, Kasztner, who always loved the limelight, assumed that the trial would "shine a light on his actions" and win him the recognition he felt he deserved. So finally he agreed to fight Grunwald, and the government filed criminal libel charges against Grunwald.[83]

The trial proved to be an unmitigated disaster for Kasztner.

Grunwald's newsletter rant had been a confused jumble of charges, but the trial judge organized them into four potential instances of libel: that Kasztner had (1) collaborated with the Nazis; (2) worked to save his own relatives and a few elite Jews while leaving the masses to die; (3) stolen money intended for rescue operations; and (4) helped Becher evade justice after the war.

The trial lasted for months and there were scores of witnesses. A good deal of the testimony focused on May 3, 1944—the day Kasztner had spent talking with the Jewish leadership in his hometown of Cluj. At issue was what Kasztner had said in those discussions. Did he simply tell the Jews about the train, or did he also warn them of the danger of deportation?

Although Grunwald was technically the defendant in the case, he had a brilliant right-wing lawyer who successfully turned the trial into an indictment of Kasztner—and by extension, of the entire Israeli political establishment for its failure to do more during World War II to save European Jewry.

In 1955, Judge Benjamin Halevi delivered a 240-page judgment that has been called "one of the most heartless in the history of Israel, perhaps the most heartless ever."[84] The judge not only cleared Grunwald of all but one of the libel charges,[85] but he took the opportunity to condemn Kasztner for having actively colluded in the Holocaust.[86] In the judge's view, Kasztner had known full well about the Nazis' extermination plans but had deliberately withheld this knowledge from the Jewish masses. Indeed, the judge found that Kasztner had made a deal with the Nazis, a quid pro quo: in order to save a small number of privileged

Jews—the Kasztner train—Kasztner had agreed *not* to warn the larger Jewish community of the true danger they were in. The judge framed this deal as a contract in which Kasztner and the Nazis had exchanged promises,[87] with Kasztner agreeing not to warn "so that the deportations could proceed without encountering panic or resistance." In essence, the judge held Kasztner responsible for the fact that some half million Hungarian Jews had gone passively to their deaths, never knowing they were bound for Auschwitz. The judge ended by drawing on two literary metaphors—he compared the Nazis' release of Kasztner's train to the idea of Greeks bearing gifts (the Trojan Horse) and Kasztner's deal with Eichmann to the legend of Faust, stating that Kasztner had "sold his soul to Satan."[88]

As I see it, the judge's opinion was not only heartless, but gratuitous. The judge could have spared Grunwald from a criminal conviction, on the grounds that the essential facts could not be established "beyond a reasonable doubt." He did not have to cruelly demonize Kasztner. Much of the judge's opinion is overblown, rhetorical nonsense. The Nazis, not Kasztner, were responsible for rounding up and slaughtering Hungary's Jews. Nothing Kasztner could have done would have saved most of those who perished. Moreover, I find it stunning that the judge blamed Kasztner alone and said nothing to condemn the behavior of the leaders of the Jewish council ("Judenrat") in Cluj. There was a great deal of testimony at the trial suggesting that these leaders urged people to cooperate with the SS and to board the Nazi trains. They were not encouraging people to flee. Moreover, some of these leaders, including Kasztner's father-in-law, probably suspected that these trains might be headed for an extermination camp.

So what explains the vicious nature of this opinion?

In part, the opinion reflects the broader attitudes in Israel in the 1950s. The Holocaust had traumatized the Jewish world. The slaughter of six million Jews raised profoundly troubling questions. How did the Holocaust happen? Why had so little been done to prevent it? Why had so many Jews died without putting up a fight? Israel, a fledgling state surrounded by hostile Arab armies, was creating a new identity as a nation of warriors who would fight for their survival. Kasztner, by contrast, could be portrayed as the old-style Jew of Europe, who would haggle and make concessions rather than take a stand.[89] As one scholar writes:

[T]he Jews who had settled in Palestine before the war and watched the Holocaust from a safe distance felt impatient with the Jews of Europe who had allowed the Nazis to drive them "like lambs to the slaughter" while the survivors from Europe, in their turn, struggled to get over the loss of their loved ones and their own sufferings. In addition, there was guilt—on one side from failing to give help when it was needed, on the other side for surviving when so many died.[90]

Regrettably, Kasztner also played a role in his own destruction. Early in the trial, he was his usual self-confident self, swaggering and strutting, enjoying being the center of attention.[91] But under cross-examination he was asked whether he had testified in Becher's favor after the war. He denied it. When his affidavit on Becher's behalf was introduced into evidence, he was caught in the trap.[92] That lie, and a few others, destroyed Kasztner's credibility in the judge's eyes on issues far more central to the case. As a result, many historians believe, the judge lost all sympathy for Kasztner's predicament.[93]

The impact of the ruling on Kasztner and his family was devastating. "Their block of flats was daubed with graffiti saying 'Kasztner is a murderer' and worse."[94] There were death threats. There was also political fallout. The Mapai party was tarnished, its coalition government lost its majority, and new elections were called. Kasztner was advised to leave the country until things calmed down, but he issued a defiant statement: "History and all those who know what really happened during those woeful times will bear witness for me. . . . I will do everything in my power to clear my name and regain my honour."[95]

The third tribunal to judge him was the Israeli Supreme Court, which reviewed the case on appeal. In 1958, the Supreme Court reversed—with a four-to-one majority—the trial court's judgment and resoundingly cleared Kasztner of collaboration with the Nazis and complicity in mass murder.[96] The majority opinion, written by Justice Shimon Agranat, criticized the trial judge for evaluating Kasztner's actions with the benefit of hindsight. The court held that Kasztner: (1) did not know for certain what the fate of the Jews not selected for the rescue train would be; and (2) had reason to hope that many more might be saved through negotiations.

Agranat's opinion was also rich with commentary. He affirmed that

Kasztner's sole intention had been to save the Jews of Hungary. Although the train was only meant for a small group, this "was just part of his goal and never became for him an exclusive objective." (The judge noted in passing that Kasztner also provided money and resources to help others not on the train escape Hungary.) Moreover, the judge wrote, Kasztner did not negotiate with Eichmann as an equal. To the contrary, Eichmann held life-and-death power over Kasztner, who behaved reasonably as a Jewish leader under the circumstances. Agranat described Kasztner as a leader with no real power who was forced to make on-the-spot decisions under conditions of extreme pressure and great uncertainty. Against such odds, Agranat wrote, "God forbid us to regard Kasztner as guilty."

This ruling should have been a vindication for Kasztner, and in some ways it was. But he did not live long enough to know that his honor had been restored. While the appeal was pending, on the evening of March 3, 1957, a member of a radical Jewish underground movement approached him outside his home and shot him at close range. Although he survived for eight days, he died in the hospital.

Eichmann was tried, convicted, and hanged in Israel in 1962.

Becher was never convicted of any war crimes. He prospered in postwar Bremen, Germany, and died a rich old man in 1995—nearly forty years after Kasztner's assassination.

ASSESSMENT

What are my own thoughts about this case? Was Kasztner wise to negotiate with the Nazis? I approach this task with reticence. Attempting to assess decisions made in such dark times is treacherous. Primo Levi, himself a Holocaust survivor and a renowned Italian author, eloquently warned that those who haven't lived in such times have difficulty grasping what life was like in what he called this "Grey Zone."[97]

I am not critical of Kasztner's initial decision to negotiate with the Nazis. Wisliceny's first response to the Relief and Rescue Committee proposal was promising. But it was hardly reliable. Like Spock, I believe it would have been wiser for Kasztner and his colleagues to begin to develop a Plan B as well—to make every effort to warn the Jews in the provinces to go into hiding or flee. Such a mixed strategy would have been optimal.

What of Kasztner's decisions in Cluj on May 3, when he obtained new information? He learned that Wisliceny's earlier promises were worthless and that Eichmann was in charge. He also learned that the Nazis were beginning to round up provincial Jews and that in all probability this was a prelude to mass deportations to Auschwitz.

This information demanded two decisions.

One was whether to continue negotiating with the Nazis, despite their lies. Kasztner decided to continue, and I don't quarrel with that. I agree that the negotiation track was still worth pursuing.

The second decision was whether to spread the alarm among the Jews of Cluj. We will never know for certain what Kasztner said or did. At the trial he testified that he issued a warning.[98] If he was telling the truth, I have no real complaint, since he would have done what wisdom required. But his testimony was contradicted by several Cluj witnesses at the trial who testified that they were unaware of the dangers of ghettoization and deportation.[99] The trial court found these witnesses more credible than Kasztner, and the Israeli Supreme Court did not reverse the trial court's findings on this factual point.[100] On balance, I am skeptical about Kasztner's testimony that he issued warnings during his visit to Cluj. My best guess is that he and his colleagues *didn't* pursue a mixed strategy, either on May 3 or in the weeks that followed.

But even if he had warned, would it have made any difference? Would it have saved more lives?

Some commentators suggest the answer is no: that what Kasztner knew about the danger facing Hungary's Jews, nearly everybody knew.[101] Additional warnings would have made no difference in people's behavior.

I don't buy the first part of this argument. Kasztner knew more—much more—about the danger than most Jews in Hungary. He knew with certainty that Auschwitz was an extermination camp, not simply a labor camp, and that there was a substantial possibility that many Hungarian Jews would be deported there—to be murdered, not to work. Other Hungarian Jews, especially in the provinces, did not know these things with certainty. They may have heard that many Polish Jews had been killed by the Nazis, but they knew far less than Kasztner about Nazi procedures with regard to trains and deportation.

Would strong warnings have saved additional lives? I believe that if Kasztner and his colleagues had acted early enough—in May 1944, just as the ghettoization process was beginning in the provinces—Plan B might have saved additional lives.[102] How many? We will never know, and certainly Kasztner could not have known at the time. And that is my point. When one is negotiating under conditions of such terrible uncertainty, it is wiser to bet on two horses, if possible, than one.

Why didn't they pursue a mixed strategy? I am sure many factors were at work. As Kasztner wrote later, events happened too fast. There wasn't an efficient mechanism to "spread the alarm" in any systematic way through the provinces. He was probably being carefully watched by the Nazis. Anything he said, especially in Cluj, to disrupt the deportation could be reported back to Nazi headquarters in Budapest.

As I see it, on May 3 Kasztner was in a very complicated and somewhat compromised position. On the one hand, he wanted to encourage some number of people from Cluj to accept the invitation to be on his rescue train. To do so, he had every incentive to make sure they understood the danger of *not* joining his train. On the other hand, he obviously realized that only a small number could be accommodated, at least on this initial train. He may have (wrongly, in my view) emphasized his hope that there would be many more trains and that maybe the "big deal" would be accomplished.

I suspect there was another factor: Kasztner's love of danger and intrigue and being at the center of the action. He was like a riverboat gambler who was willing to take chances, and who probably thought of himself as rationally calculating the opportunities and risks of various "bets." Indeed, he often described his activities in terms of gambling—roulette, poker, etc. In assessing the costs and benefits of alternative strategies, how realistic was Kasztner?

Kasztner didn't fall into any of the negative traps I discussed in chapter 3. He was always prepared to negotiate with the Nazis, and he had no illusions about the regime being evil. And he was far too cynical to fall into the "positive" traps that push people into negotiating when they shouldn't. But in analyzing the costs and benefits of his alternatives, his apparent failure to pursue a mixed strategy may have been the result of three other common cognitive errors that psychologists suggest can distort decision-making.

1. Kasztner's primary focus was on the train and on the lives that would be lost if the train project didn't work. Because of

the phenomenon known as "loss aversion," Kasztner may have
given less weight in his decision-making to the number of
lives that might have been saved had there been a mixed
strategy that encouraged flight, hiding, etc.[103]

2.   The people listed for Kasztner's train were individual human
      beings who could be identified. Those who might have been
      saved with a better warning could not be identified in
      advance but were instead nameless "statistical lives." In
      decision-making, saving a few identified people counts for
      much more than saving more statistical lives. There is
      research suggesting that more money will be spent more
      readily to save an identified worker trapped in a mine than
      a similar amount on mine safety measures that might save
      many more (unidentified) miners in the future.[104]

3.   Kasztner may have also fallen into the trap of overconfidence—
      he may have exaggerated the chances of his own success in
      pulling off the "blood for goods" negotiation.[105]

How did Kasztner himself evaluate the prospects that he and Brand
could pull off Eichmann's proposal of exchanging trucks and war materiel for hundreds of thousands of Jewish lives? Certainly, he should
have recognized all along that the deal was nearly inconceivable. It
would require the full cooperation of the Western Allies. Spock would
have ridiculed the notion that somehow World Jewry might persuade
the Western Allies—in the middle of a war in which Roosevelt and
Churchill had called for "unconditional" German surrender—to allow
the Nazis to receive war materiel. It seems highly unlikely that Hitler
had any intention of allowing a large number of Jews to escape.[106]

A better rationale for Kasztner's negotiation was that it might buy
time and slow down the deportations. Abstractly, this is plausible. Why
not try? Moreover, I applaud him for shrewdly linking the "small plan"
(the train) to the "big plan" (blood for goods), and for his skill in persuading Eichmann to expand the number of Jews allowed on the train.

But as time went on, this second rationale became less and less persuasive. Eichmann flatly refused to stop or slow down the deportations.
Boxcars were leaving the provinces daily. In other words, *Kasztner's
plan wasn't working.* Yet he refused to give up: he continued to go to

Eichmann's office, smoke cigarettes, tell lies about Brand's "progress" in Istanbul, and argue that Eichmann should stop the deportations. He never lost his focus or shifted his attention to another strategy. In a sense, his persistence was heroic. In another sense, it was perhaps willful blindness. Did he start to believe his own arguments that World Jewry could pull off the deal?[107] Did he fool himself into thinking that if he just talked long enough, he could persuade Eichmann to stop the deportations? I suspect that he got so caught up in the intensity of the negotiation that he exaggerated its potential, even to himself. He was negotiating with Adolf Eichmann, after all. The scope of the deal was huge. Foreign governments were involved.

When the dream ended, Kasztner was devastated. Porter writes: "When it seemed clear in Budapest that Joel [Brand's] mission had been a failure, only Hansi managed to remain calm. Rezso wept like a child. She cradled his head in her arms and kept repeating that they could not give up."[108]

Kasztner wrote a revealing, nearly contemporaneous letter to a friend on July 12, 1944. He acknowledged that *"the dream of a big plan is finished, the hundreds of thousands went to Auschwitz in such a way that they were not conscious until the last moment what it was all about and what was happening. We who did know tried to act against it . . . without our being able to do anything of importance to prevent it."* He added that *"we did not forget the flight to Romania, to Slovakia and attempts at hiding people."* But *"the speed of the collapse was so wild that help and actions of succor and rescue could not keep up with it; even thoughts were too slow."*[109]

This last phrase is especially poignant, for it suggests that in retrospect Kasztner may have felt that he had not thought things through carefully enough—that his "thoughts were too slow." And whose "dream of a big plan" could he have been referring to, if not his own?

Did Kasztner sell his soul to the Devil? Absolutely not. But he may have been outsmarted. One scholar argues that Eichmann pursued a brilliant strategy that distracted and beguiled not only the Jewish Councils, but Kasztner and the Relief and Rescue Committee as well.[110] By dangling bait such as the rescue train, the Nazis raised false hopes and kept the Jewish leaders in a constant state of turmoil. Once there was a train, there was a "list" that had to be drawn up—which created bitter conflicts that consumed and divided the Jewish community. Perhaps Kasztner, too, was drawn in. He thought he was Eichmann's equal, and this may have blinded him to the fact that he was being toyed with and bought off for a modest price. I am not persuaded that the Nazis were quite as diabolically clever as all that, but I find the argument intriguing.

In sum, from a cost-benefit standpoint, I think Kasztner's decision to bargain with Eichmann was wise but his apparent failure to pursue a mixed strategy was not.

———

What about the charges that Kasztner's actions were immoral?

The trial judge accused Kasztner of making a devil's bargain—that in exchange for the Nazis' sparing the lives of those on the train, Kasztner had promised not to urge resistance or flight.[111] It's entirely plausible that Kasztner would make such a promise to Eichmann. My view is, so what if he did? Kasztner would promise Eichmann anything if he thought it would help save Jews. The critical question isn't whether he *made* such a promise, but whether he honored it.

As noted, the historical record is far from clear. But let's assume the worst. Suppose Kasztner made a vow of silence and kept it—that is, he chose not to warn in order to maximize the chance that the train would succeed. Would that be immoral? In my view, no. Such a choice would be morally culpable only if Kasztner *knew or should have known* that he would save more lives by making the opposite choice. At the time, there was no way for Kasztner to know which strategy would save more lives: negotiating with Eichmann or urging escape. It is simply preposterous to claim that Kasztner was morally responsible for hundreds of thousands of deaths because, in hindsight, he may have failed to make the very best decision under conditions of such extreme uncertainty.

The second moral issue also relates to the train: Was the selection process fair? Whatever its flaws, these cannot be laid at Kasztner's door. Many people played a role in the process, and a reasonably diverse group of Jews ended up being chosen.[112] The selection process wasn't perfect—it wasn't a lottery—but under the circumstances, it could not have been perfect. Certain groups were overrepresented, mainly wealthy Jews, prominent Jewish leaders, and Jews from Cluj, including members of Kasztner's family. But was it so terrible for

Kasztner's relatives to be included? Perhaps a saint would refuse to do so, but if I had been in Kasztner's place I would have made sure my family members were on the train. What could be more human than favoring your own family?[113]

This dilemma is similar to "Sophie's choice" in the William Styron novel of that name. In the novel, a Nazi tells Sophie that he will permit her to save only one of her two children—she has to choose which child or the Nazi will kill both children and Sophie as well.[114] Eichmann and the Nazis, not Kasztner, deserve moral condemnation for forcing such a choice on Kasztner and his colleagues.[115] Kasztner and his colleagues deserve sympathy.

A third moral issue relates to lying, and I find it the easiest. Having decided to negotiate with a devil, is it morally permissible to lie in order to save lives? One of Kasztner's strengths was his ability to lie, bluff, evade, and mislead. In less extreme contexts, one might persuasively argue that it is wrong to lie, even if the lie has beneficial results, because if everybody lies the social fabric falls apart; people stop relying on each other to keep promises. But what moral or social fabric existed in the Nazi regime? None. Even those philosophers with a very strict view, who broadly condemn all sorts of lies, acknowledge certain exceptions to interactions between oppressor and oppressed, especially if necessary to save lives.[116]

Several lessons can be drawn from this inquiry.

- If you bargain with the Devil, develop alternatives. You will need them if the deal doesn't work out.

- If you bargain with the Devil, you'd better win big. Otherwise you may be harshly judged by history—and by your own people. You may even be demonized.

- If you lie to the Devil, don't get seduced by your own lies.

I am pleased that more sympathetic accounts of Kasztner's rescue efforts are now emerging, after years in which he was vilified and then largely forgotten.[117] I admire his courage. But I must confess to some ambivalence about his style of negotiation.

I don't fault Kasztner for lying to Eichmann. But I find troubling that at his trial he lied under oath about helping Becher. I wonder whether Kasztner was someone who lied, apparently without moral qualms, whenever he thought it was expedient.

Kasztner's style of negotiation is definitely not the approach that I teach and practice. My hunch is that Kasztner would claim that lying in negotiation—like bluffing in poker—is an appropriate part of the game. You must simply be clever enough not to get caught. I disagree. I can typically achieve good results—as good as someone like Kasztner—without lying. Getting caught can ruin your reputation and have long-term consequences that outweigh any benefits. Besides, it's wrong. This is what I teach my students.

But this case strains the limits of any notion of principled negotiation.

If you were dealing with a devil like Eichmann, who would you want to negotiate on your behalf—a negotiator like me who hates to lie, or someone like Kasztner, who lies persuasively because he's had lots of practice?[118] The answer is pretty obvious and it troubles me.

FIVE

Winston Churchill: May 1940— Should Churchill Negotiate?

Early in World War II, in May 1940, British prime minister Winston Churchill met with a large group of his cabinet-rank ministers and announced a fateful decision. He told them: "I have thought carefully in these last days whether it was part of my duty to consider entering negotiations with That Man."[1] That Man was, of course, Adolf Hitler. At the meeting, Churchill did more than announce that he would not negotiate with Hitler. With the rhetorical flair so characteristic of his wartime speeches, Churchill declared that Great Britain must fight to the finish: "If this long island story of ours is to end at last, let it end only when each of us lies choking in his own blood upon the ground."[2]

This chapter tells the story of Churchill's decision and the secret deliberations that preceded it. For three days, Churchill and the members of his War Cabinet debated and wrestled with the question of whether to pursue peace negotiations with Nazi Germany. Later in the chapter, I will assess the wisdom of Churchill's refusal to negotiate. Should he instead have tried to negotiate a compromise peace with Hitler?

Today, many would find this question absurd. Of course Churchill's decision was wise. No regime in history was more evil than Hitler's. If there was ever a time to reject compromise, this was it. Of course, we know the rest of the story: the British endured the Nazi onslaught during the Battle of Britain, the United States and the Soviet Union eventually joined the war effort, and the Allies crushed Hitler's regime. Most historians—and laymen—see Churchill's refusal to negotiate as not only right, but heroic.[3]

However, Churchill's decision seems obvious only in hindsight. What if we go back in time to May 1940?

In his own magisterial, six-volume history of World War II, Churchill did not even acknowledge that extended War Cabinet discussions had taken place, much less that the cabinet had seriously considered opening a channel for negotiations with the Germans.[4] Lord Halifax, his foreign secretary, also denied it. But the secret minutes of these cabinet meetings—long classified—reveal a much more complex reality and an intense debate.[5] As we shall see, it was a close call.[6]

The War Cabinet was made up of five men, including Churchill, who formulated Britain's war policy. As prime minister, Churchill had appointed the other four members: Edward, Lord Halifax, his foreign secretary; Neville Chamberlain, the former prime minister; and two leaders of the Labor Party, Clement Attlee and Arthur Greenwood. Neither Attlee nor Greenwood plays a critical role in our story.[7] Halifax, Chamberlain, and Churchill do. Their deliberations and struggle in May 1940 occurred against a backdrop of earlier differences among the three men about Britain's prewar foreign policy of appeasement.

Today *appeasement* is a dirty word. But it can be defined in more neutral terms as "the policy of settling international quarrels by admitting and satisfying grievances through rational negotiation and compromise, thereby avoiding the resort to an armed conflict which would be expensive, bloody, and possibly dangerous."[8] While the notion of appeasement now carries a "shameful and even craven"[9] connotation, quite the opposite was true in Great Britain during most of the 1930s. At that time, "the policy of appeasement . . . occupied almost the whole moral high ground. The word was originally synonymous with idealism, magnanimity of the victor and a willingness to right wrongs."[10]

When Hitler began annexing territory in the mid-1930s, many in

Great Britain thought he was simply trying to right the "wrongs" of Versailles. The Versailles Treaty of 1919 had transformed the map of Europe after World War I, carving up old nations, creating new ones, and literally cutting Germany down to size. Germany lost vast amounts of territory to France, Belgium, Poland, and the entirely new nation of Czechoslovakia. By the 1930s, many in Britain had come to believe that Versailles had treated Germany unfairly.

Other factors favored the British policy of appeasement. After the horrors of World War I, many Britons felt that another war in Europe should be avoided "at almost any cost."[11] As a practical matter, Britain was totally unprepared to fight another war. And some conservatives viewed the fascists in Germany and Italy as bulwarks against communism, which was seen as a far worse menace.

So in 1936, when Hitler violated Versailles by reoccupying the demilitarized Rhineland—Germany's own "backyard"—Britain did nothing to stop him.[12] Churchill, then a Conservative backbencher, was the only one in British politics who "wanted to call Hitler's bluff"[13] with a display of force. He was ignored. Throughout the 1930s, Churchill would remain one of the very few voices warning of the dangers of German rearmament.

Chamberlain became prime minister in 1937, and both he and Halifax are associated with appeasement because of their failure to resist German aggression in the late 1930s. Hitler's next target was the Sudeten region of Czechoslovakia, which included a significant German-speaking population. Hitler launched a vitriolic propaganda campaign, threatening the Czech government and claiming that the Sudeten Germans were being horribly mistreated under Czech rule.

In late 1937, Chamberlain sent Halifax to Germany—on the pretext of attending a hunting exhibition—to meet personally with Hitler and convey a respectful, nineteenth-century message: that Britain understood Germany's concerns about the treatment of German minorities and was not necessarily opposed to changes in the European order, *as long as they were made peacefully*. In a high water mark of appeasement, Halifax complimented Hitler on "performing great services in Germany" and expressed Britain's hope that any modification of the Versailles Treaty would come through "peaceful evolution."[14]

Chamberlain later declared that Halifax's visit was a great success in "convinc[ing] Hitler of our sincerity."[15] Soon afterward, Halifax became foreign secretary.

In fact, Halifax and Chamberlain had completely misread Hitler, who was not playing by Marquess of Queensbury rules. The visit convinced Hitler of something else entirely—that the British were so desperate to avoid war that he could maneuver freely in Europe without risk of their putting up a fight. He moved quickly. In 1938, he marched into Vienna and incorporated Austria into his Reich without firing a shot. Next he demanded that the Sudetenland be annexed to Germany and that all non-German Czechs leave the region.

Trying to avert war, Chamberlain hastily arranged a four-power conference in Munich that excluded the Czech government. The result was a historic shift in the European balance of power. The Munich Agreement among the four great powers—Britain, France, Italy, and Germany—allowed the Nazis to absorb the Sudetenland in return for Hitler's promise to allow an international commission to settle any other German claims over Czech territory. The Czechs were presented with a fait accompli. At Chamberlain's request, Hitler also signed a piece of paper—soon to prove worthless—in which Germany and Britain promised to resolve their differences peacefully. Chamberlain returned to England, "peace treaty" in hand, proclaiming "peace with honor" and "peace for our time."

The British public rejoiced when they heard the news, but Churchill proclaimed it a "total and unmitigated defeat" and a "disaster of the first magnitude" for both Britain and France. Speaking before the House of Commons, he said, "Do not let us blind ourselves to that. It must now be accepted that all the countries of Central and Eastern Europe will make the best terms they can with the triumphant Nazi Power. The system of alliances in Central Europe upon which France has relied for her safety has been swept away, and I can see no means by which it can be reconstituted."[16]

He said he did not blame the British people for their "natural, spontaneous" outburst of relief that war had been averted for the moment.

But they should know the truth. They should know that there has been gross neglect and deficiency in our defenses; they should know that we have sustained a defeat without a war, the consequences of which will travel far with us along our road; they should know that we have passed an awful milestone in our history, when the whole equilibrium of Europe has been deranged, and that the terrible words have for the time being been pronounced against the Western democracies:

"Thou are weighed in the balance and found wanting."

And do not suppose that this is the end. This is only the beginning of the reckoning. This is only the first sip, the first foretaste of a bitter cup which will be proffered to us year by year unless, by a supreme recovery of moral health and martial vigour, we arise again and take our stand for freedom as in the olden time.[17]

Once again, Churchill was proven right. Six months later, in March 1939, Nazi troops marched into Prague and seized what was left of the country. As a consequence, Czechoslovakia disappeared entirely as a nation.[18]

That was the end of appeasement as British policy—a humiliating failure from which the reputations of Chamberlain and Halifax would never fully recover. Both men became completely disillusioned with Hitler, adopted a tougher policy of deterrence,[19] and began to mobilize Britain for war. As Hitler began to make ominous threats toward Poland, parts of which had substantial German-speaking minorities, Britain and France guaranteed Poland's security through a treaty,[20] in effect warning Hitler that if he invaded Poland, there would be war.

But it was too late for warnings. Hitler was not to be deterred. On September 1, 1939, the Nazis invaded Poland. Two days later, Britain and France declared war on Germany.

The outbreak of World War II brought about rapid changes in British leadership. Churchill, thoroughly vindicated, became first lord of the Admiralty. Poland was overrun in a month.[21] Chamberlain's credibility ebbed and Churchill's grew. In 1940, when Hitler overran Denmark and Norway, British public opinion turned decisively against Chamberlain. Germany had been neither appeased nor deterred, and British mobilization had failed to meet the Nazi challenge.

Chamberlain decided he should resign. Both he and King George VI wanted Halifax to replace him. But, for reasons that were never publicly explained, Halifax turned the job down. Winston Churchill became prime minister on May 10, 1940.

———

At the pensionable age of sixty-five, Churchill was thrilled at long last to become prime minister. From his youth, he had been persuaded that he was a man of destiny. He also held "a high romantic view of the monarchy and the empire"[22] that can be easily understood from his background.

He was the grandson of the Duke of Marlborough and the son of Lord Randolph Churchill, a Tory politician, who died young and had an unrequited dream of becoming prime minister himself. Winston's American-born mother, née Jennie Jerome, was a famous and passionate beauty. Both were distant and indifferent parents, and Winston's nanny was the "central emotional prop of [his] childhood."[23] After boarding school at Harrow, Churchill attended the Royal Military Academy at Sandhurst. The year he graduated, he was commissioned as an officer in the Royal Hussars.

As a young officer, Churchill saw combat in India and the Sudan. He was seen as flamboyant and impatient, with a "dominating desire . . . to attract the greatest possible attention to himself, both on the local and the world scene."[24] An extraordinarily fluent writer, he "lived by phrase making"[25] and supported himself financially during most of his life as a war correspondent and author. By the age of twenty-five, he was already a celebrity because of his capture, imprisonment, and escape during the Second Boer War in South Africa, which he chronicled as a foreign correspondent.

As a politician, he was self-centered, self-confident, and nakedly ambitious. By twenty-six, he was a Conservative member of Parliament, but his independent views soon forced him to switch parties and become a Liberal. By thirty-three, he was a cabinet minister, and during World War I he held a variety of important posts. He became chancellor of the exchequer in 1924 under a Conservative prime minister and formally rejoined the Conservative Party the following year. "[A]nyone can rat," he quipped, "but it takes a certain amount of ingenuity to re-rat."[26]

The Tories hardly welcomed him back as a prodigal son. To many of them, Churchill's "wit and oratorical ability were not enough to overcome severe doubts about his judgment."[27] Many saw him as "unscrupulous, unreliable and unattractively ambitious"—a "political turncoat" who had twice changed his party affiliation. His personal eccentricities only alienated them further. He spoke with a lisp and a stutter. He wore loud suits and bow ties. His bowler hat and cigar seemed like theatrical props. He gambled and consumed great quantities of alcohol. By 1929, his political career hit the skids and he entered his "wilderness years"[28] as a Tory backbencher with trivial influence.

Eleven years later, when he finally shook off the dust of wilderness and moved into 10 Downing Street, he knew that his support in Parliament was still thin, especially in his own Conservative Party. "The strange dress, ridiculous hats, heavy drinking and pronounced speech impediment did little to encourage the Tory old guard to respect him for much more than having been proved right about the German threat."[29] Indeed, they considered him dangerously impulsive and apt to get carried away by his own rhetoric. Would he lead from the head or the heart? They feared the latter. Many in the Tory establishment saw Churchill as a "Rogue Elephant" whom the "wise old elephants"—Chamberlain and Halifax—might not be able to control.[30]

———————————

During Churchill's first two weeks as prime minister, the war went from bad to worse. Hitler conquered the Netherlands, invaded Belgium, and surged into northern France. Britain had sent troops to the continent to support the French, but they were unable to stop the German army. The United States was standing on the sidelines, rooting for Britain and France but doing little to help. Churchill wrote several personal letters to President Franklin Delano Roosevelt pleading for assistance, but none came.

Worst of all, by May 23, 1940, the German army had surrounded the Allied troops near the French-Belgian border. Some 250,000 British soldiers appeared to be trapped, along with a roughly equal number of French troops. The British public had no understanding of just how bad things were.[31] Churchill knew he would have to "prepare public opinion for bad tidings. . . . [W]hat was now happening in Northern France would be the greatest British military defeat for many centuries."[32] It was against this desperate backdrop that Churchill and his War Cabinet were forced to consider negotiating with Hitler.

It was Edward, Lord Halifax who pressed for the possibility of negotiation. Like Churchill, Halifax was an English aristocrat but one with very different values and temperament. Born Edward Wood on April 16, 1881, he was the fourth son of a viscount and eventually inherited his father's title because his three older brothers had died of childhood diseases.[33] He was born without a left hand, but his life was not much affected by it.[34] His family was enormously wealthy, largely because a huge seam of coal lay under a portion of their lands. Educated at Eton and Oxford, he was personally rich by the time he graduated from university because of large inheritances from a number of uncles and aunts.

In 1909, Halifax went into politics and stood for a seat in Parliament. Thereafter, he pursued a "bright and successful" career as a Tory politician. An "intensely private man," he was genuinely modest and "found it hard to lose his temper."[35] Like his father, he was a devout High Church Anglican who exuded moral rectitude. Most of all, he was respectable.

Halifax's nickname became "The Holy Fox" because he was both religious and cunning. He believed deeply in original sin. "Far from a pious blindness to the evils of the world, Halifax was [all] too keenly aware of men's failings. He was if anything more guilty of cynicism than monkish innocence."[36] He saw himself as a pragmatist, not an ideologue. His diplomatic and political career demonstrated a willingness to "[c]ompromise, a degree of guile, and an awareness of the realities of life" that, to him, were fully consistent with his spiritual values.[37] As he would later write, "Many of our intellectual difficulties come from an attempt to think that the Kingdom of God and the Kingdom of this world are concerned with the same problems. . . . [I]n a very vital sense they are not."[38]

Halifax's values and prejudices, however, were those of his class. He saw the world through the eyes of an English landed aristocrat, whose political goals were to safeguard Britain's independence, continuing imperial role, and honor.[39] Roy Jenkins, in his biography of Churchill, wrote that Halifax had a "resigned desire to preserve as much as he could of the England he knew and loved . . . the landscape, the ordered hierarchical society, the freedom from oppression or vulgar ostentation."[40] All of these factors attracted him to the possibility of a negotiated peace that would honorably get Great Britain out of a terrible war.

That possibility arose on May 25, 1940, when Halifax held a pivotal meeting in London with the Italian ambassador to Great Britain, Giuseppe Bastianini. Halifax's purpose was to explore whether Italy might be induced—that is, bribed—to stay out of the war. Although Italy was officially a noncombatant, it had signed a "Pact of Steel" (an alliance) with Nazi Germany and amassed twenty thousand troops on the French-Italian border. There was reason to think Italy might soon join the Nazis, invade France, and claim some booty. Perhaps, Halifax thought, Italy could be bought off at a reasonable price.

Churchill knew about this meeting in advance and asked only that it be kept secret and that Halifax do nothing to suggest a lack of resolve on the part of Great Britain.

But I suspect that Halifax, the "Holy Fox," went to the meeting hoping delicately to explore a second and even more far-reaching possibility—one that he had not disclosed to Churchill or the War Cabinet. Might Mussolini play a role as mediator in facilitating negotiations aimed at *ending* the war? Halifax left no incriminating fingerprints, so it will never be known whether he went into the meeting wanting to plant this seed. But by the end of the meeting the idea had sprouted.

Halifax's written report of the meeting suggests that the Italian ambassador planted the idea. According to the report, Italy agreed to discuss its relationship with Great Britain only in the broader context of a "just and enduring European settlement." Was Britain interested, the ambassador asked, in discussions that might include this "greater framework"? Such a conversation would involve "other countries"—which, of course, would include Germany.[41] Halifax, using the double negative so favored by wily diplomats, gave the ambassador permission to inform Mussolini that "His Majesty's Government *did not exclude the possibility* of some discussion of the wider problems of Europe" (emphasis added).

Halifax presented this hot potato to the War Cabinet the next day. For three days, they would be forced to discuss his plan.

THE DELIBERATIONS

Sunday, May 26, was anything but a day of rest for the War Cabinet. Churchill began by reporting the dire military circumstances on the ground. Belgium was about to capitulate.[42] The French were close to collapse, and 250,000 British soldiers were cornered in northern France.[43] Soon Britain might be facing both Germany and Italy alone.

Against this backdrop, Halifax told the War Cabinet about his meeting with the Italian ambassador. In light of the desperate military situation, he said, British war aims had to be narrowed: it was no longer a matter of "imposing a complete defeat upon Germany but of safeguarding the independence of our own Empire and if possible that of France."[44] He thought that Mussolini wished to secure peace in Europe and that the Italians might be open to facilitating a discussion about a "general European settlement," but that the discussion would have to include Germany.

From the outset, Churchill was deeply skeptical. In his view, Hitler would never accept any negotiated deal unless it allowed Germany to dominate Europe, which Britain "could never accept" because it would threaten Britain's security. "We must ensure our complete liberty and independence," he said. But nothing was decided, and everyone left the meeting knowing the discussion would continue.

When the War Cabinet met again in the early afternoon, the differences between Churchill and Halifax came into sharper focus. Halifax argued strongly in favor of an approach to Italy, saying that "the last thing Signor Mussolini wanted was to see" a Europe dominated by Hitler. Churchill was still skeptical, but he conceded that "the matter was one that the War Cabinet would need to consider."[45] Halifax began the first of several attempts to pin Churchill down. Given that Britain's security and independence were in such danger, he said, "we should naturally be prepared to consider any proposals that might lead to [restoring that security], *provided our liberty and independence are assured*" (emphasis added). Then he asked the key question: If Churchill was "satisfied that matters vital to the independence of this country were unaffected," was he "prepared to discuss such terms?"[46]

Churchill did not say no. In fact, he appeared to say yes. He said he would be "thankful to get out of our present difficulties on such terms, provided we retain the essentials and the elements of our vital strength *even at the cost of some territory*" (emphasis added). But he went on to add that he did not believe that such a deal was possible.

The third meeting that day took place around dinnertime. In the interim, Churchill had met with the French prime minister, Paul Reynaud, who confirmed that the French military situation was all but hopeless. Churchill's response to him was typically pugnacious: "We would rather go down fighting," he said, "than be enslaved to Germany." [47]

He brought that defiant attitude back to the War Cabinet that evening, where his debate with Halifax became increasingly tense. If France collapsed, Churchill declared, Britain must not go down with her. The two nations had mutually pledged not to make a separate peace with Germany, but Churchill now wanted to release France from this treaty obligation. "If France could not defend herself, it was better that she get out of the war rather than drag us into a settlement which involved intolerable terms," Churchill said. Churchill predicted that Hitler would demand the most outrageous terms possible—including British disarmament. There was "no limit to the terms that Germany would impose on us if she had her way." [48]

Halifax was not so sure. He saw no evidence that Germany wanted to "enslave" Britain. In fact, he didn't think it was in Hitler's *interest* to insist on outrageous terms. Halifax believed that Hitler's primary goal—as stated—was to unite all German-speaking peoples under one roof and to create "Lebensraum" ("living room") in the east for expansion. In order to accomplish that goal, Hitler wanted territory in Eastern Europe, not Britain. Therefore, Halifax thought, Hitler might want to stop fighting on the western front so he could focus his military power on the Soviet Union. Halifax may even have thought, why not push him in that direction? The one thing Britain and Germany shared was their hatred of the communists.

Halifax was a balance-of-power strategist who no doubt believed that this war, like most wars, would eventually end with a negotiated agreement in which territorial concessions would be made to the stronger party. Some concessions would have to be made to Hitler, and Mussolini would expect a little pourboire for his own helpful behavior, [49] but this could be accomplished by some horse-trading among colonies. So Halifax pressed his point: How could you know that Hitler would insist on outrageous terms if there was no discussion? Moreover, Britain's interests could be declared in advance. "[W]e might say to Signor Mussolini that if there was any suggestion of terms which affected our independence, we should not look at them for a moment." And Mus-solini might well be alarmed by Hitler and "look at matters from the point of view of the balance of power."[50] Why not find out? Where was the harm in trying this approach?

Churchill's response suggested that he saw Hitler as a bully with boundless ambitions. "Herr Hitler thought that he had the whiphand. The only thing to do was to show him that he could not conquer this country."

Where was Chamberlain in all of this? He did not say a great deal at this meeting, and in historian John Lukacs's view he "now sat on the fence."[51] But his diary entry that evening suggested he was leaning in Churchill's direction. Chamberlain summarized the prime minister's outlook: "[I]f we could get out of this jam by giving up Malta and Gibraltar and some African colonies he would jump at it. But the only safe way was to convince Hitler that he couldn't beat us."[52]

Let's step back for a moment and ask how Spock might assess the Churchill-Halifax debate to this point. The issue was: What would Hitler insist upon in peace negotiations? Churchill was assuming the worst and presenting it as fact. Although the record doesn't show him saying this directly, he saw Hitler as a megalomaniac bent on nothing less than world domination. Churchill's instincts had been terrific in the past, and his predictions about Hitler had so far been accurate, but he had not even come close to explaining why he thought Hitler had a vital interest in enslaving Britain and destroying its empire. Halifax, by contrast, was sticking to the known facts: The situation on the ground was dire, and it was unknown what the Germans would agree to. Why wouldn't it be wise, and indeed honorable, to see if a settlement could be achieved on reasonable terms? Spock would consider that a logical question.

Moreover, Spock would ask rhetorically, what was the alternative to negotiation? Continued fighting—in which the Germans would direct their formidable airpower against Britain and perhaps invade. In May 1940, the outcome of such a fight was highly uncertain. In fact, the odds were pretty clearly against Britain.

So it was easy to *imagine* a negotiated deal that might serve both sides' interests better than continued war: the Germans would get de facto control of Europe, including France, while Britain would keep its independence, its military, and nearly all of its empire (after ceding a few territorial crumbs to the Italians). There were three questions: Would Hitler agree to such a deal, would an agreement with Hitler be worth the paper it was printed on, and would the costs of that deal, including the loss of sovereignty for most of Europe, be acceptable to the British? Through bitter experience, Halifax and Chamberlain had come to share Churchill's view that Hitler was a completely unreliable negotiating partner. Even if the war ended now, Hitler might attack Britain later.

Spock would agree that this was a significant risk. But he would ask: Which nation, Germany or Britain, would *benefit more from a hiatus in the war*? Britain was not yet fully mobilized. If Hitler headed east and attacked Russia, as expected, it would absorb vast amounts of German manpower and materiel. That could only be good for Britain, which needed time to reach full strength.

Of course, in those desperate days in May 1940, the War Cabinet meetings were too chaotic to allow for a Spock-like discussion at this level. But Halifax's argument was strong enough to force Churchill to take another tack.

Churchill's second argument was that Britain must not be forced into the weak position of going to Mussolini and Hitler and asking them to "treat us nicely. We must not get entangled in a position of that kind before we had been involved in serious fighting."[53] In other words, this was *not the right time* to pursue negotiations because Britain had not yet proved it could put up a real fight. A willingness to engage in negotiation now would signal weakness. But perhaps after a few months of heroic fighting, Churchill suggested, the time would be ripe.

To Halifax, this was supremely illogical: In three months, Britain might be bombed to a smoking ruin. Where would its bargaining power be then? Was Churchill seriously willing to take that risk? This was just the kind of emotional argument that Churchill's critics dreaded. Halifax was aghast. If Britain could "obtain terms which did not postulate the destruction of our independence," Halifax insisted, "we should be foolish if we did not accept them." In other words, he was arguing that it would be stupid, given the situation on the ground, to turn down a negotiated deal that provided for continued British independence.

Here again, I think Spock would say that Halifax was making more sense than Churchill. In fact, I suspect the issue of timing was a makeshift argument on Churchill's part. True, one could always fight now and negotiate later, but Churchill had not explained why he felt justified in taking such a huge risk. Frankly, I think Halifax had Churchill on the ropes. If the analysis were to stop here, one might well conclude that wisdom would *obligate* Churchill to explore the possibility of negotiation by using the Italians as an intermediary.

Perhaps sensing this, Churchill backed off and the cabinet agreed that Halifax should prepare a draft of his proposal. By the end of the evening, Halifax had produced a document that was a masterpiece of obfuscation: "If Signor Mussolini will co-operate with us in securing a settlement of all European questions which safeguard[s] the independence and security of the Allies, and could be the basis of a just and durable peace for Europe, we will undertake at once to discuss, with the desire to find solutions, the matters in which Signor Mussolini is primarily interested."[54] This was to be coupled with a backchannel request that the United States make the first approach to Mussolini, not Britain or France. Roosevelt would inform Mussolini that the French and British would consider Italian territorial claims only if Italy stayed out of the war.

Note that this document conflates two goals: buying Italy off to keep it out of the war, and persuading Mussolini to mediate peace. As several scholarly commentators have noted, there is an obvious tension between them. "Buying off Italy facilitated the war against Germany, Italian mediation meant its end."[55]

What was Halifax up to? I believe he was pursuing both goals and knew he had to tread carefully. The entire cabinet supported the first goal: keeping Italy out of the war. The problem was the second goal, to which Churchill was adamantly opposed. Halifax may have hoped that by emphasizing the first goal, he might keep the door open to the second.

Monday, May 27

Before the morning session, Halifax was in despair. He told a colleague, "I can't work with Winston any longer."[56] A showdown was inevitable.

But it would have to wait. The morning meeting focused on the terrible military situation on the continent. British troops were still trapped in northern France, and the prospects for evacuating them from Calais or Dunkirk were not promising. Churchill doubted he could save more than fifty thousand men. But preparations were under way. "Around the coast of Southern England, hastily improvised flotillas of small ships, trollers, tug boats, tiny motor launches—anything that was serviceable—were being assembled and setting sail to try and do their bit in rescuing the stranded army." [57]

In many ways it was the "worst day of the entire Dunkirk saga," according to Lukacs. "The Germans ruled the air, with relatively little interference from the Royal Air Force . . . [The German dive-bombers were attacking] the columns of the British and French retreating along the dusty roads and lanes toward the town and port . . . [T]he British were systematically destroying their vehicles, stores, ordnance and other equipment" [58] to prevent their use by the German army.

With the collapse of France imminent, it was far from clear whether Britain could fight on alone. A top secret report, commissioned by Churchill, indicated that Great Britain could successfully resist the Germans, provided that it maintained air superiority and the United States gave it substantial economic support. But both conditions were open to serious question. The United States had provided virtually no help and could not be counted on. [59] Little wonder that Alexander Cadogan, an invited guest to the War Cabinet meeting that day, summarized the session as follows: "Cabinet at 11:30—as gloomy as ever. See very little light anywhere." [60]

The War Cabinet didn't take up Halifax's proposal until late afternoon, by which time the ground had shifted. A key piece of news had arrived. The British ambassador to Rome had cabled that Mussolini would soon declare war on France and that "nothing we could do would be of any value at this stage, so far as Signor Mussolini was concerned." [61]

Halifax was in a real bind. He could see that Italy probably could not be kept out of the war. But even so, Mussolini still might serve as a mediator, and Halifax was determined to keep this idea alive. French prime minister Reynaud, still desperately hoping to buy Italy off, had begged Halifax to present to the War Cabinet a plan for an even bolder and more concrete offer to Mussolini, one that specified with "geographical precision" exactly what would be given to Italy to stay out of the war.

Halifax brought Reynaud's proposal to the War Cabinet and argued that something should be done to show support of France. Chamberlain agreed, saying that "the proposed French approach to Signor Mussolini would serve no useful purpose" but that he was willing to do so anyway in order to prevent the French from later claiming that Great Britain had stubbornly "been unwilling even to allow them the chance of negotiations with Italy."[62]

Churchill would have none of this. He scorned the Halifax-Chamberlain argument as suggesting that "nothing would come of the approach, but that it was worth doing to sweeten relations with a failing ally."[63]

At this point, an invited guest chimed in and explicitly gave Churchill the broader argument he had been searching for—one that rejected any approach to Italy for either of Halifax's purposes. Archibald Sinclair, the air minister, was a Churchill supporter and, more important, head of the Liberal Party. During the previous evening's debate, Churchill had shrewdly persuaded the cabinet to include Sinclair in the discussion of Halifax's proposal. Sinclair now contended that an approach to Italy would be worse than futile: it would be actively harmful to British interests. Even *appearing* to be willing to negotiate would be disastrous. "Being in a tight corner, any weakness on our part would encourage the Germans and the Italians, and *would tend to undermine morale both in this country and in the Dominions. The* suggestion that we were prepared to barter away pieces of British territory *would have a deplorable effect that would make it difficult for us to continue the struggle that faced us.*" (Emphasis supplied.) Attlee and Greenwood warmed to this argument. Soon Greenwood was declaring that "[i]t would be heading for disaster to go any further with those approaches."

Halifax felt compelled to clarify and explain: He was not supporting the French plan of specific concessions to Italy. Instead, he was simply proposing to keep the lines of communication with Italy open.

Churchill, perhaps sensing that he had been given his strongest argument and that the tide within the cabinet was running in his direction, boldly vowed that any approach to the Italians "*would ruin the integrity of our fighting position in this country.* . . . Even if we did not include geographical precision and mentioned no names, everybody would know what we had in mind." With great passion he then went further: "[L]et us not be dragged down with France. If the French were not prepared to go on with the struggle, let them give up. . . . The best help we could give to M. Reynaud was to let him feel that, whatever happened to France, we were going to fight it out to the end."

Perhaps fearing that the conflict between Churchill and his foreign secretary was about to spin out of control, Chamberlain tried to calm things down. He offered a compromise: "to keep the French in a good temper . . . our reply should not be a complete refusal." Why not defer any response to France until Roosevelt first contacted Mussolini? But Churchill ignored the suggestion and instead made an even more provocative claim: "If the worse came to the worst" and Britain had to face Hitler alone, "it would not be a bad thing for this country to go down fighting for the other countries which had been overcome by the Nazi tyranny."

Now this was crazy. Did it make any rational sense for Britain to sacrifice itself in a *losing* battle on behalf of occupied Europe? Did Churchill have any right, as a national leader, to sacrifice his countrymen on such a basis? In my opinion, absolutely not.

At this point Halifax was fed up with Churchill's florid rhetoric. He pointed out that Churchill was contradicting himself right and left. The day before, Churchill had said "he would be thankful to get out of our present difficulties" on terms that preserved British independence, "even at the cost of some cession of territory." Now Churchill was saying that "under no conditions would we contemplate any course except fighting to the finish." The day before, Churchill had indicated that he wasn't opposed to negotiation in general, as long as the timing was right. Now he was reneging on that, too.

Churchill softened somewhat, perhaps recognizing that he had gone too far. "If Herr Hitler was prepared to make peace on the terms of the restoration of German colonies and the overlordship of Central Europe, that was one thing," he soothed. "But it was quite unlikely that he would make any such offer."

In trying to placate Halifax, Churchill had created a new ambiguity, which Halifax went after. Was Churchill saying that he was simply waiting for *Germany* to make an offer? In Halifax's view, such a scenario was not so hypothetical. "Suppose the French Army collapsed and Herr Hitler made an offer of peace terms," Halifax challenged. "Suppose Herr Hitler, being anxious to end the war through knowledge of his own internal weaknesses, offered terms to France and England, would the Prime Minister be prepared to discuss them?" In effect, Halifax was pressing Churchill: Would he "consider any peace terms, at any time?"

Thanks to Halifax's probing, Churchill finally clarified where he stood on peace negotiations: "He would not join France in asking for terms; but if he were told what the terms offered were, he would be prepared to consider them." Nor was he prepared at this time to enter into any process in which Great Britain would appear to be signaling a willingness to negotiate peace terms with Hitler.[64]

At this point Halifax may well have been considering resignation. As he would confide to his diary later that night, "I thought Winston talked the most frightful rot, also Greenwood, and after bearing it for some time I told them exactly what I thought of them." He then added, "If that was really their view, and if it came to the point, *our ways must separate.*"[65]

Churchill must have realized how close Halifax was to the edge, because he asked Halifax to join him for a private walk in the garden. There was not any record of what exactly was said, but Halifax's biographer suggests Halifax again threatened to resign and that Churchill "was full of apologies and affection."[66] The biographer concludes, "However much annoyance he had shown, though, Halifax had no intention of resigning. Indeed, the more Churchill hectored, the more convinced he was of the necessity for him to stay. Eventually, he contented himself to confining his exasperation to his diary: 'It does drive me to despair when [Churchill] works himself up into a passion of emotion when he ought to make his brain think and reason.' "[67]

Tuesday, May 28

On Tuesday morning, the news from the continent remained so bleak that the minister of information asked Churchill to make a public statement. For the first time in a week, Churchill appeared before the House of Commons and addressed the nation.

"The troops are in good heart," he reported. "And are fighting with the utmost discipline and tenacity." He provided no specifics but promised to offer a "detailed report" in about a week, "when the result of the intense struggle now going on can be known and measured." In the meantime, "the House should prepare itself for hard and heavy tidings." But he ended his speech with a rousing flourish that was typical of his wartime speeches: "nothing which may happen in this battle can in any way relieve us of our duty to defend the world cause to which we have vowed ourselves; nor should it destroy our confidence in our power to make our way, as on former occasions in our history, through disaster and through grief to the ultimate defeat of our enemies." [68]

When the War Cabinet met shortly afterward, Halifax and Churchill crossed swords again. Their brief exchange returned to the core question. Halifax thought peace talks might still be possible if Britain sent a "clear indication that we should like to see mediation by Italy." [69] Churchill retorted that the whole idea of peace talks was a ruse by the French, who "were trying to get us on to the slippery slope" of negotiating with Germany. Churchill did not respond further. He had made up his mind. He knew he had the support of everyone in the War Cabinet except Halifax, who was isolated.

At this point, Churchill staged what several commentators have characterized as a "coup." He adjourned the War Cabinet meeting until 7 P.M. and didn't say where he was going. In the interval, he met with the approximately twenty-five members of the Outer Cabinet—all of his ministers *except* those in the War Cabinet. It was to this group, not the War Cabinet, that Churchill announced his decision: that he had considered negotiation with "That Man" and firmly rejected it.

"It was idle to think that if we try to make peace now we should get better terms from Germany than if we went on and fought it out," Churchill told the ministers. "The Germans would demand our fleet—that would be called 'disarmament'—our naval bases, and much else. We should become a slave state," with a "puppet" British government under Oswald Mosley, the founder of the British Union of Fascists, or some similar Nazi sympathizer. Instead, Churchill proclaimed: "We shall go on and we shall fight it out . . . and if at last the long story is to end, it were better it should end, not through surrender, but only when we are rolling senseless on the ground." [70]

His speech had an electrifying effect on his listeners. He received enthusiastic support, and not a single minister objected. Churchill would later describe how pleased and surprised he was that "twenty-five experienced politicians and Parliament men, who represented all the different points of view" about Britain's policy toward Germany, would now be so supportive. "Quite a few seemed to jump up from the table and came running to my chair, shouting and patting me on the back." [71]

When Churchill returned to the War Cabinet, he announced what he had done. He described—no doubt with great drama—the scene that had just unfolded before the Outer Cabinet: his ringing announcement that he would not negotiate with Hitler, his vow that "there was no chance of our giving up the struggle," and the fervent support of the ministers. He expressed the "greatest satisfaction" at their response, saying he "did not remember having ever before heard a gathering of persons occupying high places in political life express themselves so emphatically" in support of Churchill's decision to fight on, and not negotiate.[72]

Halifax offered no further dissent. Nor did he resign. Had he done so, especially if Chamberlain had joined him, there would have been a political crisis within the Conservative Party that might have threatened Churchill's ability to remain prime minister.[73] But Churchill had skillfully avoided that risk.

Later that year, Churchill sent Halifax to the United States as ambassador, essentially sidelining him for the rest of the war.

———

The evacuation from Dunkirk was far more successful than Churchill had any reason to expect.[74] Nearly two hundred thousand troops were safely brought back to England.[75] France fell as predicted, and Britain had to fight on alone. But through the Lend-Lease program, the United States began providing important materiel aid. During the summer and fall of 1940, the Royal Air Force maintained air superiority and Churchill maintained public morale during the Battle of Britain. As a result, Hitler gave up any thought of invading Great Britain and instead turned east and invaded the Soviet Union. This gave Britain an ally— the Soviets. By the end of 1941, the United States joined Great Britain and the Soviet Union in their fight against Germany. Eventually the Allies prevailed.

ASSESSMENT

Churchill's speech to the Outer Cabinet was eloquent and stirring, and it epitomizes the rhetorical use of negative traps: he demonized Hitler's regime and called his ministers to battle by invoking tribal loyalty. His later war speeches to the British people were equally stirring.

Earlier in the book, I said that if you're a leader, you have an obligation to engage in rational analysis. You don't have the right to act solely on your gut feelings or personal moral beliefs. You have to think things through, to consider the costs and benefits of your alternatives. Does Churchill's decision pass this test?

My hunch is that without the benefit of the War Cabinet discussions, Churchill would never have thought through carefully whether to pursue the negotiation path. Even *considering* making a deal with Hitler was difficult for Churchill. It would have been completely inconsistent with his sense of self and his consciously crafted political identity. Churchill had warned of the dangers of German rearmament and Hitler's megalomania long before others realized it. He was asked to become prime minister because he wanted to fight, not negotiate. To back down now and negotiate with a cruel enemy like Hitler, especially when Hitler was winning the war, would be publicly humiliating—even if some sort of reasonable deal could be struck. If, at some point, Churchill had come to believe that negotiation with Hitler would better serve Great Britain, he would have resigned and let others—such as Lloyd George—handle the negotiations.[76]

Churchill was strongly motivated by his personal moral beliefs and gut feelings. He saw Hitler and his Reich as evil. On a visceral level, he found the very idea of negotiating with Hitler to be repugnant. He believed that this kind of evil should be resisted, almost no matter what the consequences. In this respect, he was much like Sharansky. I think he started with an emotionally based gut feeling of what was right and then used his reason to justify the decision. And again like Sharansky, he used the negative "traps" to keep himself (and his constituents) committed to a strategy of resistance.

Earlier, I concluded that Sharansky's refusal to negotiate with his Soviet captors, notwithstanding the pragmatic benefits of negotiation, was wise because he alone would suffer the consequences if he made the wrong choice. I also said that leaders have an obligation to act on the basis of a pragmatic assessment of the expected benefits and costs of the alternatives, not simply on moral intuitions or gut feelings alone. Sometimes the better part of wisdom is to negotiate, even when you don't want to. Even with an enemy who is evil.

As I read the minutes of the War Cabinet discussions, I was powerfully struck by how hard it was for Churchill to translate his intuitive convictions into a persuasive argument. I also gained a respect for

Halifax that I had not felt before. Halifax played an important role in the process by pushing Churchill to explain why his intuitions were sound enough to act on. He really put Churchill through his paces, almost as Spock might have done if he had been present. This underscores an important lesson: In deciding whether to enter into negotiations with a despised adversary, you can guard against a hasty rejection based simply on your gut instincts by discussing the matter with a colleague who disagrees. Being pushed to give reasons for your inclinations may sometimes lead you to change your mind. And even when it doesn't, it will force you to think through more rationally which course of action makes the most sense.

In the end, the War Cabinet's discussion persuades me that Churchill's refusal to enter into negotiations was wise. Churchill and Halifax had different perceptions of Hitler's wartime aims and interests—in effect, different predictions amid great uncertainty. We will never know what Hitler might have demanded from Great Britain if negotiations had begun in the middle of 1940. Halifax may have been right, but Churchill's prediction was equally plausible: that Hitler would make unacceptable demands because he was winning the war. That is just the problem: you can't rely on hindsight to know whether you're making a wise decision. A wise decision can turn out badly; it happens all the time. And a stupid decision can have a good outcome; you can be lucky. So the test of wisdom cannot be whether you're proven right in the end. The test is, *Did you think it through?*

With Halifax's help, I think Churchill passed that test. He was surely right in his implicit premise that it would be impossible to keep secret any sort of international conference about ending the war. If peace negotiations failed, they would fail publicly. He was also right that in May 1940, few in Great Britain knew how profound the risks were and how difficult it would be to resist Hitler alone. He was surely justified in being concerned, along with Sinclair and Greenwood, that if the negotiation route failed—and failed, moreover, *in the middle of a war which the British were losing*—British morale would have been seriously damaged. Britain had gone to war very reluctantly. Now she was the underdog and was taking a terrible beating. That was disheartening enough for the British people. Peace talks would raise hopes that further bloodshed could be avoided, and Churchill believed they were false hopes, which, once dashed, might leave the British too demoralized to fight to the finish. This was not an unreasonable prediction, particularly from a charismatic leader who understood when his rhetorical magic worked and when it did not.

Halifax never rebutted Churchill's argument that if the negotiations failed, British morale would have been undermined. By refusing to negotiate, Churchill signaled his determination that Britain would fight on. This signal was sent not just to Germany and other countries but, most importantly, to the British people themselves. He understood that entering into the negotiation process itself is not costless and can create risks. Wise decisions must take these into account.

Let me conclude by coming back to the subject of heroism. I must confess that there is something deeply appealing for me about the way Churchill resisted Hitler. And something disturbing about Chamberlain and Halifax's prior policy of appeasement. Churchill is one of my heroes. Chamberlain and Halifax are not. Even I, a strong proponent of negotiation, am not immune to the notion that fighting evil is heroic—and sometimes even thrilling.

What, after all, is a hero? A hero is someone who acts on behalf of a principle greater than himself, without regard to his own well-being. Consider the legends in every culture: A hero doesn't negotiate. He fights. To the death if necessary! A hero is willing to risk it all.

Negotiating with an evil enemy, by contrast, doesn't seem very heroic. It may be *prudent* to negotiate and make concessions, but it is rarely romantic or thrilling. It doesn't get the blood going. Nor, I must admit, is the process of negotiating typically exciting. It is often slow and tedious. It drags on and on.

But such simple dichotomies can be misleading. The very word *appeasement* now automatically evokes the story of Chamberlain and Halifax, and the moral of that story is plain: Never try to placate an enemy. The example of Churchill evokes a different narrative: It is heroic to resist evil, especially when standing alone. These are two very powerful narratives, but they can be dangerous because they invite knee-jerk reactions, not careful thought.

Can it be heroic to negotiate with evil? I think it can, and the next chapter explains why.

SIX

Nelson Mandela:
Apartheid in South Africa

Sitting in his isolated prison cell late in 1985, Nelson Mandela asked himself: Is it time to change my strategy? For nearly forty years, as a leader of the African National Congress (ANC), he had been fighting the South African government and its apartheid regime. By the time our story opens, he had been sitting in prison for twenty-three years, serving a life term for treason. Nominally sidelined from the struggle, he had, in fact, become the most famous political prisoner in the world. He was seventy-one years old, still thinking deeply about strategy and tactics, often a step ahead of his more cautious colleagues. In the solitude of his cell, he pondered: Should I try to initiate secret negotiations with the Devil?

There were signs that the time might be ripe, that perhaps it was time to talk. The ruling National Party was under increasing pressure to change its racist policies. The ANC had succeeded in discrediting apartheid throughout the world. An international trade boycott was crippling the country's economy. Within the black townships, the ANC was making good on its threat that black South Africa would become ungovernable without deep reform. Every year, the clashes with police were getting uglier and deadlier. An outright civil war would cause "both sides to lose thousands if not millions of lives," Mandela thought. He felt that some within the government understood this as well.

But after so many years of conflict, he knew that his initiating a "talk" would be a momentous step. Both sides viewed negotiation as a sign of "weakness and betrayal." Both sides had declared that they

would not "come to the table until the other made significant concessions." This is a classic problem in prolonged conflicts. Adversaries establish preconditions to negotiation that require the other side to
sacrifice most of its bargaining power before talks can even begin. Naturally, neither side agrees to this and the conflict simply persists. This
was the case in South Africa.

Throughout his time in prison, Mandela had refused on principle to
negotiate with the regime. He often received feelers from the government offering to release him from prison if he would renounce the use
of violence. But, much like Sharansky, Mandela had refused to compromise any principle that would weaken the movement. And he was very
public about it. For example, in rejecting the government's latest offer
of freedom, he had written a defiant speech that had been smuggled out
of prison and read aloud at an ANC rally. In it, Mandela had vowed *not*
to negotiate, saying, "Only free men can negotiate. . . . I cannot and
will not give any undertaking at a time when I and you, the people, are
not free."

The government's precondition for talks was that the ANC renounce
violence. Mandela had already staked his reputation on saying no.[1] The
ANC's preconditions were that political prisoners be released, exiles be
permitted to return, and the ban on the ANC be lifted. The government, of course, was nowhere near agreeing to these demands.

So how in good faith could Mandela offer to negotiate? If he reached
out to the enemy, he would essentially be waiving his own side's
preconditions—a colossal betrayal of the cause and his closest friends.

He faced other pitfalls behind the table. What authority did he have
to make such a momentous decision on behalf of the ANC? None. The
ANC was run collectively; no single leader could make decisions by
fiat. Moreover, Mandela wasn't even the president of the organization.
Oliver Tambo was. And Tambo was one of Mandela's oldest and closest
friends—the last person he would want to betray. Tambo had been
leading the ANC from exile for some twenty-five years; its headquarters were in Lusaka, Zambia.

So Mandela pondered his dilemma. Should he send a note to Tambo?
Over the years, Mandela and Tambo had developed ways to communicate with each other by passing messages through intermediaries. But
this process was difficult and slow. Mandela knew it might take months

to communicate with Tambo—and he couldn't be sure that Tambo would agree with him.

Another alternative was to consult with his fellow ANC prisoners. Three senior colleagues were serving terms in the same prison, including Walter Sisulu, Mandela's mentor.[2] Their cells were just three floors above Mandela's and there were reasonably frequent opportunities to meet and communicate. But actually . . . Mandela didn't want to consult with them, either. He knew what they would say. "[M]y colleagues upstairs would condemn my proposal, and that would kill my initiative even before it was born."

So Mandela decided to take the first step toward negotiations on his own. He would write to South Africa's minister of justice, Kobie Coetsee, offering to meet with him in secret to discuss how negotiations between the ANC and the government might begin. "I chose to tell no one what I was about to do. Not my colleagues upstairs or those in Lusaka," he later wrote in his autobiography. "There are times when a leader must move out ahead of the flock, go off in a new direction, confident that he is leading his people the right way."

When I think of Mandela at this moment of decision, frankly, I don't think of bucolic metaphors involving shepherds or flocks. I think of a man standing alone at the edge of a chasm, deciding to toss a steel cable across the divide, hoping that by some miracle someone will catch it and secure it on the other side. In this case, on one side of the chasm were the political aspirations of the black majority. On the other was a terrified white minority with a death grip on political power. Mandela understood this and tossed the cable, and by some miracle Coetsee caught it. Within a matter of months, the two men began a clandestine conversation that would continue for four years and lay the groundwork for building a bridge across the abyss.

———

Nelson Mandela's journey began in the tiny South African village of Mvezo, far removed from white society. The year was 1918, and the ANC was already six years old. But in the vast Transkei region where Mandela was born, there were hardly any white people and the ANC was largely unknown. As Mandela later wrote, "I thought little if at all about the white man in general or relations between my own people and these curious and remote figures." Life in the village was essentially controlled, as it had been for centuries, by tribal custom. But two seeds—advantages planted at Mandela's birth—would shape his identity and help him move far beyond the tribe.

Mandela's father was a chief, and his family was closely connected to the Thembu royal house, a tribe that was part of the Xhosa nation. When Nelson was nine, his father died of tuberculosis and the Thembu regent became his guardian. Nelson moved into the royal residence, called the Great Place, and was raised as a brother to the regent's son and heir, named Justice. By custom and blood, Nelson was expected someday to counsel the rulers of his tribe. From his earliest days, he was treated as someone special and he understood that he was being groomed to be a leader.[3]

The second advantage was planted by his mother, a Christian convert, who arranged for him to receive a British missionary education. He was baptized as a Christian and sent to a succession of ever more demanding schools established by British colonials hoping to cultivate a native black elite who held Western values. Nelson first attended a mission school near home,[4] then two elite boarding schools farther away, and finally the super-elite University College at Fort Hare. "For young black South Africans like myself, it was Oxford and Cambridge, Harvard and Yale, all rolled into one."

Both the tribe and the mission schools were powerful influences. "My later notions of leadership were profoundly influenced by observing the regent and his court," he writes. The regent presided over tribal meetings that lasted for hours. He would open the meeting, thank everyone for coming, explain the issue at hand, and listen in silence until everyone else had spoken. Then he would summarize the points made and search for a consensus. Mandela followed these principles for the rest of his life. "I have always endeavored to listen to what each and every person in a discussion had to say before venturing my own opinion." He was particularly impressed by the regent's pastoral metaphor for leadership, which he would later adapt to suit his own style. "I always remember the regent's axiom: a leader, he said, is like a shepherd. He stays behind the flock, letting the most nimble go out ahead, whereupon the others follow, not realizing that all along they are being directed from behind."

As for white people, he heard nothing positive about them. Within the tribe, they were demonized. One elder told him that the white men, with their "fire-breathing weapons," had "shattered . . . the fellowship of the various tribes" and been "greedy for land." Another elder tried to explain the racial situation in terms the young Nelson could understand. White people believed that the "true chief" of black South Africans was "the great white queen across the ocean," the elder said, but in truth, the white queen "brought nothing but misery and perfidy to the black people, and if she was a chief she was an evil chief."

It was through the missionary schools that Mandela first came to understand that whites could offer benefits to blacks through education. He appreciated these benefits and began to develop a lifelong fondness for British culture. In fact, he may have been well on his way to becoming a "black Englishman"—a pejorative term used by South African blacks to describe a member of the black elite who held British values and wouldn't make trouble. But when he was about nineteen, in his last year of boarding school, his universe became more complicated. "An event occurred that for [Mandela] was like a comet streaking across the night sky."

A great Xhosa poet came to visit the school. The entire school, including both black and white members of the school staff, gathered in the dining hall to hear the great man speak. All eyes turned to the end of the hall, where a door led to the home of Dr. Wellington, the white headmaster. As far as the students knew, the only person who ever stepped through that door was Dr. Wellington.

> Suddenly, the door opened and out walked not Dr. Wellington, but a black man dressed in a leopard-skin kaross and matching hat, who was carrying a spear in either hand. Dr. Wellington followed a moment later, but the sight of a black man in tribal dress coming through that door was electrifying. . . . It seemed to turn the universe upside down.

Even more stunning to Mandela was what the poet said in mixed racial company. The poet drew a sharp distinction between African culture, to which Mandela had not given much thought, and European culture. He informed the boys that the former was "indigenous and good," while the latter was "foreign and bad." Then he declared: "We cannot allow these foreigners who do not care for our culture to take over our nation. I predict that one day, the forces of African society will achieve a momentous victory over the interloper."

As the poet continued in this vein, Mandela writes,

> I could hardly believe my ears. His boldness in speaking of such delicate matters in the presence of Dr. Wellington and other whites seemed utterly astonishing to us. Yet at the same time, it aroused and motivated us, and began to alter my perception of men like Dr. Wellington, whom I had automatically considered my benefactor.

In the aftermath of this event, Mandela found himself disturbed and confused. "I saw that an African might stand his ground with a white man, yet I was still eagerly seeking benefits from whites, which often required subservience."

How was he going to reconcile these ideas? Such questions incubated in his mind for three years. In the meantime, he started college at Fort Hare, the best possible "passport" for an ambitious black in South Africa. He aspired to be a civil servant, "a glittering prize for an African, the highest that a black man could aspire to." With a secure income, he hoped to buy his mother a comfortable house and "restore to [her] the wealth and prestige that she had lost after my father's death."

But when he was twenty-two, about halfway through college, this inner conflict seemed to demand action. In a very short span of time, he rebelled against both British and tribal authority.

The first rebellion took place in college and foreshadowed many political decisions he would make in later life. The catalyst was hardly an issue of great significance: the quality of the food in the Fort Hare dining hall. Mandela had been nominated to the student council but, along with many other students who found the food "unsatisfactory," he decided to boycott the election as a protest. Six student representatives (including Mandela) were elected, but most in the class had refused to vote. All six "elected representatives" immediately resigned on the grounds that most of the students had not voted and that the election was illegitimate.

This set off a battle of wits between the principal, Dr. Kerr, and the student rebels. The next day, Dr. Kerr called a second election—this time in the college dining room at dinnertime, to make sure all the students attended. (Mandela saw this as a "clever" attempt on Kerr's part to legitimate the election.) Once again, most of the students boycotted and only a small number of students submitted ballots. The same six students were elected.

But this time, the other five representatives were willing to take office. Mandela was not. Most of the students still hadn't voted, he argued, so "it would be morally incorrect to say that we enjoyed their confidence." He was the only one who resigned.

Kerr called Mandela into his office and asked him to reconsider. Kerr was "a greatly respected man," Mandela writes, "virtually the founder" of the college. Kerr warned that if Mandela insisted on resigning, Kerr would be forced to expel him. "He told me to sleep on it and give him my final decision the following day."

Mandela did not sleep that night. He was torn. Should he stand on principle or stay in college? He believed that his stand was "morally right." He felt he had an "obligation" to the students who had boycotted the second election. He was acutely aware of his reputation with his peers: "I had taken a stand, and I did not want to appear to be a fraud in the eyes of my fellow students." On the other hand, were these concerns important enough to throw away his academic career?

Mandela returned to Kerr's office the next morning and said that he could not "in good conscience serve." Kerr reluctantly expelled Mandela in November 1940.

Now here was a question for Spock. Was this a wise choice on Mandela's part? Spock surely would have questioned Mandela's decision-making process. Even Mandela later called it a "foolhardy" decision. But this choice at the age of twenty-two bears all the trademarks of the later Mandela: an acute self-consciousness about himself as a leader, an obsession with legitimacy, a passion for moral rectitude, and a flair for martyrdom—with a dash of sanctimony and self-importance. It also presages later decisions in which he would demonstrate courage and integrity. "[A]t the moment I needed to compromise, I simply could not do so," he writes. "Something inside me would not let me."

In that spirit, he went home for the summer to the Great Place at Mqhekezweni. The regent was "furious" when he heard what Mandela had done. In fact, the regent decided that both Nelson and his own son, Justice, needed to settle down. A few weeks later, the regent called both young men to a meeting. "[B]efore I journey to the land of the ancestors," he said solemnly, "it is my duty to see my two sons properly married. I have, accordingly, arranged unions for both of you." The ceremonies were scheduled to take place shortly. (Mandela was to marry the daughter of the local Thembu priest.)

Mandela was horrified, and Justice was no happier with the situation, so they plotted an escape—they would run away to Johannesburg. They financed their trip by selling two of the regent's prize oxen. The regent and his minions pursued them for many days but never quite caught them. After a series of hair-raising adventures, they arrived in Johannesburg in April 1941.

In Johannesburg, Mandela learned how to deal with the white power structure. Walter Sisulu, a black estate agent, got him a job as a clerk in a progressive white law firm.[5] The job brought him into "regular contact with whites for the first time." It also introduced him to black role models who were assertive with whites. Mandela was greatly impressed by the firm's only other black employee, a clerk named Gaur Radebe, who was a member of both the ANC and the Communist Party. "Gaur was his own man," Mandela recalls. "He did not treat our employers with exaggerated courtesy, and often chided them for their treatment of Africans."

After working at the law firm for a few months, Mandela's career ambitions soared. He no longer aspired to be a civil servant; now he wanted to become a lawyer. This was no simple task in South Africa, even for whites. It required years of work as an "articled clerk" in a law firm and a law degree from a university. There were thousands of black teachers and civil servants in South Africa, but hardly any black lawyers. The 1946 census indicates that there were only thirteen articled clerks and eighteen African lawyers in the entire country.[6]

Mandela would become one of them. He completed his B.A. by correspondence, got a job as an articled clerk at the law firm, and enrolled as a part-time law student at the University of Witwatersrand, perhaps the top English-speaking university in South Africa. There he finally met many white people his own age.

His political education was overseen by Sisulu, Radebe, and a college acquaintance named Oliver Tambo. These men introduced him to the

ANC. Founded in 1912, it was the oldest political organization in the country, committed to securing full citizenship rights for blacks. Mandela soon took a leadership role, helping to launch an ANC youth affiliate. He also searched for a political philosophy and was powerfully drawn to "Africanism," which emphasized black self-determination and encouraged blacks to think of themselves as Africans first, not members of a particular tribe. For Mandela, the appeal of Africanism was that it was a nationalist movement that sought to restore pride in African culture.

> I, too, had been susceptible to paternalistic British colonialism and the appeal of being perceived by whites as "cultured" and "progressive" and "civilized." I was already on my way to being drawn into the black elite that Britain sought to create in Africa. . . . But it was an illusion. Like [others,] I came to see the antidote as militant African nationalism.

The year 1948, when Mandela was thirty, was a turning point for South Africa. The political landscape underwent a seismic shift in which apartheid became, for the first time, an explicit national policy. To understand the meaning of this shift, some historical background is important.

South Africa has two distinct white cultures, which have been in conflict since the early nineteenth century. The larger group, about 60 percent of the white population, speaks Afrikaans, a Dutch dialect. They descend from European settlers who arrived in the mid-seventeenth century as part of a colony established by the Dutch East India Company. By the late eighteenth century, this group no longer identified with Holland or even Europe. They thought of themselves as Afrikaners—white Africans (or Boers)—with their own special culture and a divine mandate to impose it in this part of Africa. For many, central to that culture was the belief that the white race was inherently superior to the black race and that the proper relationship between the two was that of master and servant.

The second group of whites (about 40 percent) is English-speaking, and most are of British origin. They came much later than the Boers. In 1815, Britain annexed the Cape Colony by military force. Soon British settlers, lured by fertile land (and later the discovery of gold and diamonds), were arriving in droves. Some were reform-minded and had more liberal racial attitudes than the Afrikaners. In 1830, well before the United States did so, Great Britain abolished slavery in the Cape Colony.

The abolishment of slavery sparked intense conflict between the two white cultures. A group of Afrikaners set out on what became known as the "Great Trek," hoping to establish new farms and settlements far away from the Cape and its British colonists. But the British were reluctant to cede control of this rich territory. What followed was a long period of three-way wars among the British, the Boers, and the native black tribes, particularly the Zulus.

An uneasy "compromise" was reached in 1910 with the creation of the Union of South Africa—a new nation subject to the British Crown but which had its own parliament and considerable autonomy.[7] The white minority, of course, controlled the government.[8] Blacks made up two-thirds of the population but were not allowed to vote.[9]

Until 1948, the English-speakers dominated the Afrikaners socially and economically; political power was shared. That political balance radically changed when the National Party came to power.

The NP was a "nationalist" party composed of Afrikaners who were fed up with being second-class citizens to the British. The party was strongly anti-British and had sympathized with the Nazis in World War II. In racial matters, it was an extreme right-wing party committed to preserving white control of South Africa at all costs. Central to its platform was apartheid, or "apartness," which required the consolidation and expansion of existing racist practices and laws into a unified national code. The party's key slogans included the *swart gevaar,* or "black danger," and *Die kaffer op sy plek,* which meant "the nigger in his place."

The NP was so extreme, in fact, that few people expected it to win the 1948 elections. When it prevailed, many in South Africa were shocked.

Apartheid was not built overnight, but over the next ten years it became what Mandela describes as a "monolithic system that was diabolical in its detail, inescapable in its reach, and overwhelming in its power." It classified everyone into racial groups: black, colored (mixed race, Indian, or Asian), and white. The groups were forcibly separated, physically as well as legally. Beginning in 1950, black and colored neighborhoods began to be moved away from white neighborhoods. Over the next thirty years, millions of nonwhites would be "resettled" to new designated areas.

Blacks, of course, fared horribly under this system. They were essentially stripped of national citizenship, divided into ten tribes, and assigned to tribal "homelands" where they were virtually quarantined. These homelands were small and economically unproductive; the best agricultural land was controlled by whites. This system made blacks akin to guest workers in white South Africa. They could not travel outside their homeland without their "pass books," which identified them and had to be signed every month by their employers. Black men from rural areas, who were permitted to work in cities, were not allowed for many years even to have their wives and children accompany them. Some were housed in all-male dormitories, others in shantytowns.

This rigid system of "political partition" controlled every aspect of life. Marriages between persons of different races were prohibited. Restaurants, restrooms, and swimming pools were segregated. There were separate universities for blacks, coloreds, and Indians. To enforce these laws, the government built up a massive, heavily armed security force.

———————

It took Mandela several years to figure out his own approach to this evil regime. The ANC leadership favored peaceful protest. But as Mandela rose through the leadership ranks,[10] he began to believe that this approach was far too timid and would never force the government to change. In 1953, long before his colleagues were ready to consider tougher measures, Mandela publicly advocated armed resistance for the first time—without seeking prior clearance. The ANC's National Executive Committee censured him for departing from its policy. Mandela loyally fell in line, but privately he believed that the ANC would eventually have to agree with him. As long as the government could repress all peaceful forms of protest, he felt, there was "no alternative to armed and violent resistance."

What ultimately helped Mandela make his case was the rise of a rival black organization known as the Pan Africanist Congress (PAC), which was willing to use much more assertive and headline-grabbing tactics. In 1960, the PAC organized a mass rally at Sharpeville to protest the pass book laws. Protesters left their pass books at home, marched en masse to the local police depot, and demanded to be arrested. The tiny police force was overwhelmed and called in reinforcements. In the melee that followed, the police killed sixty-nine blacks, most of whom were shot in the back while fleeing. The "Sharpeville Massacre" made headlines around the world.

Not to be outdone, the ANC orchestrated a *national* strike and pass-burning demonstrations. The escalating rivalry between the two black organizations created so much disorder that the government quickly declared a state of emergency and banned them both.

Tambo went into exile, set up ANC headquarters in Lusaka, and began to organize foreign support. Mandela and other leaders stayed in the country and went underground. Mandela popped up from time to time, making well-publicized appearances to demonstrate that the ANC was still alive and well.

Mandela proved to be a master at generating publicity. In 1961, appearing at a conference before some fourteen hundred delegates, he issued a public challenge to Prime Minister Hendrik Verwoerd. He demanded that Verwoerd call for a national constitutional convention in which representatives of all races would "sit down in brotherhood" and create a "new nonracial democratic constitution." If the prime minister failed to act, Mandela said, he would call for a three-day national strike. To make sure he got his point across, Mandela put his challenge in writing—better for the press to quote accurately from it—in a follow-up letter to Verwoerd. Verwoerd never acknowledged Mandela's letter, but the government responded on a scale never seen before in South Africa. To inhibit the strike, police arrested and detained some ten thousand black people.

This massive display of repressive force shocked even some leaders of the ANC, and it was precisely the evidence Mandela needed to persuade them that they had to permit some forms of violence or risk becoming irrelevant. Finally, with the leadership's blessing, Mandela established a military arm of the ANC: Umkhonto we Sizwe, "The Spear of the Nation." Its initial policy was to carry out acts of sabotage against government installations and facilities, and not target people. But if sabotage proved not to be enough, Mandela was prepared to "move on to the next stage: guerrilla warfare and terrorism."

Where all this would lead, he didn't know. If Spock had asked him,

"What's the end game? A civil war?" Mandela probably would have answered, "I hope not. But without armed resistance, the regime will never change."

He spent the next year learning how to lead a guerrilla army. He read about Che Guevara, Mao Tse-tung, and Menachem Begin. He studied guerrilla armies in Kenya, Algeria, and the Cameroons. He traveled across Africa to meet freedom fighters and to learn how to secure arms. He also went to London to meet with Tambo—and perhaps to acquire some tailored English suits. As Mandela wrote:

> I confess to being something of an Anglophile. When I thought of Western democracy and freedom, I thought of the British parliamentary system. In so many ways, the very model of the gentleman for me was an Englishman. Despite Britain being the home of parliamentary democracy, it was that democracy that had helped inflict a pernicious system of iniquity on my people. While I abhorred the notion of British imperialism, I never rejected the trappings of British style and manners.

As a gentleman-terrorist, however, Mandela's days were numbered. He never had a chance to engage personally in any guerrilla attack or terrorist activity. Shortly after he returned to South Africa in 1962, he was arrested and ultimately linked to terrorist activities. He and several colleagues were charged with treason.

Mandela's trial attracted international attention and helped make him a star. The fact that he faced the death penalty only heightened the interest of the media, which he used skillfully. In a remarkable address to the court, Mandela practically pleaded guilty to treason. He admitted that he was one of the founders of Umkhonto we Sizwe, that it was a guerrilla organization, and that he had played a "prominent role" in its activities, including planning acts of sabotage. He also offered a powerful justification of his decision to lead a violent movement. Because it is so characteristic of his thinking and personal style, it is worth quoting at length.

> I did not plan it in a spirit of recklessness nor because I have any love of violence. I planned it as a result of a calm and sober assess-

ment of the political situation that had arisen after many years of tyranny, exploitation, and oppression of my people by whites.

We of the ANC . . . shrank from any action which might drive the races further apart than they already were. But the hard facts were that fifty years of nonviolence had brought the African people nothing but more repressive legislation, and fewer and fewer rights.

He issued no calls to battle. He did not demonize the regime. Instead he made a "calm and sober assessment." In fact, he sounded a bit like Spock. As long as the government used violence to repress peaceful protest, he continued, he and his comrades saw only two choices: outright civil war, which would be a complete bloodbath; or guerrilla warfare, which would risk *fewer lives on both sides*. This was the language of cost-benefit analysis.

But his oratory could also soar.

During my lifetime I have dedicated myself to this struggle of the African people. I have fought against white domination, and I have fought against black domination. I have cherished the ideal of a democratic and free society in which all persons live together in harmony and with equal opportunities. It is an ideal which I hope to live for and to achieve. But if needs be, it is an ideal for which I am prepared to die.

Mandela instructed his lawyers that no matter what the verdict— even the death penalty—he would refuse to appeal it, because in his view the South African court system had no legitimacy. In June 1964, along with several of his comrades, Mandela was convicted and sentenced to life in prison. True to his word, he took no appeal.

Mandela would be imprisoned for twenty-six years. For the first eighteen, which he calls the "Dark Years" in his autobiography, he was held on Robben Island, a hellhole which, like Alcatraz in San Francisco Bay, now stands as a gloomy tourist attraction. I visited the place in 2005. About a thirty-minute boat ride from Cape Town's harbor, the island lies in the far reaches of a beautiful bay. The prison itself is appalling. I saw Mandela's cell, so small that a man his size could not lie down without touching two of the four dank walls. There was one small window at eye level. My guide, a former political prisoner who served time on Robben Island with Mandela, showed me the courtyard where the prisoners had crushed rocks.

How did Mandela survive?

He got into the habit of "negotiating with the enemy"—the guards and prison authorities. This was a radical departure from the Sharansky mode of prison survival. From the very beginning, he became the leader of Robben Island's political prisoners, and he told them that the "struggle" in prison was no different from the struggle outside. With characteristic dignity, he insisted on proper treatment from his jailers and taught the other political prisoners to do the same. He complained about the inadequacies of the prison blankets, clothing, and food, but not in an adversarial spirit. He and his fellow prisoners "adopted a policy of talking to the wardens and persuading them to treat us as human beings. And a lot of them did, and there were lots of things we could talk about. And the lesson was that one of our strongest weapons is dialogue. Sit down with a man [and] if you have prepared your case very well, that man . . . will never be the same again."[11]

By getting to know his jailers, Mandela also had a longer-term motive: preparing for future negotiations with the white power structure. In college he had learned how to box, and he remembered this training as he sparred with the wardens. "This is a boxing match that I know how to handle," he thought. "I know how to fight against these fellows. I know how they feint, I know how they move, and I feel confident in this arena."

Meanwhile, outside the prison walls, violent confrontations between blacks and the government were escalating. In 1976, a protest in Soweto had left more than six hundred dead.[12] By the early 1980s, the ANC was setting off bombs at government facilities. People were dying.[13] Mandela was prepared for this. He knew it was the price of the armed struggle he had insisted on launching. On the bright side, the ANC was increasingly popular among blacks and well-known internationally. World support for the anti-apartheid movement was growing. The government was under pressure. All these were promising signs.

In 1982 the government moved Mandela and three of his comrades to a new facility, Pollsmoor Prison, near Cape Town. The government never explained this move, but it was the subject of much speculation. The four senior ANC prisoners received special treatment from the beginning—they were separated from the other prisoners and housed in a spacious room with real beds and other amenities. Because it was situated on the top floor of the prison, Mandela called it the "penthouse."

He didn't think it was a pure coincidence that the government seemed to be sending him more serious "feelers" during the next three years. The new minister of justice, Kobie Coetsee, began to allow prominent foreign visitors to meet with him in prison, where they freely discussed politics with him, fell under his spell, and presumably reported back to the government.

This was the context in which Mandela decided that it was time to send out a feeler of his own. He thought he finally had enough bargaining power to start talking directly with the government.

Coetsee did not initially respond to Mandela's secret letter sent in 1985. But a few weeks later, when Mandela underwent routine surgery at a local hospital, he received a surprise visit from Coetsee. The minister simply "dropped by the hospital unannounced as if he were visiting an old friend who was laid up for a few days," Mandela writes. They discussed little of substance; it was a social visit. "Though I acted as though this was the most normal thing in the world, I was amazed," Mandela recalls. "The government, in its slow and tentative way, was reckoning that they had to come to some accommodation with the ANC. Coetsee's visit was an olive branch."

Mysterious events continued to happen. When Mandela returned to prison, he was not led back to his old cell. Instead he was escorted to a "palatial" three-room suite several floors away from his ANC comrades, where he was told that he would now live alone. No explanation was given. At first Mandela resented the separation from his comrades, but then he realized the freedom it gave him to negotiate with the government without being observed. "If we did not start a dialogue soon, both sides would be plunged into a dark night of oppression, violence and war. My solitude would give me an opportunity to take the first steps in that direction, without the kind of scrutiny that might destroy such efforts," he wrote. "I would have to adopt a strategy that would enable me to confront people with a fait accompli. I was convinced that was the only way." [14]

Mandela was aware, however, that this move ahead of the flock would be riskier than his previous forays. The flock had no idea that contact had been made. If they heard the news from anyone other than himself, there would be big trouble in the pasture—that is, behind the table. Indeed, there was a significant risk that the government would try to place a wedge between Mandela and his colleagues by leaking the news itself. Mandela wanted to prevent this at all costs. Thus, after his hospital meeting with Coetsee, he sent for his legal advisor, George Bizos. [15]

As Bizos recalled, "He asked me to try to get to Oliver Tambo in Lusaka and assure him that nothing would happen without their approval." [16]

In sending this message, Mandela was shading the truth. Something quite significant had happened. But he got away with it. Tambo, having only the "sketchiest idea of what was going on," conferred with a small circle of ANC leaders and sent back the message that Mandela could go ahead and make contact. [17] Having received this belated green light, Mandela wrote to Coetsee a second time, to "propose talks about talks."

Coetsee did not respond, however, and violence continued to climb. In 1986, President Pieter Botha ordered air raids on ANC bases in Zambia, Zimbabwe, and Botswana. [18] In response, the Commonwealth countries imposed sanctions on South Africa [19] and the ANC leadership turned up the heat. "Oliver Tambo and the ANC had called for the people of South Africa to render the country ungovernable," Mandela recalls, "and the people were obliging." As black protests surged throughout the country, the government imposed another state of emergency.

Sensing an opportunity, Mandela requested another meeting with Coetsee. "In every outward way, the time seemed inauspicious for negotiations," he writes. "But often, the most discouraging moments are precisely the time to launch an initiative." This time Coetsee obliged. The two spoke for more than three hours and directly addressed the issues that separated the ANC and the government. At the end of the talk, Mandela told Coetsee that he would like to meet with President Botha.

Botha did not accept Mandela's invitation, but he told Coetsee to keep the talks going and report back. This was another step in the right direction: Coetsee and Mandela were now meeting with the express permission of the president. They began to meet more frequently, and in May 1988, Coetsee suggested that their secret talks be expanded to include a Special Committee of senior government officials.[20] Mandela agreed, thinking this was a favorable development.

But he had no control over the membership of the committee, and he was in for some unpleasant surprises. One member turned out to be Niel Barnard, the head of the secret police. To the ANC, Barnard was viewed as evil incarnate—a man who had personally committed evil acts. "It was like asking [Soviet dissident] Andrei Sakharov to talk to the head of the KGB," Mandela thought.[21] Another member was the director general of prisons, Fanie van der Merwe.

Mandela again pondered how much to tell his ANC colleagues. They would never approve of his meeting with a committee that included Barnard. And yet Barnard could prove helpful in persuading the prime minister.

Mandela resolved the quandary in the usual way, with partial (and misleading) disclosures to his ANC prison mates. He decided to "seek their counsel about the idea of having talks with the government without mentioning that an actual committee had been formed." By working in this oblique way and withholding key details, Mandela received the qualified—if uninformed—support of his prison mates.[22]

No sooner had he covered his flanks on one side than he was exposed on another. He received a note from Tambo, who "thought I was making an error in judgment" in having further contact with the government at all. Mandela immediately wrote back and explained that he was talking to the government "about one thing and one thing only: a meeting between the National Executive Committee of the ANC and the South African government."

Again, this assurance was truthful in one sense but evasive in another. Mandela would be talking about far more than some future meeting between the ANC and the government. As his autobiography makes plain, he had already discussed substantive political issues at length not only with Coetsee but also with two men with day-to-day responsibility for investigating and imprisoning black protesters. Ultimately, Mandela met with the Special Committee forty-seven times.

Mandela felt that these meetings were essential in earning the trust of the Afrikaners. He knew that the white officials were afraid of what he represented and of what the future might hold for them as a white minority. He treated them with respect and worked to make them comfortable. Indeed, by all accounts he dazzled them. At the first meeting between Mandela and Barnard, for example, the latter confessed: "I am not able to express myself in English as one is able to do in one's mother tongue." Mandela immediately put him at ease by saying, "I can follow Afrikaans quite well. If I don't understand something, I will ask you."[23] He also tried to establish a "personal link" with each member of the committee. The commissioner of prisons, Van der Merwe, was surprised and flattered that Mandela remembered him from some thirty years before, when they had argued opposite sides of a case. The trust Mandela earned with these simple gestures "counted for far more than Mandela's policy position on any particular issue."[24]

The policy disagreements were profound. There were four central issues: "the armed struggle, the ANC's alliance with the Communist Party, the goal of majority rule, and the idea of racial reconciliation." Mandela made no concessions, but neither did he make threats. Instead he talked about peace, his interest in a negotiated settlement, his understanding of their concerns, and his commitment to racial reconciliation.

At the end of 1988, to facilitate these meetings, the government moved Mandela to plush new quarters at Victor Verster Prison. He was given his own small cottage on the prison grounds, complete with furnishings, a swimming pool, and a personal cook. Naturally, some members of Mandela's own party, especially the younger and more radical ones, began to get suspicious.[25] What was Mandela promising the government? Was he selling out?

To allay these fears, Mandela occasionally invited young black leaders to his cottage for a meeting or a meal. "They came in pilgrimage to their legendary leader, and he made each of them feel special. He knew the names of wives and children; had followed the career of each one with attention; he awed them with his grasp of the South African political situation. They left under the same spell of seduction as their enemies."[26]

But the person Mandela most wanted to seduce was Botha. Mandela spent months writing a detailed memorandum that spelled out what he saw as the terms of an honorable peace. He felt that peace would only come with democratic majority rule, but he acknowledged that this goal would have to be reconciled with white fears of black domination. This subject would need to be addressed through negotiations.

On July 5, 1989, shortly before Botha resigned as president, the two men finally met in the presidential office. This meeting, too, was carried out in the utmost secrecy; Mandela was "smuggled" in. They did not discuss the substance of Mandela's talks with the Special Committee. Botha treated Mandela with great courtesy and poured the tea. Mandela drew "parallels between their rival nationalisms"—the Afrikaner nationalism and its rebellions, which pitted white brother against brother, and the ANC's nationalism, which involved a struggle "between brothers who happen to be different colours."[27] "While the meeting was not a breakthrough in terms of negotiations, it was one in another sense," he writes. "Mr. Botha had long talked about the need to cross the Rubicon, but he never did it himself until that morning. . . . Now, I felt, there was no turning back."

In August 1989, Botha resigned as president of South Africa. The following day, F. W. de Klerk was inaugurated to fill the empty seat. De Klerk had not been involved in the secret talks and Mandela had no idea what to expect of him, but there was little reason for optimism. According to the journalist Patti Waldmeir, de Klerk was "almost genetically predestined to defend white rule." His father and uncle had been important NP leaders, and de Klerk himself had never "knowingly strayed from the party line."[28]

Although de Klerk did not immediately respond to Mandela's request for a meeting, he proved to be an altogether different leader from Botha. He was "a pragmatist," Mandela discovered, "a man who saw change as necessary and inevitable." Mandela began to use the Special Committee as a channel for sending direct messages to the new president. For example, Mandela urged de Klerk—through the committee—to prove his "good intentions" by releasing senior ANC prisoners unconditionally. In return, Mandela guaranteed that his men would display "disciplined behavior." Within weeks, de Klerk announced the unconditional release of eight high-profile political prisoners, including Walter Sisulu. This move was praised both at home and in the international community and signaled a significant step toward reconciliation. (Through the committee, Mandela sent his thanks to de Klerk. In effect, the two leaders were already negotiating.)[29]

When Mandela finally met with de Klerk in late 1989, he was impressed. "Mr. de Klerk listened to what I had to say," he remembers. "This was a novel experience. National Party leaders generally heard what they wanted to hear in discussions with black leaders, but Mr. de Klerk seemed to be making an attempt to truly understand." Among the topics they discussed that day was the issue of Mandela's freedom. Mandela knew that his imprisonment was a stain on the National Party's reputation and that his release could help the NP. He was in a strong position to negotiate the terms of his own release and he drove a hard bargain. It made no sense, he told de Klerk, to release him while the ANC was still officially illegal. Mandela had no intention of going into retirement, so the government would just have to arrest him again. The best plan, he said, was for the government to release the remaining political prisoners, allow exiles to return, lift the official ban on the ANC and other political organizations, and end the state of emergency. *Then* it could free Mandela.

De Klerk made no promises, but Mandela was heartened by his visit. He told his colleagues that de Klerk "was a man we could do business with."

About a month later, on February 2, 1990, de Klerk stunned the country by announcing a set of decisions that met most of Mandela's conditions for release. He lifted the ban on the ANC and several other political organizations, freed prisoners arrested for nonviolent activities, suspended capital punishment, and lifted many of the restrictions associated with the state of emergency. As de Klerk told the South African people, "The time for negotiation has arrived."

He neglected to mention, of course, that the two sides had been secretly negotiating for four years.

"It was a breathtaking moment," Mandela writes, "for in one sweeping action he had virtually normalized the situation in South Africa." Mandela knew it would not be long before he too would be free.

But the logistics of his release sparked tension between the two men. De Klerk had not yet learned with whom he was dealing. On February 9, just a week after his speech to Parliament, de Klerk informed Mandela that he would be released the next day. De Klerk had mapped out the entire plan without consulting Mandela, who was not pleased.

Mandela wanted to leave prison as soon as possible, "but to do so on such short notice would not be wise." In true Spockian fashion, he wanted to think it through. He wanted to prepare his family and the ANC leadership—and no doubt himself—for this momentous occasion, which he rightly feared could degenerate into chaos.

Thus began a negotiation that might have been amusing had it not been so serious. Mandela demanded to stay in prison for another week; de Klerk insisted that he be released immediately. Mandela wanted to walk out the prison gates and thank his guards personally; de Klerk wanted to fly Mandela to Johannesburg and preside over a huge media event there. Ultimately they reached a compromise. The release could not be postponed, de Klerk said, because the foreign press had already been told of the plan. But the release would take place at the prison.

The following day, after twenty-seven years in prison, Mandela ended his long confinement. As biographer Tom Lodge explains:

> By the end of 1989 it was obvious to South Africa's rulers that only their most famous captive could render any settlement legitimate. This realisation was very substantially the product of Mandela's diplomacy. In "talking to the enemy" he had become more than the master of his fate, because he could now profoundly affect the political destiny of his compatriots.[30]

———

With his release, Mandela had obviously scored some important points in his boxing match with the National Party. He'd won some early rounds. The government had acknowledged the need to negotiate. Everyone knew that apartheid was dying and would soon be buried. The ANC had won a dominant political role in South Africa and, as far as the world was concerned, Mandela was its leader.

But Mandela's task was far from over. In fact, in some ways it became more difficult. Apartheid might be dying, but what political and economic structures would replace it? On the big issues, the ANC and the National Party had irreconcilable differences. Behind the table, there were deep divisions, not just within the two major parties but more broadly within the black and white communities. For the next four years, Mandela and de Klerk would struggle—and often fail—to control the interplay between the action across the table and the action behind it. I will not attempt to describe the full complexity of the peacemaking process.[31] Suffice it to say that it was violent and often out of control.

Mandela's immediate task behind the table was to consolidate his authority among his colleagues and prove that he hadn't sold out. Two weeks after his release, he met with the ANC leadership in Lusaka. "I could see the questions in their eyes," he recalls. "Was Mandela the same man who went to prison twenty-seven years before, or was this a different Mandela, a reformed Mandela? Had he survived or had he been broken?"

Candor was the only way out. For the first time in five years, Mandela told the leadership everything he had done in his secret talks with the government. His colleagues responded positively and elected him deputy president of the ANC. (Actually, they had little choice. Oliver Tambo had suffered a stroke the year before and was not in good health. As Tambo's successor, Mandela was so revered that he had no real competition.)[32]

Across the table, there were profound problems. The central political dispute was how to distribute power between the 80 percent black majority and the 20 percent white minority. To Mandela, the principle of "one man, one vote" was not negotiable. But the NP could not conceive of ever making this concession. De Klerk assured his constituents that "[w]e are not sellouts of anyone"[33] and promised a political system that would retain either a white veto or "group rights" to protect the white community from black rule.[34] "Group rights" was seen as essential for the survival of the Afrikaner community and culture. Gerrit Viljoen, the NP's minister of constitutional development, told an interviewer during this time, "Those who want to live, worship, work, or play in specifically defined communities should have the right to do so in the new South Africa, but without laws making [integration] compulsory."[35]

Economic questions also loomed. If the ANC came to power, what would happen to private property, most of which was owned by whites? The National Party had spent decades lambasting the ANC as a communist front. By 1990, these fears had largely ebbed—the Berlin Wall had fallen, the Soviet Union had collapsed, and de Klerk could see that a South Africa, even if governed by the ANC, was not going to become a communist satellite.[36] But the whites were still worried about their property. The ANC had an openly socialist agenda: it had consistently called for nationalization of the mines, greater governmental control of the means of production, and substantial redistribution of property.

The first official talks between the ANC and the government, held in May 1990, did not tackle any of these fundamental issues. Instead the parties focused on simply getting to know each other. To Mandela, the sight of long-standing enemies shaking hands was "extraordinary." The ANC delegates explained that historically their party had always wanted to negotiate with the government, and de Klerk made another of his astonishing statements. As Mandela recalls, "Mr. de Klerk, for his part, suggested that the system of separate [racial] development had been conceived as a benign idea, but had not worked in practice. For that, he said, he was sorry, and hoped the negotiations would make amends. It was not an apology for apartheid, but it went further than any other National Party leader ever had."

These talks, which lasted three days, had a powerful psychological impact on the participants. It was a first step in reversing their mutual demonization: as an ANC participant later told reporters, "each side had discovered that the other did not have horns." In a modest and very carefully worded agreement, both sides pledged a commitment to the peaceful process of negotiation. Mandela did not explicitly end the ANC's armed struggle; he walked right up to the line but could tell his constituents he had not stepped over it. In return, the government promised to lift completely the state of emergency.

Outside the meeting room, however, this conclave had little impact. In fact, the summer of 1990 was a disaster for the peace process. The black community was being ravaged by internal warfare. Within the Zulu community, the ANC and a rival organization, Inkatha, were embroiled in mutual slaughter, particularly in the region of Natal.[37] Mandela wanted to meet with the other group's leader and negotiate peace, but militant members of his own party would not allow such a meeting.

By July, more than fifteen hundred people had died in political violence in 1990. "Our country was bleeding to death," Mandela writes.

That same summer Mandela's own credibility with de Klerk took a major hit. The government arrested forty members of the ANC and discovered documents that appeared to describe a Communist Party plot to overthrow the government. The incident was a terrible embarrassment for Mandela, who knew nothing about it,[38] and for de Klerk, who had just lifted the state of emergency and now had to calm his constituents' fears that the ANC was planning a violent takeover.[39]

To mitigate the damage and keep the talks moving forward, Mandela decided to make a concession. De Klerk, Mandela wrote later, "needed to show his supporters that his policy had brought benefits to the country." So Mandela told his own supporters that it was time to suspend the armed struggle. Not *end* it, he emphasized, just *suspend* it. This was a very tough sell behind the table. Although the Umkhonto we Sizwe, the military arm, had been quiescent for more than a year,[40] "the aura of the armed struggle had great meaning for many people," Mandela writes. Many of them thought the ANC was giving up too much bargaining leverage.[41] But Mandela prevailed, and, in August 1990, the ANC promised to suspend the armed struggle. This concession was widely praised internationally and brought the ANC significant political and financial support.[42]

But continuing violence in the black townships took a heavy toll on Mandela's relationship with de Klerk. Mandela came to suspect that the National Party, and perhaps de Klerk himself, was purposely fomenting black-on-black violence to weaken the ANC's credibility as a party that could someday lead the government.[43] Here was Mandela trying to make the case for majority rule, and the "majority" was rioting and looting. This was all too convenient for the NP, which claimed to be the only party capable of maintaining order. Mandela became increasingly convinced that there was a "hidden hand behind the violence[,] . . . a mysterious 'Third Force,' which consisted of renegade men from the [white] security forces who were attempting to disrupt the negotiations." He repeatedly asked de Klerk to explain why the police were failing to control the Inkatha rampages; the police rarely made arrests and often seemed to encourage the violence. De Klerk never provided an answer.

Mandela's suspicions were later confirmed when a newspaper investigation revealed that the police had been secretly financing Inkatha.[44] Although de Klerk denied any personal knowledge of such a "third force," Mandela never got over the feeling that he was somehow complicit.[45] I suspect that neither Mandela nor de Klerk could completely control their most militant followers—not to mention people outside their own parties. Some of the looting, rioting, and gang warfare was carried out by thugs whose motivations were not even political. But the resulting carnage had a destructive and lasting effect on the peace process.

For the next two years, it was all Mandela and de Klerk could do to keep the negotiations alive. The dynamic among the rival black groups and the white security forces was just too destructive. The talks lurched, faltered, and broke down several times.[46] As Mandela told his supporters in July 1991, "[T]he struggle is not over, and negotiations themselves are a theater of struggle, subject to advances and reverses as any other form of struggle."

It is often dangerous when talks bog down. Each party blames the other and the anger needs an outlet.[47] The summer of 1992 proved to be the most terrifying period of the peace process. Despite Mandela's misgivings, the ANC resolved to pursue a campaign of "rolling mass action"—a wave of strikes, boycotts, and other protests—to pressure the government to make concessions. Mandela feared the demonstrations could get out of hand and lead to further violence and loss of life. And he was right. But many of his followers were impatient with the lack of progress at the table and he relented. The campaign began on June 16, the sixteenth anniversary of the Soweto uprising, and would culminate in August with a national strike.[48]

But before this campaign was even twenty-four hours old, the country was shaken by yet another debilitating spasm of black-on-black violence. It was the fourth in a week, killing forty-six ANC followers, mostly women and children.[49] Again, the police made no arrests. For Mandela, this was the "last straw." In a rare display of anger, he publicly compared the NP to the Nazis in Germany and withdrew from the negotiations.

His followers, too, had lost faith in the peace process. One day, he arrived at a mass meeting of the ANC and found an anonymous note waiting for him on the podium. "No peace, do not talk to us about peace. We've had enough. Please, Mr. Mandela, no peace. Give us weapons. No Peace." Mandela threw away his prepared text and in his "most regal manner" exercised his moral authority:

> [W]e must accept that responsibility for ending the violence is not just the government's, the police's, the army's. It is also our responsibility. We must put our house in order. If you have no discipline you are not a freedom fighter. If you are going to kill innocent people, you don't belong to the ANC. Your task is reconciliation.

When some in the crowd shouted their objections, Mandela said, "Listen to me! Listen to me! I am your leader. As long as I am your leader,

I am going to give leadership. Do you want me to remain your leader?" The crowd roared back that it did. "Well," he declared, "as long as I am your leader, I will tell you, always, when you are wrong." [50]

The summer culminated in a tragic incident. A group of ANC militants planned a demonstration in Bisho, a black homeland that was known to be hostile territory for the ANC. Unwisely, they included women and children in the protest and failed to control their own ranks. When some protesters tried to climb through an opening in a fence and take a different route to town, twenty-nine people were gunned down by untrained homeland police.

The Bisho massacre strengthened Mandela's hand behind the table. Within the ANC, the balance of power shifted back toward Mandela and others who favored reaching an agreement through negotiation. [51] Although the police were condemned for their part in the massacre, the ANC was condemned as well for irresponsibly failing to control a provocative demonstration.

Around the same time, Mandela realized that the violence was destroying the South African economy. After receiving a briefing by the ANC's head of economics, Mandela said, "[I]t appears to me that if we allowed the situation to continue . . . the economy is going to be so destroyed that when a democratic government comes to power, it will not be able to solve." [52]

The Bisho massacre, in the words of Allister Sparks, forced Mandela and de Klerk "to stare into the abyss in order to recognize their mutual dependency." [53] They resumed their negotiations and the two parties began to work together in earnest. During the next fourteen months, a deal was finally hammered out. In June 1993, the parties set a firm date for elections based on universal suffrage. In November, Mandela and de Klerk reached agreement on the interim constitution.

On the core political issues, Mandela prevailed. It was a classic liberal constitution providing for three branches of government, an independent judiciary, and a bill of rights protecting individual human and property rights. The new South Africa would be a parliamentary democracy based on one man, one vote. There would be no white veto of any sort, no "group rights." For five years, there would be a transitional government in which all significant political parties would be represented. Thereafter, a government would be formed on the simple basis of majority rule. De Klerk agreed.

Why did de Klerk make so many political concessions? In part because it was pragmatic for him to do so, and in part because Mandela helped make these concessions bearable. For one thing, Mandela guaranteed de Klerk a role in the transition. Although it was understood that the ANC would get the most votes and Mandela would head the interim government, he agreed that de Klerk would be a deputy president. As Mandela told de Klerk, "I've always acted on the basis that you're needed and that you have a role to play."[54]

Another reason, of course, is that on the core economic issues, de Klerk essentially prevailed. Nothing would be nationalized. Private property would remain protected. And the jobs and pensions of white civil servants were guaranteed.

Finally, Mandela helped the cause of peace by reaching across the table to white political leaders who were far to the right of de Klerk. These stakeholders had to be brought around and de Klerk couldn't do it alone. The Volksfront, for example, was an extremist Afrikaner party headed by General Constand Viljoen. Mandela built a relationship with Viljoen by inviting him to his home and talking openly with him. Viljoen was impressed by Mandela and appreciated his candor. At one point Mandela told him, "If you want to go to war, I must be honest and admit that we cannot stand up to you on the battlefield . . . [but] you cannot win because of our numbers: you cannot kill us all."[55] Ultimately, Viljoen and his party supported the interim constitution.

These negotiations transformed South Africa. By 1994, apartheid was dead. In a free election based on one man, one vote, Mandela was elected the first president of the new South Africa. Soon thereafter, he signed a new constitution that guaranteed equal rights for blacks and whites.

ASSESSMENT

Mandela's achievement is unique in modern history, largely because of his extraordinary personal characteristics. But even for us ordinary mortals, there are negotiation lessons to be drawn from his story. In this chapter I will focus on three tensions that are common to many conflicts, and which I think Mandela managed brilliantly.

The first tension is between what is going on *across the table* with your adversary and what is happening *behind the table* among your constituents. Robert Putnam has called this a "two-level game" in which a leader must negotiate in both directions.[56] This requires enormous skill. History is full of political leaders who have failed this test, especially when dealing with violent ethnic conflicts. The tension is also common in business contexts, as we will see later in this book.

The second tension is between *pragmatism* and *principle,* which you will recognize from previous chapters. It relates to the clash between "rational" and "intuitive" thinking, between utilitarian and moral concerns. It is the tension that usually causes Spock to make an appearance.

The third tension is so fundamental that I teach it as part of my basic negotiation course. We encounter it often with friends, relatives, co-workers, and strangers. It is the tension between *empathy* and *assertiveness,* and its mastery requires two different kinds of skills. Empathy requires good listening skills and the ability to demonstrate an understanding of the other side's needs, interests, and perspectives, without necessarily agreeing. Assertiveness requires the ability to state clearly and confidently the interests and perspectives of one's own side. A good negotiator has to do a lot of both, no matter how strong the emotions or how high the stakes. This can be surprisingly difficult, even when the stakes are low and the bargaining power is more or less equal—for example, when we're negotiating with a spouse, a friend, or a business associate of similar status. When the stakes are high and one party clearly has the upper hand, the tension is even more difficult to manage. For black South Africans of Mandela's generation, very little in their lives prepared them to negotiate effectively with the white power structure, either to understand the whites' perspective or to assert their own.

In praising Mandela, I don't mean to minimize the role of F. W. de Klerk. Mandela needed someone he could do business with, and de Klerk was that man. De Klerk found a way to end white rule without surrendering white prosperity.[57] He made some excruciatingly painful decisions that required a great deal of courage. He made far more concessions than Mandela ever thought about making. And he was a highly skilled leader. In Waldmeir's words, he managed "to keep his party together, with no significant defections, from the day that he unbanned the ANC to the day he agreed to hand power over. He had dragged his party from the backwater of ethnic politics into the modern world. It was an extraordinary achievement."[58]

But Mandela's achievement strikes me as far more extraordinary. In fact, I would award him the title of the greatest negotiator of the twentieth century.

You have seen his patience and tenacity. When negotiating with his adversaries, he was respectful but never fawning or sycophantic. He demanded respect in return. You've seen his pragmatism. He hated violence but was not a pacifist. He was one tough hombre. He understood the power of violence and used it strategically—to force the government to negotiate. He rejected the simple-minded notion that one must either negotiate with the Devil or forcibly resist. He did both. He was willing to make concessions, but not about what was most important to him. With respect to his key political principles, he was unmovable.

But the most important lesson goes to the core of this book: We must reject as foolish the categorical claim that it is wrong to negotiate with an evil adversary. Mandela hated the apartheid regime, which most people would agree was evil. But he didn't demonize whites, including those who participated in the oppressive regime.

Paradoxically, Mandela's attitudes toward these whites softened during his years of incarceration. "In prison, my anger toward whites decreased, but my hatred for the system grew. . . . I hated the system that turned us against one another." Instead he saw his political adversaries as individuals; he avoided easy generalizations. Mandela came to appreciate many of his white guards. "Men like Swart, Gregory and Warrant Officer Brand reinforced my belief in the essential humanity even of those who had kept me behind bars for the previous twenty-seven and a half years." Mandela was able to separate the people from the problem.[59] The contrast with Sharansky is striking. Recall that in order to maintain his resolve, Sharansky found it necessary to distance himself from—and even demonize—his captors. Sharansky feared that trying to understand them, and learning about their families and children, would subvert his will.

Mandela understood that the goal of negotiation is to persuade your adversaries. He ultimately achieved through negotiation an outcome that could never have been accomplished solely through violence or resistance. Moreover, he did this without making any concessions with respect to his core political beliefs. Why was he so persuasive? I don't want to claim that the implicit threat of black violence played no role. But fear of civil war does not fully explain why de Klerk and the Afrikaners were able to make concessions to Mandela.

The explanation lies in the fact that Mandela was a negotiator to whom one could make concessions and yet maintain one's self-respect. Mandela worked hard to establish and maintain a personal, human connection with Afrikaner leaders whose life experiences and attitudes were radically different from his own. These leaders came to see that Mandela really believed in racial reconciliation. They saw that his vision for South Africa included them.

"Peace was made," Waldmeir concludes, "because Mandela was able to persuade such Afrikaners that he had the best interests of the nation—their nation, his nation, the South African nation—at heart. They learned to trust him with their fate."

I am not saying that Mandela was perfect. I wish I could say he avoided completely the trap of demonization. But he didn't. He never forgave de Klerk for his failure to mitigate the violence in the townships. Mandela was all too aware of his own difficulties controlling his own followers, but he doesn't seem to have given de Klerk the same benefit of the doubt. I think Mandela may have held that grudge too long. It led to a two-year impasse in the peace process, during which many people, primarily blacks, were killed.

The two men were jointly awarded the Nobel Peace Prize,[60] but their personal relationship never healed. In naming them "Men of the Year" for 1993, *Time* noted that their "mutual bitterness" was palpable. *Time* asked rhetorically, "How could these two have agreed on anything— lunch, for instance, much less the remaking of a nation?"[61]

The answer is that both men recognized that they were stuck with each other. With few exceptions, neither man allowed his personal feelings to stand in the way of doing business. When it was pragmatic to negotiate, they negotiated—even though they didn't *feel* like it. As Mandela once confessed to friends, "My worst nightmare is that I wake up one night and that de Klerk isn't there. I need him. Whether I like him or not is irrelevant, I need him."[62]

As we will see in Parts III and IV, parties in protracted business and family conflicts also find themselves stuck with adversaries they don't much like.

PART III

Business Devils

SEVEN

Giant Software Wars: IBM vs. Fujitsu

I had often spoken to large audiences, but I had never addressed a press conference in a ballroom with a live feed to Japan. Nor had I ever helped resolve a dispute with so much at stake. It was September 15, 1987, and I was standing with my co-arbitrator, Jack Jones, on a stage in the Villard Ballroom at the Helmsley Palace Hotel in New York City, about to announce a major turning point in the legal war between IBM and Fujitsu.

IBM was the biggest computer company in the world, Fujitsu was its biggest competitor, and their dispute dealt with software that was essential to both of them. The parties still despised each other—that hadn't changed. Jack often joked that they couldn't agree on anything, even the color of a stoplight. The news was that Jack and I, with the help of the parties, had found a creative solution.

But our story was complicated, involving arcane computer technology, an undeveloped area of law, and a solution that had never been tried before. The core issue was whether Fujitsu had illegally copied IBM's operating system software.[1] This was back in the days of mainframe computers—gigantic machines used by banks, insurance companies, and other large institutions. IBM had long dominated this market, but Fujitsu had made inroads by selling computers that were "IBM-compatible"—that is, capable of running applications originally written for an IBM. The problem, from IBM's point of view, was that Fujitsu had not created its own operating system from scratch. It had copied IBM's programming materials.

In the view of IBM and its proud engineers, this was stealing—

hitching a free ride on decades of hard work and financial investment. But to what extent did copyright law protect IBM's software? The law wasn't clear.

In 1983 these two rivals had themselves negotiated a settlement, but within a year it had broken down, destroying any hope of cooperation. They were like two spouses in a bitter divorce whose settlement had fallen apart. When IBM discovered that Fujitsu was still poaching, or so it believed, the top brass at IBM exploded. "This time, when we caught Fujitsu copying, our cup boiled over," recalls Dan Evangelista, former general counsel of IBM. "We assumed that they would behave honorably. From then on, we didn't trust anything they said or did."[2]

Fujitsu, believing it had honored the agreement, was equally enraged by what it viewed as IBM's disrespectful claims and arrogant demands. Takuma Yamamoto, the CEO of Fujitsu, had been a pilot during World War II and had been assigned to go on a suicide mission just before the Japanese surrendered. He had seen himself as a guardian of Japan's honor during the war and had transferred these feelings to Fujitsu. Yamamoto had put *his* trust in IBM in reaching the prior settlement. When IBM refused to work things out in what he understood as a civil manner, he felt Fujitsu had been betrayed. "A betrayal is the worst thing in life," another Fujitsu executive explained to me recently. Fujitsu "could never trust IBM again. IBM was not simply a competitor, it was an *enemy*."[3]

Jack and I were determined to keep this mutual demonization under strict control during the press conference. As a result, we had orchestrated it down to the smallest detail. There would not be one moment of spontaneity in it.

As we gazed out over the ballroom, we saw grim-faced executives from both sides sitting in stony silence. For their own good, we had put them under a gag order. Left to their own devices, each side would spin the story not simply as a "win" for themselves but as a big loss for their rival. That wouldn't be accurate: our solution would protect the interests of both firms, not to mention their customers, who needed to know that their business would not be disrupted because these two giants were brawling over the scope of intellectual property law. Therefore, Jack and I would be the only ones speaking at the press conference.

We had hired Burson-Marsteller, one of the biggest public relations firms in the world, to help us hone the message. Because of the significance of the story in Japan, we had arranged to have the event beamed live by satellite to Tokyo (the first such telecast in history) so the news could be reported simultaneously in both countries. We had taken out full-page ads in the *Wall Street Journal*, the *New York Times*, and Japan's leading newspapers, summarizing our decision in our own words so there could be no question about what we were saying. Finally, Jack and I had spent the last three days being drilled by a team of media coaches until our presentation was as sharp as we could make it. (I was not a natural. My coaches kept telling me not to be so professorial. Or perhaps the word was *didactic*.)

We opened the press conference and explained the key points. We had created a framework—and *just* a framework, we emphasized—for resolving all past and future disputes between these two companies. With regard to past disputes, we would order Fujitsu to pay IBM a single lump sum—in effect, a "coerced license"—for its previous use of IBM programming materials. In return, Fujitsu and its customers could continue to use all of Fujitsu's existing software without fear of legal challenges. Going forward, we would establish a set of standards, accompanied by strict and elaborate safeguards, that would define precisely what Fujitsu could do with IBM materials in the future—and the price Fujitsu would pay for it. (We had not yet determined the total dollar amounts, but IBM would collect nearly $1 billion between 1983 and 1995.)

The beauty of this regimen, we thought, was that it would liberate the parties from the realm of ordinary intellectual property law, which wasn't developed enough to be of much use to them in this conflict. Instead, it empowered Jones and Mnookin to create private law that would apply only to the relationship between IBM and Fujitsu. And we would not leave them unsupervised to get into further trouble. We would retain jurisdiction for another decade and resolve all future software disputes between them. There would be no appeal. If we did our job well—and much remained to be done to flesh out and implement our framework—these two giants would compete in the marketplace, not the courtroom.

We answered reporters' questions for about an hour and gave individual interviews to CNN and other stations. All three U.S. networks reported the story that evening, and the next day it would be front-page news around the world. When the last reporter had left, Jack and I retired to the hotel bar and enjoyed a few rounds of drinks. We looked at each other with amusement and a certain amount of disbelief. Jack clinked my glass and grinned: "Who would have thought a farm boy from Iowa and a Jewish kid from Kansas City would end up doing something like this?"

Jack's question was a good one. How did we come to be responsible for solving this enormously complicated problem?

In my case, it was a fluke. In the late spring of 1985, as I was sitting in my office at Stanford Law School, I got a call from Dave Nelson, a senior partner at Morrison & Foerster, a large law firm based in San Francisco. At the time I was a forty-three-year-old professor.

I knew Dave Nelson but not well. I hadn't seen or spoken to him in five years, not since I'd left the law faculty at the University of California at Berkeley to join the faculty at Stanford. (When I lived in Berkeley, we had both served on the board of the private school my daughters attended.) Nelson said that he was representing a client involved in a major software dispute with another large company, and it looked like the conflict was headed for arbitration. He couldn't disclose the name of either party, but soon his client would have to nominate someone to serve as its designated arbitrator on a three-person panel. Nelson had thought of me because he had recently read an article of mine in the *California Bar Journal*.

Life takes strange turns. The short article that had reminded Nelson of my existence was so trivial that I hadn't even bothered to put it on my résumé. Titled "Spreading the Word about Spreadsheet Software,"[4] the article explained how electronic spreadsheets could be useful in a variety of legal contexts. At most, the article showed that I was an early adopter and reasonably sophisticated user of spreadsheet software (which was unusual for a lawyer in those days).

I told Nelson I had no expertise in software programming and only a little experience as a mediator or arbitrator. The field of "alternative dispute resolution" (ADR) was still in its infancy and I was hardly a big name in it.

Nelson brushed aside these disclaimers and invited me to San Francisco to talk with his partner Bob Raven, who would handle the case if arbitration proved necessary. I accepted the invitation. I was curious. Who was this secret client? What was the fight all about?

The next week I drove to San Francisco for my first meeting with Raven, one of the brightest stars in California's legal galaxy. He was then about sixty years old, a physically imposing man of at least six-foot-three with a full head of gray hair. With his rugged features and confident air, Raven looked as if he would be just as happy wearing jeans and riding a horse as wearing a suit and tie and sitting in a conference room. (I later learned he owned a ranch.) He was an easy man to like, exuding an appealing combination of energy, strength, and warmth. But behind his charm was a fiercely competitive and ambitious temperament, which I would also come to appreciate.

Raven asked about my background and seemed particularly glad to hear that I had studied economics and taught antitrust law. (I would later learn why.) But when he asked about my knowledge of computer programming and intellectual property law, I trotted out my disclaimers again. I told him that if he wanted a real expert in these fields, he should talk to two of my Stanford colleagues who were far more qualified.

I enjoyed the interview and left persuaded that nothing more would come of it.

To my surprise, about two weeks later Nelson called again and asked me to come back to San Francisco. It was at this second meeting that I finally learned the identity of the client, Fujitsu, and its opponent, IBM. (Given IBM's dominance, I suddenly understood why Raven had been so interested in my background in antitrust.) Raven told me only the bare bones of the dispute—that it involved operating system software for mainframe computers—because if I were appointed as an arbitrator I would be serving a quasi-judicial role. But he did tell me that IBM would be represented by Tom Barr of Cravath, Swaine & Moore.

When I heard Barr's name, I realized that the stakes in this conflict had to be enormous. In terms of big-case commercial litigation, Tom Barr was a five-star general. He had successfully defended IBM in a massive antitrust suit brought by the U.S. government and scores of private plaintiffs. By enlisting Barr in this fight with Fujitsu, IBM was signaling to the world that it would spend whatever it took to prevail.

After confirming that I had had no conflicts of interest in the case,

Raven popped the question: Was I interested enough to go to Japan and let the client look me over? He would send Mike Jacobs, a young associate, to keep me company. (I was amused. Did I need a chaperone? It was the first sign that Fujitsu, too, was sparing no expense.) Perhaps I could give an academic talk of some sort to Fujitsu employees, but that wasn't critical. The point was that the company's senior executives wanted to meet me in the flesh before they nominated me.

I asked for a couple of days to think it over. Raven had said the case would take about half my time for the next eighteen months—little did we know how off the mark *that* guess would turn out to be—and that I'd be well compensated for my time. I thought it all sounded extremely interesting, but I worried that the whole exercise might be a distraction from my academic career. Fortunately, my Stanford buddy Ron Gilson stepped in and told me I'd be crazy not to do it. This assignment would put me in the middle of an important high-tech dispute between two giant companies represented by superb lawyers. I would learn a great deal about dispute resolution, an emerging interest of mine. "Stanford is in the middle of Silicon Valley. You have tenure," Gilson urged me. "The dean would surely grant you half-time leave. Do it!"

So I said yes. Mike Jacobs and I flew to Japan. We spent a day visiting Fujitsu's executive headquarters in Tokyo, a large, modern office tower overlooking the Imperial Garden. I was given a tour of several museum-like rooms that traced the company's phenomenal growth. In 1949, it had been an obscure company that made telephone switching equipment and had about 2,300 employees. (That was the year that Takuma Yamamoto, the company's future CEO, graduated from Tokyo University and was steered to Fujitsu by a professor. As Yamamoto later confessed in his memoir, he was "totally crushed" when the professor placed him at Fujitsu because Yamamoto had "never even heard" of the tiny company.[5]) By the time of my visit in 1985, Fujitsu was Japan's largest computer company, with annual revenues in the billions of dollars.

As requested, I gave a thirty-minute talk in English to some software engineers and mid-level managers. It was a bit of a farce. Although Yuri Morita (then a young manager) ably served as translator, the engineers had no clue what I was talking about, or even why I was there. Those who managed to stay awake were impeccably polite. The real point of the trip was for the top executives to meet me in person. I remember having a rather elegant lunch in an executive dining room and being introduced to a number of distinguished-looking, extremely polite men, none of whom had attended my lecture. (Morita again served as translator.) I learned that all had spent their entire careers at Fujitsu and were extremely proud of the company's growth.

The man who made the strongest impression on me was Michio Naruto. Voluble and self-confident, younger than the other top executives, he was a member of the Fujitsu board and in charge of international operations. I would later learn that this charming and outgoing man was independently wealthy (his family owned vast forestlands in Japan) and had a passion for golf. Naruto traveled the world and played whenever he could. He owned at least three matched sets of clubs and kept one in California, another on the East Coast, and a third in Europe so he could play during his travels. He said nothing to me about Fujitsu's conflict with IBM except to underscore the arbitration's extreme importance. I responded that if I were appointed, I would work very hard to resolve this conflict.

About a week after my return to the United States, Nelson called to tell me that the trip had gone well. Fujitsu wanted to nominate me as an arbitrator. I was pleased but puzzled by Fujitsu's decision-making process. What had Fujitsu learned of importance about me during my visit? Nelson later told me that I was hired because Naruto liked my face.

———

I first met my co-arbitrator, Jack Jones, in the lobby of the Ritz hotel in London. We had flown there as part of a large entourage, including Raven of Morrison & Foerster and Tom Barr of Cravath, to interview candidates for the position of chair of the arbitration panel. The parties' earlier settlement required them to resolve disputes by arbitration—a common commercial practice. Substantial international arbitrations are typically resolved by a panel of three arbitrators, one chosen by each party and a third who acts as chair. Fujitsu had chosen me, IBM had chosen Jack, and now our group had to complete the panel by selecting the third arbitrator.[6]

Why London? Because Fujitsu had refused to accept an American chairperson and IBM had refused to accept one who was Japanese. Because the proceedings were going to be in English, the parties had decided to focus our search in the United Kingdom and Canada.

The night before our first interviews, Jack and I met in the bar to get acquainted over a couple of drinks. He was not a lawyer and had never been involved in an arbitration case, but he knew a lot about computers and had served as a witness for IBM in the antitrust suit brought by the U.S. government. As the executive vice president of the Norfolk Southern Corporation, he was in charge of purchasing millions of dollars' worth of computer equipment. He bought a lot of IBM machines, but he bought from many other companies as well. He personally used an Apple computer, which he adored.

As he talked, I remember thinking, "This guy would be a hell of a witness." He was an impressive-looking man, about sixty years old, who seemed comfortable in his own skin and completely credible. He was articulate and straightforward. His manner was relaxed. He obviously was very knowledgeable about computers and software, but he avoided the use of jargon. His stature was imposing—both tall (about six-foot-four) and big-boned. Best of all from IBM's point of view, he didn't always buy equipment from IBM. He could make the case that IBM was not a monopoly and had plenty of competition. That was how Jack had gotten to know Tom Barr, who had chosen him for this arbitration.

I soon discovered that Jack and I were both from the Midwest, but that was about all we had in common. He drank bourbon; I drank scotch. He liked country and western music, and Willie Nelson was his favorite. I preferred classical music, especially Bruckner symphonies. More important, Jones had grown up on a small family farm in Iowa, the only child of Lutheran parents of German ancestry. He had been the first in his family to go to college—choosing nearby Luther College in Decorah, Iowa, a tiny church-affiliated school. His big break was a scholarship to MIT, where he got a master's degree in electrical engineering with a minor in mathematics. I had grown up in Kansas City as a rather privileged kid from an assimilated Jewish background. I spent my high school years in a private boys' school and went off to Harvard College without considering it all that unusual.

Nor did Jack and I share much in way of recreational interests. He loved to hunt and fish. I didn't. He asked me if I had ever gone to a pig roast, grinning at the question: he knew I had not. He had a huge pig-roasting pit in his backyard, and nothing pleased him more than staying up all night roasting an entire pig for a party. His home was a huge log house in the middle of fifteen acres of woods outside Chesapeake, Virginia. Jack had little interest in foreign travel with one exception: every year he would take his wife, Nancy, and their entire clan of seven grown children and spouses to Munich for Oktoberfest. Year after year they would stay at the same hotel, drink beer in the same beer gardens, and sing the same songs. Much of this struck me as charming but completely alien. I could not imagine the Mnookin clan going on an annual pilgrimage to Munich, much less to drink beer and belt out German drinking songs. I'd never met anyone like Jack before.

Over the next twelve years Jack and I would become something of an odd couple, partners who grew very close but couldn't be more different. Looking back, I realize that our knowledge and talents were complementary. I knew a lot about law and process; he knew a lot about computers. I was talkative and intense; he was laconic and very calm. I was an academic who fretted over nuances of language and loved to analyze everything to death; he was an executive who, to my endless admiration, could make decisions quickly and never look back.

In London, our group interviewed five candidates who looked promising on paper. Most were prominent English barristers, called Queen's Counsel, who were experienced in international arbitration. One candidate, a crusty old lord and retired judge, disqualified himself within minutes. After greeting us, he said, "I've heard of IBM. But this other company . . . Fujitsu? Or is it Jujitsu? What is it?" Another barrister assumed he'd already been picked and took over the interview. He didn't make the cut, either. Nor did the others. None seemed very technologically sophisticated, and Tom Barr saw several of them as stuffy and pretentious.

This was my first exposure to Barr, who was not a bit stuffy. I discovered that he, too, was from Kansas City. Rather short and slightly stocky, partial to elegant suits that might well have been hand-tailored in London, he exuded supreme self-confidence. At fifty-four, he was at the very pinnacle of his career.

I had heard all kinds of stories about Barr, whose defense of IBM in the antitrust cases was legendary. The battle had started in the late 1960s, when IBM customers and competitors, claiming that IBM was a monopoly, sought billions of dollars in damages. In 1969, the U.S. government joined the attack and sought to break it up into several separate companies.

IBM fought back in a fierce legal campaign that lasted some thirteen years. (A top IBM executive quipped that during these years the IBM legal team had no budget, but every year exceeded it.[7]) Tom Barr was its commanding general and ultimately triumphed,[8] in what one commentator dubbed "the most brilliant and sustained legal representation in history."[9]

Barr had served in the Marines, he was proud of the Corps, and the experience had shaped his view of litigation as all-out combat. He hated to lose cases and rarely did. He was once quoted as saying, "I never know exactly what people mean by the 'theory of the case.' My theory of the case is 'We're right and the other guy's wrong. We're going to win and the other guy is going to lose.' "[10] He demanded total commitment from his troops, which were famous for working harder, preparing more thoroughly, and fighting more aggressively than any opponent. In Barr's office hung a poster depicting a scowling Marine drill sergeant with veins popping out of his neck. The caption read, "We Don't Promise You a Rose Garden."

I didn't see this aspect of Barr in London. He and Raven, who already knew each other on a first-name basis, were very friendly not only to Jack and me but to each other. They shared an interest in finding a third arbitrator they could agree on.

Although they found no one to their liking in London, they ultimately found the man they were looking for in Donald Macdonald, a Toronto lawyer with extraordinary credentials. He had been a member of the Canadian Parliament and had held five cabinet posts in the first government of Pierre Trudeau. When we three arbitrators met for the first time in the fall of 1985, simply to organize ourselves and establish a schedule, I found Macdonald equally impressive in person: urbane and polished, as tall as Jack and as well dressed as Barr. At my suggestion, we made an important decision about our roles as arbitrators—that all three of us serve strictly as neutrals.[11] Later I would be very glad we had taken this course.

What exactly were these two computer giants fighting about? Boiled down to its essentials, the fight was about operating system software and other sophisticated software programs, sometimes called "middleware," which work in close cooperation with the operating system. Some background is necessary to see why this was such a big deal for both companies.

An operating system is an organized collection of software used to manage the flow of work inside the computer and provide services to other programs. Middleware is software that works closely with the operating system, using its services and providing specialized services to application programs. Software applications, such as programs to manage a company's payroll, inventory, or customer orders, are written to run "on top of" a particular operating system and associated middleware programs. Today, for example, the operating system for PCs is typically some version of Microsoft Windows. If you own a PC and use Word or Excel, those applications are written to run "on top of" your Windows operating system.

In 1969, IBM completely dominated the mainframe market, selling about 70 percent of all computers in the world.[12] The overwhelming majority of applications for mainframes were written to run on the IBM operating system.[13]

In the early 1970s, the Japanese government aimed to get a piece of the action for Japanese computer manufacturers, especially in Japan, which was by then the second-largest computer market in the world. As a matter of industrial policy, the powerful Ministry of International Trade and Industry ("MITI") decided to develop the Japanese computer industry into a force capable of taking on IBM. It encouraged two companies, Fujitsu and Hitachi, to manufacture and market "IBM compatible" computers.[14] These machines would be virtually interchangeable with IBM machines, able to run any application written for an IBM mainframe.

The big question was what to do about the operating system. In retrospect, Fujitsu could have saved itself a world of trouble if it had simply let its customers license an operating system from IBM.[15] Instead, Fujitsu made the fateful decision to develop its *own* operating system, which would be IBM-compatible and contain special features of its own. At the outset, Fujitsu may have believed this would not be overly difficult. Throughout the 1970s, IBM distributed to its customers the source code for the IBM operating system. With the source code, a programmer could figure out just how IBM had programmed its software.[16]

Copyright constraints weren't an obvious concern back then. (IBM didn't claim copyright protection for its software until 1977, and even then no one knew whether copyright law applied.) But as Takuma Yamamoto would confess in his memoir, developing a compatible operating system "posed a challenge of far greater and more severe dimension" than Fujitsu had anticipated[17] and would "sow the seeds of the software dispute destined to be fought farther down the road with IBM."[18]

In the short run, the compatibility strategy appeared to pay off. In 1976, Fujitsu sold its first IBM-compatible mainframe, the M Series. Six years later, Fujitsu mainframes were outselling IBM's in Japan—the first time any company had outsold IBM in a major market.

But IBM had long suspected that Fujitsu and Hitachi were copying its technology, and in 1982, it got the goods on each of them.

Hitachi fell first, in a "sting operation" in California that received worldwide attention. Several Hitachi employees were caught on videotape trying to buy IBM hardware design manuals. Criminal indictments followed for the individuals caught in the sting and for the company.[19] The scandal was humiliating for both Hitachi and the Japanese nation: a tremendous loss of face. A Japanese cabinet official was quoted as saying that Japan had been "slapped in the face."[20]

All this took place against a backdrop of intense economic rivalry between the United States and Japan. American firms were alarmed because Japanese firms were undercutting them in the marketplace, often through industrial espionage. Japanese firms feared that America would adopt discriminatory trade policies toward Japan. Waves of xenophobia swept both countries. American commentators claimed the Japanese were engaging in "sneak attacks." Shortly after the Hitachi incident, a Japanese newspaper reported that an anonymous American IBM engineer had made the following boast: "Guess you've been reading about what IBM did to those Japs in California. We sure got them good. It took a little time, but we made sure they knew who was boss. . . . [I]n a sense we are at war with Japan all over again."[21]

Later that year, IBM caught up with Fujitsu as well, after acquiring a Fujitsu mainframe and some of its software. Operating software contains hundreds of programs, but IBM had to analyze only a few of these to confirm its worst fears. There was a vast amount of copying. (This was not a criminal matter, but a potential civil case of copyright infringement.)

The news immediately went to the very top of IBM. The concern was: How many more programs had Fujitsu copied—and placed in the hands of its customers? IBM had reviewed only a tiny sample. There was no telling how far the damage had spread. What was clear was that Fujitsu's copying had to be stopped.

The first shot was fired in October 1982, when the president of IBM wrote directly to the president of Fujitsu to declare that Fujitsu had infringed IBM's copyrights. He demanded that Fujitsu pay for these offenses and clean up its software development process.

Fujitsu parried these claims with equal vigor. First, it said, IBM hadn't even bothered to copyright its operating system until 1978, well after Fujitsu had started selling compatible computers. Second, Japanese copyright law did not apply to operating system software.[22] Third, IBM so dominated the mainframe market that its operating system had become the de facto standard; therefore, Fujitsu had every right to develop and maintain a compatible operating system.

The legal conflict had begun. Eight months of arduous negotiations ensued.[23]

On June 29, 1983, the parties signed a pair of documents—the "1983 Agreements"—that attempted to square the circle. But as you already know, these contracts didn't solve the problem and in some respects made the relationship worse. Because they play such a prominent role in our story, I will explain a bit about them here.

The first document, called the Settlement Agreement, tried to get a grip on the copying problem. The parties appeared to have three simple goals: to identify Fujitsu's "tainted" programs, to compensate IBM for their use, and to prevent further copying disputes. But because the contract language is quite complex, some paraphrasing may help nonlawyers understand it. IBM had the greater bargaining power, so imagine IBM saying the following to Fujitsu:

"Okay, let's start by making a list of all the programs that arguably contain copying. *You* compile the list, because we don't know how many programs are affected. Include as many programs as you want—anything you're worried we might sue you for. We will sell you immunity for those programs. We'll call them 'Designated Programs'—'DPs' for short—a nice neutral term so you don't have to admit to copyright violation.

"You will pay us a lump sum of $65 million. In exchange, we promise not to sue you—or your customers—for having used these programs in the past.

"As for the future, well, we *could* make you call up all your customers and pull the programs off the market, or we could sue your customers who are using your tainted software. But that would be terribly inconvenient for them—and you. We understand. So we'll let you leave the programs in your customers' hands, but only on one condition: you pay us a license fee twice a year, equal to what we charge our customers for the corresponding IBM program." (These semiannual fees would soon dwarf the $65 million lump-sum payment.)

That addressed the first two goals of the Settlement Agreement. The third related to Fujitsu's future programming activities and its new programs. To what extent could Fujitsu use IBM programming materials? And, what use, if any, could Fujitsu make of its DPs in future programs?

Here's where things got a little vague. Fujitsu promised to "refrain from infringing the copyright and other legally protectable rights [of IBM] under applicable law." But the scope of these rights was not defined. Fujitsu promised to adopt an internal protective procedure to make sure its programmers didn't have access to IBM programming materials and wouldn't do any more copying. But there were important exceptions to this rule that were poorly defined.[24] Fujitsu promised to make copies of all its new software available in a special depository so that IBM could inspect them for compliance. But exactly what material it would provide, and when, weren't spelled out. What was spelled out was the stiff penalty for cheating: Fujitsu would have to pay three times the normal license fee and immediately withdraw the program from its customers.

Moreover, as murky as the Settlement Agreement was, the second contract was even murkier and would later cause IBM untold grief. Blandly titled the "Externals Agreement," it was Fujitsu's consolation prize—and gave Fujitsu hope that it might remain compatible as IBM technology changed. At the time both Fujitsu and IBM made available to their own customers certain interface information that allowed the customer to write their own application programs that would work with the operating system.[25] The parties called this "external" information. In this second agreement, the two companies promised to provide, upon request, the other with external information in exchange for a license fee.

At the time, IBM may not have thought this Externals Agreement was of much consequence. IBM had no interest in licensing information pertaining to Fujitsu's operating system. But Fujitsu felt this second agreement, and a license to use IBM interface information, was essential if it was to maintain IBM compatibility. And it was willing to pay for this information.

But the Externals Agreement didn't define in any detail what counted as external information. Nor did the parties even bother to fill out the exhibits, which should have listed the programs covered by the contract—and the price.

They were on a collision course of their own making.

It wasn't long before IBM once again found what it considered flagrant evidence of copying, and it showed no mercy. IBM demanded that Fujitsu pay triple fees for *all* the offending programs and pull them off the market immediately. Fujitsu couldn't possibly agree to these terms, which would have dismantled much of its software base. There were confrontations, even yelling and screaming.[26]

Later on, Jack and I would often ask ourselves: How could sophisticated parties represented by counsel be foolish enough to think that the 1983 deal could possibly have resolved this conflict? I am now more sympathetic. With the benefit of hindsight, I think many factors played a role, including different cultural perceptions of the obligations created by contract.[27]

For an American company, the details of a contract are critical. In IBM's view, the Settlement Agreement created specific obligations that were legally enforceable. IBM had caught Fujitsu breaking its word, the contract spelled out the remedies, and IBM was entitled to them. Period!

In Japanese culture, the precise words of a contract are far less important than the underlying spirit, which should be interpreted with an eye to preserving relationships. For Fujitsu, the purpose of the 1983 Agreements was to repair a damaged relationship and create a new one in which both parties would behave reasonably. In Japan, litigation over contracts is rare. Fujitsu assumed that if new disputes arose, the parties would sit down and work out their concerns in a reasonable way. Instead, what was IBM doing? Impugning Fujitsu's honor and issuing ultimatums. Its behavior was insulting and its demands humiliating. To meet them would be economically ruinous.

As the feelings of betrayal mounted, each side viewed the other's behavior as increasingly outrageous. Fujitsu belatedly offered to add a slew of additional programs to the DP list, even ones that IBM hadn't complained about. IBM thought this was sneaky and disingenuous. IBM said, in essence, "Too late! Read the Settlement Agreement! You missed the deadline. You owe us triple fees for these programs and you have to pull them off the market."

IBM's hard line never softened. In IBM's view, it was losing both hardware and software profits because Fujitsu had copied. In June 1985, it sent Fujitsu a "Final Report" of its alleged offenses, coupled with a nonnegotiable demand: If Fujitsu didn't withdraw *all* offending programs from the market and pay damages amounting to hundreds of millions of dollars, IBM would seek to impose these remedies in arbitration.[28]

As I've since learned, President Yamamoto saw the Final Report as a declaration of war—the final betrayal of the new relationship he had hoped to create with the 1983 Agreements. Those agreements had been terribly one-sided, in his view, but Fujitsu had shown its good faith by paying IBM vast sums of money—more than $150 million in fees since the agreements were signed. Now IBM was coming back with new demands that threatened the very survival of his company. Under a Japanese code of honor, you didn't negotiate with such an enemy. You said through gritted teeth: "I will fight you; my son will fight your son; and my grandson will fight your grandson."[29]

Both parties had chosen war. Was this wise? What would Spock have said? I will return to this question later.

———————

The panel decided to hold the first formal arbitration hearing in Palo Alto, California, conveniently located between Tokyo and New York (it is also the home of Stanford University). The parties booked a conference room in a local hotel and made the necessary arrangements. Meanwhile, I hired Jonathan Greenberg, a former law student of mine, to work half-time with me on the arbitration as my law clerk. A gifted lawyer (and playwright), Jonathan would become an indispensable part of the process and later serve as counsel to the Arbitration Panel.

On the appointed day in February 1986, I met Jack Jones and Don Macdonald in the hotel lobby, and we entered the conference room precisely at 9:00 A.M.

I was stunned by what I saw. There were at least a hundred people in the room, probably more, arranged in two hostile phalanxes like the armies of Athens and Sparta. In the front row on one side sat Tom Barr, accompanied by his lieutenants: Cravath partners and Dan Evangelista, soon to be the top in-house lawyer from IBM.[30] Behind them sat their troops: associates and paralegals wielding huge black litigation briefcases. Behind them glowered a platoon of IBM executives and managers, each wearing the uniform—suit, tie, and white shirt—specified by the IBM dress code.

On the other side of the aisle, Raven commanded an army that looked even bigger than Barr's. I guessed that Raven had told his clients something along these lines: "I know from earlier battles that IBM will spare no expense. They will try to beat you into submission by outspending you. Your only hope is to demonstrate that you will match them man for man—that you have the will and resources to fight all the way. Open your checkbooks. If they put 1,000 men on the battlefield, you should field 1,100."

Fujitsu had done just that. Among the Japanese troops I recognized Michio Naruto, the gregarious golfer, and his immediate boss, Shoichi Ninomiya, a taciturn chain-smoker whom I had also met during my Tokyo visit. I spotted Yuri Morita, the young man who had served as our translator. Many of the other Japanese men looked familiar to me because they had been forced to sit through my lecture on American law.

Every seat in the room was equipped with a headset that could be set to either Japanese or English. The room teemed with translators. A glass booth at the back of the room had been provided for the simultaneous translators, whose murmurings would provide a constant babble during the hearing. In addition, each side had its own translator, and there was one "neutral." A court reporter was there to create a transcript in English. Perhaps she consulted with the neutral. Who knows? A table for the panel had been placed at the front of the room. I took a seat on Macdonald's right; Jack sat on his left.

The hearing lasted about two days and focused mainly on procedural matters. The Palo Alto weather was miserable. A cold, torrential rain wrapped us in a gloom worthy of *Bleak House*, the Dickens novel about the grotesque inefficiency of the English chancery courts. My most vivid memory was when the arbitration panel allowed Tom Barr to question Ninomiya. We all perked up because we thought something interesting was about to happen. Ninomiya was Fujitsu's top executive for hardware and software development and had made many decisions central to the case. Barr wanted Ninomiya to describe exactly how Fujitsu was currently using IBM's programming materials in its software development.

It should have been a moment of high drama. Barr was a great courtroom lawyer and no doubt had looked forward to this confrontation. Instead he found himself moving in slow motion with a stone-faced enemy who wouldn't engage. He would ask a question of Ninomiya. It would be translated from English to Japanese. Ninomiya would then mumble some short answer in Japanese. One of the translators would translate his response into English. Another translator would sometimes object to the first translator's translation. All three translators would then get into a dispute while the rest of us sat there impatiently. Barr would then characterize the answer as unresponsive and ask the same question again, phrased somewhat differently.

This went on for hours. It was excruciatingly boring. The high point came as Barr was trying to get Ninomiya to explain how Fujitsu had decided which programs belonged on the DP list. Barr wanted to force Ninomiya to acknowledge in front of the panel that the DPs contained copied material. But Ninomiya parried with a double negative that gave the translators quite a workout. As I recall, the English version was something like, "Fujitsu put a program on the DP list when it could *not* be concluded that the program had *not* been influenced by an IBM program." Even in translation, it was obvious that Ninomiya had been well coached by counsel. (Note the words "influenced by" rather than "copied.") Recently I learned that one of the young Morrison & Foerster lawyers had nicknamed him "Garbo" because he was so elusive.

———

During the next ten months, like a traveling circus, we met in various cities around the United States, Japan, and even Canada. The parties fought about everything. For example, the panel needed some education on operating system software and the technology underlying the conflict, but these seminars were difficult to arrange because the parties so deeply distrusted each other and worried we would somehow be brainwashed in this process. Although our instructors were always neutral experts who weren't affiliated with either party, the lawyers fought about who would educate us and they fretted about what these experts might say. Each side insisted on having a representative present at every session so they could carefully monitor everything we were told.

The parties also submitted an astounding volume of letters, memoranda, documents, and exhibits to educate us about their conflict. The parties' submissions also gave us a much clearer sense of the legal questions we would need to address, although the answers each proposed were diametrically opposed. Fujitsu argued that it had broad rights to IBM information under the Externals Agreement, and IBM argued that its obligations were extremely narrow. IBM argued that copyright law provided very broad protection for its software, while Fujitsu claimed that copyright law applied narrowly, if at all, to IBM's operating system software.[31]

Unfortunately, copyright law itself didn't provide much guidance. For one thing, it wasn't clear whether U.S. or Japanese law applied. But either way, the case posed very difficult questions about the scope of protection.

If copyright law applied to operating system software at all—and we assumed it did—it obviously prohibited line-by-line copying. IBM's Final Report gave some compelling examples of this. (One "smoking gun" involved a subroutine, or loop, which an IBM programmer had named after his wife, Lucy. The corresponding Fujitsu program included the very same loop—also named "Lucy.") But we didn't know how important those examples were in the context of the full program. In other instances, IBM claimed that Fujitsu had simply paraphrased the IBM material. This, too, would be a violation.

But we had a growing sense that the heart of IBM's case involved a much more subtle claim: that Fujitsu had copied the "structure, sequence and organization" of an IBM program without actually quoting or paraphrasing any lines of IBM code. When, if ever, would this be enough to prove the "substantial similarity" required for infringement? Deciding this issue would require us to apply the most elusive doctrine found in copyright law, the distinction between "ideas," which are not protected, and "expression," which is.

Even with literary works, it can be hard to draw that line. The following hypothetical is often used in law school copyright courses: Imagine that the descendants of William Shakespeare still owned a copyright on his play, *Romeo and Juliet*. Would the Broadway musical *West Side Story* violate the copyright? The actual words in the two productions are entirely different. But the story line in *West Side Story* was plainly copied from Shakespeare's play. The plots are similar. (Two families are feuding. Boy from one feuding family falls in love with girl from the other. They decide to secretly marry and run off together. After a series of mishaps, all ends tragically with death of both.) How similar do the two plots have to be before the later work violates the copyright of the original? Many years ago Learned Hand, a distinguished federal circuit court judge, said that drawing this line requires an "ad hoc judgment" based on a careful comparison of the two works. There's no rule to tell you how to do it. It all depends on the particular facts and a detailed comparison of the two works.

And there was the rub. IBM had brought scores of claims against Fujitsu, each concerning a different software program. To draw the line between idea and expression, we'd have to conduct a detailed analysis of each disputed program and its IBM counterpart. How similar would the sequence, structure, and organization have to be to prove a violation? Each program contained hundreds of thousands (in some cases millions) of lines of code. Would we have to examine each program, function by function, data area by data area, line by line? That would take years.

IBM hoped to limit this process by delivering a knockout blow in the form of a motion for summary judgment, but to my mind this hope was nearly delusional. One of the requirements for summary judgment is that no material facts are in dispute. The idea/expression distinction and most of Fujitsu's other defenses clearly involved "mixed questions of law and fact." So we denied IBM's motion[32]—*and* its request for triple license fees, which we held to be punitive—and ruled that we would have to analyze the disputed Fujitsu programs one at a time, by comparing each with its IBM corresponding program. We told the parties that a detailed comparison of the first pair of programs would be due in forty-five days.

The parties immediately began to fight about which pair of programs to compare first. There were three pairs under consideration. On behalf of IBM, Barr argued that the panel should start with a pair that he thought would reveal blatant line-by-line copying. Fujitsu, naturally, wanted to start with a pair that was deep in the gray area, involving similarities in structure, sequence, and organization. The third example had features of both.

While the panel was struggling with this issue, Barr suddenly changed course. "Why choose now, before you've seen the evidence?" he asked the panel. "IBM can submit detailed memoranda on *each* of the three Fujitsu programs comparing them to the corresponding IBM program. You can choose later, after you've read our analysis and anything Fujitsu wants to submit," he purred. Perhaps, fearing that the panel was about to choose the wrong set of programs, he wanted to make sure we saw the worst of Fujitsu's copying before we made a decision. Whatever his motives, I saw jaws dropping in horror among his troops. Barr was improvising. He obviously hadn't discussed this offer with the enlisted men and women who would actually be looking at millions of lines of code. From their ashen faces, I figured some of them wouldn't be seeing their families for a while.

Meanwhile, I had my own, more basic concern. Was conventional arbitration a sensible way to resolve this conflict? While we were looking backward at old disputes, new ones were cropping up. IBM was still investigating Fujitsu's alleged misdeeds and adding claims, and Fujitsu was *still developing new programs*. I feared the new conflicts would multiply faster than we could dispose of the old ones. I thought, This is crazy. Like Sisyphus with his boulder, the panel might never reach the end of its labors. Moreover, a case-by-case process would miss the forest for the trees.[33] It wouldn't directly answer the core question: To what extent can Fujitsu use IBM programming material *in the future*?

I began to believe that the most effective way to help the parties was to adopt a radically different approach, one that looked forward as well as backward. But designing a new process was not part of an arbitrator's job description.

I have never been good at hiding my impatience. Even when I'm not speaking, my facial expressions often give me away. Shortly after the panel denied summary judgment, we held a session at a beautiful Japanese resort in Hakone National Park, in the shadow of Mount Fuji. During a break in the hearing, I decided to take a walk in the woods nearby—and ran into Tom Barr. I may have made some offhand comment to the effect that we all had "our work cut out for us." If I didn't say it, that certainly was what I was feeling. Barr may have sensed my frustration with what lay ahead, and perhaps even shared it.

In any case, he said something that would change the course of the entire proceeding: "Why don't you and Jack put your heads together and figure out some more efficient way to cut through all this crap and get this matter resolved?"

I was stunned by his directness but leaped at the opportunity. "Do you mean IBM would be open to some sort of mediation process, with Jack and me helping the parties see if some kind of deal might be negotiated?"

Barr said, "Yes! I can assure you IBM would participate."

I found this an appealing prospect. Barr didn't say why he had not included Macdonald in his suggestion, but that made sense to me. It would protect Macdonald, who, after all, had been chosen by both parties. It is highly unconventional—and some would say improper—for a sitting arbitrator to change roles and become a mediator. The two roles are completely different. The former is a decision-maker who imposes a solution on the parties; the latter is a facilitator who helps the parties negotiate a solution with each other. If this mediation didn't work, either party could probably disqualify Jack or me from returning to an arbitral role. Leaving Macdonald out of the mediation process was the solution: he could carry on as arbitrator.

I immediately went to find Jack. He liked the idea. The two of us went to Macdonald and told him about Barr's suggestion. Macdonald thought the whole thing was a bit unorthodox and probably doomed to failure, but worth a try—as long as Fujitsu was willing.

I naïvely thought, Of course Fujitsu will be willing. It's obviously a great idea to look for a global solution that doesn't require comparing scores of programs! But to my surprise, it wasn't that easy.

When Jack and I first proposed mediation to the Morrison &

Foerster team, we told them that the idea had initially come from the other side. Bob Raven and Dave Nelson listened with poker faces and solemnly said they would consult with their client and get back to us. Eventually Fujitsu agreed to participate, on one condition: that they not be required to meet or negotiate directly with IBM. They would participate only if Jack and I met with both sides separately, generated proposals for the parties, and refined those ideas through shuttle diplomacy.

As a mediator, this is not my preferred method of mediating. I prefer working primarily with the parties and their lawyers together, in the same room. That way, each side hears directly from the other side their story of what happened in the past and what their needs and future interests are. In most cases, I believe, this is the best way to solve hard problems and promote mutual understanding.[34]

But here, I was forced to realize that was impossible. We had one party that was very cautious—indeed, fearful that somehow IBM was going to trick them again. From Fujitsu's perspective, they had already been burned once in a negotiation with IBM: the 1983 Agreements had resolved nothing and IBM had used them to assault Fujitsu. Now here was IBM suggesting mediation. How could that be good for Fujitsu?

Looking back, I realize that the entire arbitration process must have seemed terribly alien and risky to Fujitsu. Fujitsu probably resented being forced to participate in a process so dominated by Americans, and in which it was so dependent on American lawyers. I recently learned from a Fujitsu executive that, in the eyes of some of his colleagues, the arbitration was "four against one": (1) IBM was an American company; (2) Cravath was an American law firm; (3) the panel consisted entirely of Americans;[35] and (4) Morrison & Foerster was an American law firm.

Nelson and Raven showed great sensitivity to this problem. They were always at pains to keep their clients fully informed and to strengthen their sense of control.

One ingenious idea helped improve the quality of communication between Morrison & Foerster and its clients. Bob Raven suggested to Fujitsu, "Lend us one of your young in-house lawyers. Have him move to San Francisco and work out of our San Francisco offices. You have my word he will be allowed to sit in on all of our internal meetings when we discuss the strategy we are developing for the arbitration. Your Mr. Katoh would be perfect." Masanobu Katoh was fluent in English and served from then on as a key link between the American lawyers and the Fujitsu top brass, most of whom were engineers. With a smile, Katoh recently told me that when he was assigned to the San Francisco post, one of his Fujitsu colleagues told him he was being sent as a "hostage" to the Americans.[36]

Cultural differences permeated the mediation process as well. For Jack and me, there was a big difference between the kinds of conversations we could have with each side. When we met with the IBM team, lawyers Tom Barr and Dan Evangelista, IBM's general counsel, had broad authority to act on their client's behalf. They and the IBM executives were comfortable exploring new ideas with us, telling us what they thought, and even making decisions on the spot. That was never the case with Fujitsu. Bob Raven and Dave Nelson attended all the mediation sessions but never claimed authority to make decisions for their client. Naruto would typically speak on behalf of Fujitsu but he would usually just report Fujitsu's reaction to what had been discussed at the last meeting. He might indicate which aspects were acceptable and which ones were not. Once I understood Fujitsu's objection, I would invariably suggest some modification and ask whether this would solve Fujitsu's problem. The Japanese would typically say nothing one way or the other. They would be completely nonresponsive. I was initially very frustrated by this. I wondered, Why can't they simply say what they think? Why won't they work with us?

After one of these sessions, in which the Japanese had once again declined to respond to one of my "brilliant" ideas, Nelson pulled me aside and gave me a coaching tip. When you are negotiating with a Japanese company, he said, don't expect movement at the table when something new is proposed. The Japanese negotiating team needs time to discuss the idea within the team and build a new consensus before they can proceed. In a Japanese organization, no one at the negotiating table typically has the authority to deviate from the position announced at the outset of a meeting. "Bob, be patient," Nelson said. "In due course, after they have discussed it internally, I suspect they will come around."

Barr was probably aware of these cultural differences and Raven's more limited authority. At one point in the mediation, Jack and I suggested that the two top lawyers get together and try to work out a couple of details. They happened to meet on Valentine's Day, in an IBM conference room that some staffer had decorated with hearts and valentines. When Barr entered the room and saw the decorations, he didn't say "Be My Valentine." He quipped, "Remember the St. Valentine's Day Massacre!" (That was when Al Capone's men lined up six members of an opposing gang and shot them.) Raven laughed. Barr went on to make a concrete proposal to deal with the questions the panel had asked counsel to work on. Perhaps wanting to needle Raven, Barr said to him, "Bob, in all seriousness, I want to assure you that the IBM Corporation has given me full authority to make a deal on the two questions we've been asked to address. What authority has Fujitsu given you?" Raven, who had a good sense of humor, grinned and said, "Tom, I want to assure you that I have full authority to report back to Fujitsu everything you say today."

What did we actually do during the mediation phase? Ultimately we designed an entirely new process that was custom-made for this dispute. Here's how we got there.

As a first step, Jack and I tackled the mess that was the DP list. This turned out to be fairly easy because the parties were now both motivated. We had already dispelled IBM's fantasy with regard to getting triple damages for the "new DPs" that Fujitsu had wanted to add. Fujitsu, meanwhile, still wanted immunity for those programs and was prepared to pay.

After less than four weeks of shuttle diplomacy, we had a deal: Fujitsu would add 295 programs to the DP list and would pay IBM a lump sum of $30 million for past use. Going forward, as with the original DPs, it would pay a semiannual license fee for each customer installation. Thus, in one fell swoop, the panel and the parties were freed from the task of slogging through those particular programs case by case.

But that was only a baby step. We had more ambitious goals.

In our meetings with each side, Jack and I had begun asking the sorts of questions that Spock would ask: What are your company's interests? Think about the legitimate interests of the other side. How might we together develop some creative options that might serve the interests of both sides better than conventional arbitration?

IBM's primary interest, clearly, was to protect its intellectual property. To the extent that Fujitsu used its technology, IBM also had an interest in being adequately paid for that use.

Fujitsu's primary interest was to stay in the compatibility business. It wanted a real shot at being able to develop compatible software through its independent development efforts.

That much was easy to figure out. But our discussions also suggested to me that the parties had a common interest in something they hadn't yet identified: *certainty*. Certainty about what materials Fujitsu was entitled to use in its development of IBM-compatible software. That clarity was what the 1983 Agreements had failed to provide. I said, "Look, for this conflict ever to end, we've got to have a set of standards. There have got to be more precise rules. Unless clear standards are established, won't you be stuck fighting for all eternity?" I asked each side, "Wouldn't both companies be better off if Fujitsu knew *in advance* what information it can use, rather than fighting these things out after Fujitsu has released a program to its customers?"

We were now deep in a Spockian process of *thinking things through—* trying to solve a hard problem with all the creativity we could muster. This was more fun than anything we had done so far. In fact, for me it was thrilling.

In my mind, the shape of a possible deal gradually emerged, one that would involve tearing up the old 1983 Agreements and starting from scratch. With the benefit of hindsight, I saw that these agreements had been doomed from the start.

One flaw related to the DP list—which had not been a bad idea in theory. Fujitsu wanted to escape the onerous burden of the continuing semiannual license fees, and the 1983 Agreement had given it an incentive to "clean up" its tainted programs by writing successor programs that somehow didn't violate IBM's rights. But without any meeting of the minds about when a successor was "clean enough" or what part of a DP Fujitsu could use in some future program, new fights were inevitable.

In actual operation, the DP scheme struck me as incredibly inefficient. Fujitsu was spending time and money redeveloping old programs to get rid of the taint. IBM was spending time and money monitoring and tracking Fujitsu's successor programs and fighting over whether the new programs were clean enough. Wouldn't it make more sense, I thought, to avoid these disputes by simply allowing Fujitsu to use the DPs any way it wanted in its future software development—for a price? I suggested to IBM, what you *ought* to care about is that Fujitsu pays you adequately for this privilege. Let's get rid of the ongoing license fee and establish a lump-sum payment that allows Fujitsu to use its own DPs freely.

This, too, took some persuasion. IBM was attached to the ongoing license fees. They liked the income stream. I also sensed that IBM valued the whole setup as a way to make Fujitsu's life as miserable as possible. I said, "Fujitsu has taken this material from your old programs. Sell them a paid-up license and let them use their DPs anyway they want. Admittedly, a fair price will need to be established for a paid-up license. You and Fujitsu will have to negotiate the amount—or the arbitration panel will have to set it—but that will only happen once. And then you're done!"

Gradually IBM came around.

A second flaw in the 1983 Agreements was its total lack of guidance with regard to the "external information." IBM was required to provide *some* information to Fujitsu, but exactly what was it? At what price? How would Fujitsu developers get access to that information and *only* that information?

This was the most difficult conundrum of all.

The simple solution, Jack and I thought, would be for IBM to write down the "external information" for each program on a piece of paper and then sell Fujitsu a license to use it. When we asked Fujitsu whether this would be acceptable, they not only rejected the idea but ridiculed it. They actually laughed. IBM would have every incentive to leave something out, they explained—something essential but not obvious. It would be like buying an expensive kit to build an elaborate model airplane. You would spend weeks trying to assemble it, only to find that an essential piece was missing and the plane wouldn't fly. And you wouldn't know which piece was missing! No, Fujitsu would only trust its own people to extract the externals.

IBM in turn found that idea ridiculous. Giving Fujitsu access to IBM source code would be like opening up the cookie jar to a child with a ravenous sweet tooth, IBM protested. No matter how strictly the rules were defined, Fujitsu would take more than they were entitled to.

Jack and I eventually found an answer, but it wasn't simple. We would come to call it, somewhat ponderously, the Secured Facility Regime.

First, we decided, we would create a precise definition of external information. "Instructions" would articulate that definition. Then we would set up a secure work site managed by an independent expert, in a location far away from all of Fujitsu's operations. "Secure" would be an understatement: the place would be tighter than Fort Knox. A handful of Fujitsu programmers would work there, isolated and under guard. They would be permitted to examine IBM programming materials, yes, but they'd only be allowed to write down (on "survey sheets") the external information as it had been defined in the Instructions. That's *all* they would be allowed to do. They would have absolutely no role in writing software and no contact with their colleagues who did. (I didn't envy the lonely souls who would end up working in our airless little capsule.) Before the survey sheets left the building, they would be vetted by IBM or an independent expert. If approved, they would be sent to the Fujitsu engineers who were writing new programs. Needless to say, that second group would have no access to anything but the survey sheets.

It was an exhausting process to contemplate, but the parties liked the concept because it offered real security to each.

But how could this scheme become operational? Many details remained to be filled in. Were the parties prepared to negotiate these issues directly with each other? Both parties said they'd try, but neither had any confidence that they would ever reach agreement. Then what?

The parties had the 1983 Agreements to fall back on, but that wasn't a big comfort. So I made a bold suggestion: Why not give the *panel* the power to make any decisions necessary to implement this new regime—but only to the extent IBM and Fujitsu were unable to agree?

Barr rather quickly responded that IBM would give the panel this sweeping power. He had only one condition: that going forward, the panel would consist only of Jack and me. He didn't say why he didn't want Macdonald to be part of the new regime, and I didn't ask. Barr did say IBM had a good deal of trust in Jack and me, largely because they knew we understood their interests.

Fujitsu, however, really struggled with this decision, I later learned. Certainty sounded good in theory, but ambiguity, after all, has its advantages. Specificity can be terrifying, especially if it forces you to accept fewer benefits and tighter restrictions than you think you are entitled to. Moreover, Fujitsu had been hauled into arbitration unwillingly, and the idea of giving the panel so much coercive authority was a bitter pill. But what was the alternative? Fighting things out under the 1983 Agreements? If they wanted to continue down the compatibility path, they were stuck. They were going to have conflicts with IBM. The only decision was whether the Jones-Mnookin regime would be better than conventional arbitration.

Fujitsu took the leap. Jack and I were willing to serve without Macdonald, and Macdonald gracefully resigned.[37]

In February 1987, the parties signed a new accord laying out this framework. (We called it the "Washington Agreement" because it was signed in Washington, D.C.) The agreement was only a few pages long and had taken only four months to create.

We gave the parties sixty days to negotiate the details. As expected, they failed.

A new hybrid process was about to begin—one in which Jack and I would each be wearing two hats. We would mediate where possible and rule when necessary. Over the summer, Jonathan Greenberg and I wrote an Opinion and Order describing the framework. (Jonathan became counsel to the panel and would remain closely involved in its work for the next ten years.)

In September, Jack and I held our first big press conference and let the world in on our secret. As you've no doubt gathered, we thoroughly enjoyed our fifteen minutes of fame.

Then the hard work really began.

During the next year, our biggest challenge was to create Instructions that defined with real precision just what information from IBM programs Fujitsu would be allowed to extract in the Secured Facility and then later use in software development.

The judgment calls were tough. Before we could define external information, we had to grapple with such metaphysical questions as "What does IBM-compatibility mean?" Or to be more precise, to what extent should Fujitsu's operating system legitimately aim to be IBM-compatible? We soon realized that compatibility was not a point, but a spectrum. Where did Fujitsu deserve to come out on this spectrum?

I can assure you the two parties fought like crazy over this issue. After briefs and argument, Jack and I decided that Fujitsu was entitled to a reasonable opportunity to maintain certain types of compatibility, but not others.[38]

There was no way Jack and I could have done this without technical help. Barr and Raven were equally clueless. To assist us, we assembled superb technical teams from both companies who did most of the heavy lifting.

These teams worked surprisingly well together, and we protected them from the litigators as much as possible. (Some of the lawyers were not happy to be sidelined and remained a bit dubious about the whole regime.) The teams were headed by Ron Alepin of Fujitsu and Bill McPhee of IBM, two software geniuses whom I could occasionally understand, and by lawyers Tony Clapes (of IBM in-house) and Mike Jacobs of Morrison & Foerster, who understood programming at a sophisticated level and could articulate the concepts in a way that could be consistently applied.

In less than a year the Instructions were completed. As you may recall, the 1983 Externals Agreement had tried to define "external information" in two sentences. Our Instructions ended up being more than forty single-spaced pages.[39] Through a rule-making process, we also ended up promulgating hundreds of pages of detailed rules providing strict and elaborate safeguards governing the operation of the Secured Facility, and ensuring that Fujitsu software programmers outside the facility did not have access to IBM programming materials.[40]

Finally, we had to resolve two conflicts over money.

The big issue was the price for the new paid-up license: how much Fujitsu would pay for the right to use the DPs in its own software development. Needless to say, the litigators were primed for a fight on this issue. IBM was asking for more than $2 billion. After receiving preliminary briefs, we announced the legal standard to be applied and the key variables we would be estimating in determining an amount.[41]

Although the financial stakes were high, Jack and I didn't find the task of determining the lump-sum payment all that daunting. Indeed, Jack had been a top executive at a huge railroad and had made lots of big financial decisions. I found his attitude comforting. "After all," he told me, "it's only money! And both companies have plenty of it." I agreed. In our view, the really important work was creating and implementing the new regime so that both companies could get on with their real business: competing in the marketplace. Setting a price for the paid-up license was just cleaning up their old mess.

But that was easy for us to say. Each company assembled vast teams of lawyers, engineers, and consultants who spent many person-years preparing massive submissions concerning the variables we had identified as relevant to the determination of the price for the paid-up license. I'm sure each party spent millions. At times the strain on the lawyers showed. A few of the younger lawyers got so caught up in the fight that they started to attack each other in letters to the panel. Personal insults were flying back and forth. Jack and I eventually lost patience with this nonsense. We warned them that if they didn't cut out the personal attacks, we would impose fines on individual lawyers. Fortunately, we never had to carry out the threat.

In the end, we found it neither difficult nor time consuming to establish a fair price for the paid-up license. While some courts might have heard months of live testimony and argument, we limited the actual hearings to one week. The only live testimony consisted of the cross-examination of each party's experts.[42] We gave counsel a chance to make oral arguments, and submit post-hearing briefs. Then we promptly made a decision,[43] setting the total price of the paid-up license at $396 million.[44]

The smaller money issue related to the annual fee that Fujitsu would pay for the "external information." (As you will recall, the 1983 Externals Agreement was useless in this regard—the parties had neglected to set a price.) After briefs and argument, we decided that for the first year in which the regime was in operation, Fujitsu would pay between $25 million and $52 million, depending on how many IBM programs it wanted access to. This gave Fujitsu an incentive to save money by accessing fewer IBM programs.

It was then again time to go public, with another carefully orchestrated round of press conferences both in New York and Tokyo. In our first round, Jack and I had simply sketched out a framework. Now we had put meat on the bones and we wanted people to see what we and the parties had created. We released an opinion, prepared with Jonathan Greenberg's able assistance, explaining the details, including the Instructions and the dollar amounts Fujitsu would be required to pay.

Again, there were hundreds of newspaper articles around the world, most very laudatory. As the *Wall Street Journal* reported, some observers hailed what we had done as "a model for resolving arcane, high-tech lawsuits." But others considered our role controversial. A Dean Witter analyst harrumphed, "This is a warning to other large companies: don't throw your fate in the hands of an arbitrator. You never know what they'll do, and they'll order you not to say anything about it. They are above the lawyers and above the courts."[45] Ah, those were the days!

In May 1989, the final piece fell into place: the Secured Facility was up and running. Of course, its location was a carefully guarded secret. In our rather quiet announcement of this milestone, we just said it was in Japan.

No expense was spared in creating this hermetically sealed chamber. If we and the parties could have put it on the moon, we would have. Instead we located it in Sakura, an obscure town about forty miles outside Tokyo, on the top two floors of an eight-story office building. Inside the building's sole elevator, you would never know that floors seven and eight even existed. We had the buttons and numbers for those floors removed from the elevator panel. You could only gain access to these floors with an elevator key, and only the facility manager and the guards had them. No one else reached the seventh or eighth floor unless their names were on a list, and even then they had to be personally escorted. There were guards on both floors twenty-four hours a day, 365 days a year. As far as we knew, no one in Sakura—or even the building—ever knew what was going on in there.

The handful of Fujitsu programmers who worked in the facility were not permitted to bring anything in or out of the inner sanctum—not a cell phone, not a wallet, not a scrap of paper. (Personal items had to be checked in a locker.) They had no access to a phone. Every time they went in or out, their movements were documented. The IBM source code was kept in a locked safe. We used security consultants to design the system, of course, and before the facility opened we hired a different security expert, whose primary client was the CIA, to check things out. He said our facility was more secure than either the Pentagon or the CIA headquarters in Langley, Virginia.

For the next seven years the regime operated without a hitch. As an extra safeguard, IBM built its own secured facility in Hampton, New

Hampshire, to inspect Fujitsu's new programs. IBM had the right to bring a claim before the panel if it found evidence that Fujitsu was breaking the rules—and I assure you, IBM looked. But it never brought a claim.

———————

Let me begin my assessment by turning back the clock to June 1985, just before the arbitration began. Both IBM and Fujitsu were awash in strong currents of demonization and tribalism. Was it wise for them to give up on negotiation and go to war? Or did they simply get caught in emotional traps?

To answer this question, let's suppose each side had been able to consult with Spock and consider his advice dispassionately. In 1985, could they have resolved their conflict through negotiation? What could they have done differently?

With regard to IBM, Spock would have pressed them on whether their hardball strategy in 1984 was wise. As you recall, Fujitsu offered to add many programs to the DP list in 1984, plainly signaling that it was prepared to negotiate a deal in which it would buy immunity for these programs. IBM refused this offer and demanded a draconian remedy: triple fees and the withdrawal of the offending software from Fujitsu's customers. It was these continued demands—and the threat of arbitration—that triggered the complete breakdown of negotiations in 1985.

Spock would have asked IBM and its lawyers, "How likely is it that an arbitration panel would grant you this harsh remedy?" Spock would have given them slim odds. He would have pointed out that the 1983 Settlement Agreement was a contract, and contract law does not allow punitive damages. He would have noted that an arbitration panel probably wouldn't order Fujitsu to pull the offending programs off the market because it would disrupt the business operations of innocent bystanders. In fact, I have a hunch that the lawyers on both sides of this case made similar assessments at the time.[46]

So was it irrational for IBM to persist in these demands? I don't think so. In fact, I think IBM would have responded to Spock, "As long as Fujitsu insists that it has the right to engage in what we see as illegal copying, why should we give up the leverage of a demand for draconian sanctions?" And I think Spock would have seen this as rational.

On the Fujitsu side, Spock would surely have focused on its strategic decision to persist with a business model based on maintaining an IBM-compatible operating system. Spock would have asked Fujitsu: "There is a long-term risk that you won't be able to sustain an IBM-compatible strategy. Even if you get the 'external information' you need, what are the odds that you can keep producing compatible operating software, given copyright constraints?" I'm sure Fujitsu asked itself the same question. Spock would have pushed Fujitsu to consider abandoning that model altogether, saying: "If you agree to leave the compatibility business after a reasonable transition period, or agree to sell IBM's software to your customers, IBM might be willing to negotiate a reasonable deal with respect to the other terms." I'm sure Fujitsu considered this possibility. But in 1985, my guess is that Fujitsu was not prepared to abandon its compatibility strategy. It had no ready alternative. Whatever the long-term risks of that strategy, I strongly suspect that Fujitsu perceived that abandoning it was even riskier. And I don't think Spock could have characterized this conclusion as irrational.

That leaves us with an interesting question. With the benefit of hindsight, we know there *was* a solution to this conflict: the Secured Facility Regime, which the panel and the parties devised jointly. Could the parties have figured this out on their own—two years earlier—and avoided warfare altogether?

To put it another way, suppose either side had offered the other a deal identical to the one we later imposed: the same lump-sum amount for the paid-up license; the same Instructions; the same annual access fee; the same Secured Facility safeguards. In 1985, would either have accepted such a deal from their adversary?

I think the answer is no—it's inconceivable. And more important, I don't think Spock would have considered either party's refusal to be irrational or unwise, even though, with the benefit of hindsight, both would have been better off with the Secured Facility Regime.

Why is this so? Why couldn't they have saved themselves all that pain?

The answer, I think, lies in the nature of uncertainty and its role in decision-making. This conflict was full of uncertainty on both sides. The legal issues were so unclear that the parties' lawyers could reasonably make very different predictions of what an arbitration panel would decide. The parties were fierce competitors and didn't trust each other, with good reason. Moreover, I suspect that within each company there were powerful constituencies that would have opposed the radical concessions necessary to create the Secured Facility.

Therefore, I am sure that IBM would never have agreed to give Fujitsu access to its source code, no matter what the safeguards. IBM would have said, "Are you crazy? Fujitsu is a major competitor. The 1983 Agreements don't give them the right to inspect our source code, and they'll never get it in arbitration. So why should we give it to them now? No way!" [47]

Similarly, I can't imagine Fujitsu accepting a deal as restrictive as the one we eventually imposed. The elaborate safeguards contained in the Security Facility Regime were highly intrusive of Fujitsu's programming practices. And we gave Fujitsu far less access to "external information" than its lawyers might reasonably have expected.

In short, both sides would probably have said, "No thanks. We'll do better in arbitration." And they wouldn't have been crazy to think so. Nor do I think they realized in 1985 how poorly suited arbitration was for their type of dispute. Even if they had been capable of such foresight and had seen that the Secured Facility Regime served their interests better than warfare, I don't think they could have made the mental leaps necessary to erect such a structure, absent the panel's coercive power.

This conclusion has implications that extend well beyond this unique case. In some conflicts, the intervention of third parties with coercive power may be necessary to overcome a host of barriers: not only distorted thinking created by psychological or ideological traps, but uncertainty and internal organizational constraints.

Moreover, the type of coercive process used, and when, can make a real difference.

A conventional lawsuit, for example, would have been a disaster in this case. The parties were right to avoid it. Can you imagine a jury trying to deal with the technological and copyright issues involved? Or even a judge, for that matter? Moreover, I doubt the parties could have agreed on venue. Fujitsu would have refused to try this case in an American court and IBM would have refused to try it in Japan. So arbitration had its advantages, including the fact that the parties could choose the decision-makers.

Once the parties were in conventional arbitration, the panel's rulings in response to the motions for summary judgment could not appropriately resolve the core copyright issue, but they did remove one of IBM's favorite cudgels, the threat of draconian penalties—nudging the parties closer to settlement.

Although many disputants do settle after summary judgment, these parties didn't. As you recall, they tried and failed. They needed a third way.

What ultimately worked was a hybrid process that started out as a conventional arbitration and evolved into something more complex—a kind of "grab bag" in which Jack and I were free to play many different roles, depending on the conflicts that arose over time. Our mind-set was facilitative: We were always eager to help the parties reach agreement, directly or indirectly, through their own negotiations. We always had in mind that the parties knew far more than we ever could about the technology and their own priorities and constraints. We always wanted to build on what they and their lawyers knew about the problem. But we had muscle in reserve. Without the flexibility of this hybrid system, we never would have resolved this case.

For example, in setting the price for the paid-up license, we used a process similar to traditional arbitration. (Indeed, it was not that different from what a court might have done, although I think it was quicker.) In creating the Instructions, we employed something akin to an administrative rule-making process. Once the regime was up and running, we acted like a regulatory commission charged with ensuring compliance. Imagine trying to mediate those issues! It would have been a nightmare. But because the parties had given us the power to use clout when necessary, they were able to capture the *efficiencies* of a coercive process without losing the tailor-made nature of the system itself.

Another lesson of this case is that a third party, acting as mediator, can facilitate voluntary settlements when it is impossible for bitter enemies even to sit down at the negotiation table together. You will recall that during the initial mediation phase of our process, Fujitsu refused to negotiate directly with IBM. But as go-betweens, Jack and I helped the parties make a deal in which Fujitsu added hundreds of programs to the DP list.

Why should it matter whether negotiations are direct or indirect? Because for a party locked in a heated conflict, direct negotiations may be perceived as imposing greater risks and offering fewer benefits. Any proposal coming directly from the enemy may be devalued,[48] and the mere act of sitting down at the negotiating table with a distrusted adversary may subject the leader to intense criticism from hard-liners. Indirect negotiations may feel much safer, both psychologically and politically. International relations provides many examples of intermediaries permitting indirect negotiations where adversaries are not willing to meet together. Switzerland acted as a go-between for the United States and Iran in 2003, and Turkey played a similar role for Syria and Israel in 2008.

Our mediation process provided Fujitsu's leaders with analogous protective cover. Fujitsu decision-makers could tell themselves—and their constituents—that they weren't bargaining with the Devil. Instead, they were working with Jones and Mnookin to explore any options we might suggest.

When mediation didn't work, Jack and I found that our ability to impose an outcome also lifted strategic and emotional burdens. It relieved one side or the other from agreeing to a compromise that might have been politically unacceptable behind the table. "I was made to do it by the panel" was a refrain that provided some psychological comfort and organizational protection.

This combination of roles—sometimes called "med-arb" because it combines the functions of both mediation and arbitration—is not only unusual but typically frowned upon.[49] There are two concerns. One is that a mediator who also has coercive powers won't really mediate at all—instead he or she will simply twist arms under the guise of being facilitative. The parties won't get the full benefit of a facilitative approach. The second concern is that the neutral will learn things during a private mediation session that may later corrupt his judgment as an arbitrator.

Both of these concerns are legitimate, but I think that sophisticated and informed disputants should have the option of choosing a mixed process in which the same person plays multiple roles. This can have obvious efficiencies. The information that Jack and I gained at each stage of the process was never wasted. Moreover, parties may grow to trust particular neutrals and want them to play a mixed role.

This hybrid process turned out to be congruent with the Japanese cultural tradition captured by the word *gaiatsu*, or "outside pressure or guidance." As neutrals, Jack and I adopted what we hoped would be a flexible, problem-solving mantra backed up by arbitral authority. In some ways such a mantra is consistent with the Japanese historical preference for informal dispute resolution mechanisms, based on well-developed relationships.

This case teaches a lesson about the role of lawyers as well. Lawyers can do more than conduct litigation as usual. The lawyers in this case played very constructive roles in designing a dispute system and getting this conflict resolved. Without the leadership and support of Raven and Barr, the clients would never have agreed to this process.

In 1997, five years before our regime was scheduled to end, the parties jointly decided that it was no longer necessary. Jack and I weren't surprised. Fujitsu had not requested access to new IBM source code for about three years. We sensed that Fujitsu had been winding down its IBM-compatible line of business and was focusing its energies elsewhere. Indeed, our regime had given Fujitsu time to make an orderly transition to a new business model that was not based on IBM compatibility. As always, the computer world was changing. Mainframes, while still important, were no longer the center of the computer universe.

The parties made their final public announcement: Their conflict was officially over, and the special regime had ended. The two companies jointly declared their return to "an ordinary business relationship" governed by ordinary law. But sometimes an ordinary thing can knock your socks off, or at least give you pause. Imagine Palestinians and Israelis announcing that they had established ordinary relations in Jerusalem.

EIGHT

Disharmony in the Symphony

The phone call came out of the blue. Steve Toben, a program officer at the Hewlett Foundation, had tracked me down during my summer holiday on Martha's Vineyard. I had known Steve for several years and I liked him very much. He headed the foundation's program relating to conflict resolution, which had helped launch both an interdisciplinary research center I founded at Stanford in the 1980s and the Harvard Program on Negotiation, which I now directed.

"Sorry to bother you during your vacation," he began. "I'm calling because the San Francisco Symphony is in deep trouble. I think you can help. Have you read about the strike?"

Steve knew I had successfully mediated a number of complex disputes. I thought I knew where he was going and I didn't want to go there.

"Steve, I have no interest in mediating a labor dispute," I interrupted. "This isn't my kind of gig. I have no experience in the labor-management area—that's a specialty of its own."

Steve politely told me that I had misunderstood the purpose of his call. He didn't want me to act as a mediator. The strike was over. A new contract had been signed.

I had violated one of my own teachings: listen first, talk second. Somewhat sheepishly, I asked Steve why he had called.

The strike had been "a real catastrophe," Steve went on. No winners, only losers. The musicians had lost two months' wages and were bitterly divided. By a narrow majority, the orchestra had ended up accepting a contract that was little better than what management had offered before the strike began. Management had suffered a public relations disaster. Ten weeks is an eternity for a business that depends on live performances. The strike had forced the cancellation of forty-three concerts, offended major donors, prompted erstwhile loyal fans to cancel their subscriptions, and elicited ridicule from the public. Inside the organization, relationships were horribly strained. People were barely speaking to each other.

Steve finally got to the point. "We need you to teach these people to negotiate. All they know how to do is fight. If they don't change their ways, they may destroy the institution the next time around."

I thanked him but declined. My fall schedule was already crammed.

Steve persisted. "We have some time. The new contract still has twenty-seven months to run. And there's no need for you to do this alone. Put a team together and the foundation will fund the work."

I said, "Look, Steve, just because the Hewlett Foundation wants these people to 'change their ways' doesn't mean they're motivated to *do* it—much less get instruction from some Harvard professor."

"That's a fair point," Steve conceded. But he was a good negotiator—persistent as hell. "Come see for yourself. After your vacation, give me two days of your time. Talk to some key people at the symphony. I'll arrange it all. No commitment on your part beyond this little visit. I'd like your assessment."

At this point I felt like a bachelor whose rich uncle was trying to set him up on a blind date. No commitment, the uncle says. Just meet her—I'll pay for dinner! I certainly wasn't looking for a new project, especially not one with a long-term commitment.

But I found it hard to keep saying no to Steve. He wasn't asking for much. And in a sense, I owed Hewlett. No foundation had done more to support the field of dispute resolution. I began to waver. I love classical music, and I attend symphony concerts regularly. Like most music lovers, I had no idea how the business side of a major symphony orchestra worked. All I knew was what I saw and heard from my comfortable seat in the concert hall: disciplined teamwork, beautiful music, everything just as it should be. Now Steve was telling me that behind the façade, people were practically breaking chairs over each other's heads. I was intrigued. I agreed to visit about a month later. In the meantime, Steve sent me some background materials and we talked further.

I began to realize that this would be no conventional blind date. I wasn't just being fixed up with a person, but with the whole crazy family! By the time I got to San Francisco I realized that the dating metaphor was all wrong. I was more like a therapist being asked to treat a horribly dysfunctional family.

On September 18, 1997, I flew from Boston to San Francisco for a two-day visit with the symphony. Steve had set up a series of appointments so I could meet separately with the parties. I would meet first with labor: several key members of the orchestra. Then I would meet with management—or more precisely, the three captains who shared responsibility for running the symphony: executive director Peter Pastreich, who ran the business side; Nancy Bechtle, head of the board of governors; and maestro Michael Tilson Thomas, the music director, whom everyone referred to as "MTT."

As my taxi headed for Davies Symphony Hall, I went over what I hoped to accomplish. One of my goals was to listen. I expected that each of my interviews would reveal a radically different perspective on the symphony's problems.

I also hoped to give everyone a sense of my own approach to negotiation and training. Slogans like "win-win," often associated with my Harvard program, are incomplete and misleading. They make it all sound too easy. I believe that effective conflict resolution requires one to manage certain tensions that cannot fully be resolved. People can learn to manage these tensions, but it is hard work. It takes motivation, especially in the context of a large institution.

So my most important goal was to assess for Steve whether the parties were motivated. The symphony people wouldn't be paying for this program, I reflected; the foundation would. It would be a little too easy for the symphony people to say yes to "negotiation therapy" and then just go through the motions. If they really wanted to learn a new approach to conflict, great! They didn't have to accept *me* as their negotiation guru; in fact, I was kind of hoping they wouldn't. I would help Steve find someone else. But if they weren't prepared to do some serious work—if they didn't genuinely want to change—I would tell Steve that there was no point in going forward.

My first meeting was with five musicians who had been elected by their peers to serve on the "Players' Committee." I didn't know what the Players' Committee was, but I'd soon find out. The musicians introduced themselves in terms of their instrument. Tom Hemphill, the gregarious committee chairman, was a percussionist. Wayne Roden played the viola. Robin McKee and Linda Lukas were flutists. I was surprised to learn that Chris Gilbert, who looked no more than five feet six, played the double bass.[1]

It was almost noon, so I suggested we have lunch together at a small café just up the street. I don't know if my excitement showed, but I was thrilled to be meeting with five members of the San Francisco Symphony (SFS)—more thrilled than if I had been meeting with, say, five players from the San Francisco Giants. I had never been on my school's baseball team, but I had played the trumpet in my school orchestra. I knew the SFS was the big leagues and that you had to be an extraordinary musician to get this far. To me, all 105 musicians of the SFS were members of an artistic elite. And now I was having lunch with what I took to be the innermost circle: the "Players' Committee."

I soon learned, however, that the Five[2] were not impressed with this honor. It was easy to get elected to the Players' Committee, they said, laughing. Hardly anyone wanted the job! The Players' Committee was a function of the orchestra's union status. The Five were essentially shop stewards, like their counterparts at an automobile plant. Their job, making sure management lived up to the terms of the contract, was a time-consuming, unpaid, and largely thankless task. Indeed, the Five described the orchestra as something like an octopus without central control, one of whose arms was always ready to strangle you. Coordinating the unruly beast was impossible, and any assertion of leadership by the committee was likely to be challenged. Most of the musicians viewed the committee mainly as a conduit for gripes and grievances: for example, that a rehearsal had gone six minutes overtime. Whenever the committee worked with management in solving a problem, some in the orchestra would condemn them as collaborators.

As part of my homework, I had asked Steve Toben to send me a copy of the latest contract. I was stunned by what I saw. More than twenty-six pages with two columns of fine print, it contained elaborate protections that were a throwback to old-style industrial labor contracts. For one thing, after a brief probationary period, every musician had tenure.[3] Nearly all earned more than one hundred thousand dollars a year.[4] Everyone enjoyed ten weeks of paid vacation and generous health and retirement benefits. What I found most surprising was the level of detail with respect to work rules. With limited exceptions for tours, there could be no more than twenty hours a week of combined rehearsal and performance time. Rehearsals were regulated down to the minute. The same went for concert scheduling (no performances during the summer or on Sunday afternoons), touring conditions ("first-class hotel accommodations in single rooms"), and even parking privileges.

The contract was renegotiated every three years, but not by the Five. That was the job of a different committee—a "Negotiating Committee"—which came into existence only for the few months of negotiation.

That brought us to the recent strike. "You have no idea how bruised everyone feels," Hemphill said, "and how much anger there is among the musicians."

A primary target of their anger was Peter Pastreich, the executive director. Although the Five held different personal views of Pastreich, they all agreed that he was his own worst enemy. One said that he couldn't resist demonstrating how smart he was by making someone else feel stupid. Another said his body language and manner often exuded arrogance and condescension. He was prone to barbs and biting sarcasm—exactly the wrong style for dealing with artists. Everyone in the orchestra saw him as a formidable adversary in contract negotiations, and many saw him as a bully who enjoyed outsmarting them in a good slugfest every three years. I was told that a significant number of musicians despised him and wanted to use the strike to get revenge and perhaps even get him fired.

Another target of their anger, however, was each other.

Nearly 100 percent of the players had voted to go on strike, but beneath that show of solidarity lay deep fissures. The Negotiating Committee had been split between two groups, which for simplicity I'll call the Hard Liners and the Moderates. The Hard Liners were the ones who were angriest at management, most committed to playing hardball, and least experienced in contract negotiation. Having a majority of three to two, they seized control of the committee and hired the toughest lawyer they could find. The two Moderates—one of whom was the bassist, Chris Gilbert—were simply outvoted.

To make things worse, as the strike dragged on, many of the rank and file lost confidence in the committee majority. The walkout ended with the committee majority urging, "Fight on!" and the orchestra narrowly overruling them and accepting a management offer.

Afterward, there was a "profound split among the musicians and tremendous bitterness and a sense of betrayal among colleagues," Hemphill said. A vocal minority thought the strike should have lasted longer, and a larger camp thought the strike had been a disaster. Some players hadn't spoken to each other in months. Even some who shared the same stand[5] were not on speaking terms.

It sounded unbearable, and I could read the distress in their faces. What about the music, I asked. How could they perform under such conditions? As I was to hear from many sources, the performances were as good as ever. As Linda Lukas said proudly, "We play our hearts out anyway."

In fact, the Five were a reflection of the orchestra and its divisions. Two of them had backed the Hard Liners and voted against the settlement. One had denounced the Hard Liners' approach as "stupid" from the beginning. The remaining two (Hemphill and Gilbert) had been Moderates, initially supporting the strike but later working to end it. For my purposes, I was just glad the Five were on speaking terms.

Chris Gilbert knew the most about the contract negotiation process. A soft-spoken and even reticent guy, he had served on every Negotiating Committee for the past fifteen years. Contract negotiation was "the one time that [management] really has to listen to you and hear what you are saying," he said. "It's the one time you really have some ability to create some change. *Force* things to change." He had often chaired the Negotiating Committee, but not during the last round, which he had found deeply frustrating and painful.

I sensed that the Five liked my basic problem-solving approach to negotiation, which I briefly described. They all clearly wanted help healing the wounds among the musicians. This was a good sign. But they seemed extraordinarily anxious at the prospect of selling a negotiation training program to the orchestra. "If the musicians think management is pushing for some new approach, half the orchestra will vote against it for that reason alone," Hemphill predicted gloomily.

"This [initiative] isn't going to happen simply because *we* recommend it. We're just going to take abuse."

I could understand the others' anxiety about getting too far out front, but Hemphill's apprehension surprised me. He was one of the reasons we had gotten this far. Hemphill, Lukas, and Pastreich had been the first to contact the Hewlett Foundation, months ago, to discuss the possibility of launching a negotiation program. And during lunch Hemphill had expressed exuberant support for negotiation training—in fact, he seemed eager to claim partial credit for the idea. So why the ambivalence? I would later come to realize that despite his flamboyant personality and desire to lead, he didn't have a thick enough skin for politics. Performing was one thing: he had once performed at a society ball dressed up in a gorilla suit so he "couldn't be ignored." But taking heat was another. At the end of the strike, he had personally intervened with Pastreich to make a modest change to management's offer, believing correctly that it would make the deal more palatable to a majority of the musicians. The Hard Liners had really beaten him up for that, and the wounds hadn't healed.

As I came away from the lunch, certain conclusions seemed obvious. Many musicians were demonizing Pastreich and engaging in a lot of zero-sum thinking. Moreover, the musicians' relationships with one another were badly strained. They were traumatized. They had no authority structure, no strong leadership, and no training in collective bargaining. No wonder they had not been effective negotiators.

My next meeting was with the alleged demon himself. Peter Pastreich had Brooklyn roots and an Ivy League education, both of which were immediately apparent. Raised in a working-class neighborhood with left-wing parents, he had gone from a public school to Yale. Now balding, energetic, and fit, he still had a slight New York accent and wore the uniform of the Yalies of his generation: a well-tailored Brooks Brothers suit and a shirt with a button-down collar. He had discovered music management as a trumpet player in the Yale band, when he had organized and raised the money for the band's first European tour. He would later tell me, "The preppies in the Yale Glee Club and the Wiffenpoofs[6] all got rich alums to sponsor tours to Europe. I thought we public school boys in the band should as well."

I already knew of Pastreich's stellar reputation in the symphony management world. When he joined the SFS in 1978, it was running a deficit, employed no full-time musicians, and didn't even have a concert hall of its own. During his tenure it recruited gifted young musicians (including Hemphill and Gilbert, both of whom joined in their early twenties), established a full-time salary for its players, and achieved national prominence. Davies Symphony Hall, a magnificent concert facility, was built during this period. Pastreich brought the SFS budget into balance, amassed an endowment, and took the symphony on international tours.

But as soon as we took our seats in his office, I began to see why the musicians found him difficult. After about two minutes of pleasantries, he began to test me. He treated me as if I were being interviewed for a job. I wouldn't play that game.

"What do you know about labor law?"

Very little, I said.

"What do you know about the orchestra business?"

Nothing.

"What makes you think you are the right person to help us?"

Good question. I'm not sure I am.

"Look, Peter," I continued, "I'm here at Steve Toben's request. I'm not looking for work. The purpose of this visit is for me to learn more about the symphony and its problems, and to share some ideas with you about problem-solving approaches to negotiation. Even if you are interested in a new approach, I may not be the right person. I'd be glad to help you and the Hewlett Foundation find somebody else."

It's fun being interviewed for a job that you really don't think you want. Fortunately, neither of us took this mano a mano jousting too seriously, and after this little contest he started educating me. I found him to be deeply perceptive about his role.

The executive director of a major American symphony, I learned, does not have nearly the sweeping authority of a corporate CEO. He runs the business side of the enterprise—setting the budget, running the hall, negotiating contracts with soloists, arranging tours—with the help of a staff of about one hundred people, about the same size as the orchestra. But unlike a typical CEO, he is one of *three* leaders with interdependent roles, and he must constantly negotiate with the other two. One of them is the maestro. The primary mission of a major symphony is artistic, not profit-driven, which means that the maestro must have enough autonomy to define the musical product. But artistic decisions can profoundly affect the bottom line, so the executive director must manage this relationship skillfully. The third power center is the board of trustees. Like most nonprofit institutions, American symphonies depend on private philanthropy for survival. That gives the trustees significantly more power than ordinary corporate directors; they are more akin to board members who own a lot of stock. An executive director has to be careful not to offend them. The result is a complex triangular relationship among the three power centers. I was beginning to see the complexity of Pastreich's world.

He also surprised me with his attitude toward unions. He had nothing against them. To the contrary, his brother was a union organizer, and he was sympathetic to the union movement. He even thought that strikes could be cathartic for the rank and file. In 1981, he had written an article saying that one should not "underestimate the value of grievances, negotiations and even strikes as a safety valve for . . . frustration. . . . Why should the musicians be denied their triennial opportunity to talk back, even shout back, to management and, through management, to the conductor and the board?"[7]

Why, then, had the last strike been so damaging? From Pastreich's perspective, three main factors had contributed to the deadlock.

One was his own relationship with the musicians. He readily acknowledged that the relationship had been deteriorating for years and that his personal style was partly responsible.

Another factor was the composition of the Negotiating Committee, which had been controlled by the "most rabid players in the orchestra," he said. "I was negotiating with a committee controlled by tough guys" and a lawyer hired "not to make a deal" but "to bloody us."

The third factor—the real killer, in his view—had been the "crazy" demands of the Negotiating Committee. Their first proposal had been a list of sixty-five demands that would have sweetened nearly every aspect of the twenty-five-page contract. In his thirty years of negotiating with unions, Pastreich had never seen anything like it.

Pastreich explained that before the negotiation had begun, he had announced that the symphony was running an operating deficit for the first time in many years. He had laid off seven members of his own staff to underline the point. Wasn't the committee paying attention?

No, apparently they were in fantasyland. The musicians didn't believe him about the deficit and accused him of cooking the books.

The actual negotiations then got off to a terrible start when Pastreich tried to discover what the musicians' real priorities were.

> *Pastreich (referring to the list of demands):* Which of these things really matter?
>
> *Musicians:* All of them matter to us.
>
> *Pastreich:* Well, wait a minute. They can't all be of the same importance. Which ones are the most important?
>
> *Musicians:* It's not our job to prioritize. . . . It is our job to deliver what [our colleagues have] asked for.

After a few rounds of this, Pastreich saw no choice but to respond in kind. He submitted a counterproposal with an almost equal number of counterdemands. In his experience, the only way to get minor items off the table was not to argue them off, but to "trade them off." He felt trapped into the following kind of conversation: " 'You want overtime to start at ten minutes? We want it to start at twenty minutes. Eventually, we'll get back to fifteen minutes, which is where it was to begin with. You want to increase radio fees by thirty-three percent? We want to decrease them by thirty-three percent.' And so on. It couldn't have been more positional. Because they've taken sixty-five positions, we've taken sixty-five counterpositions." In the end, "[t]he only way to see what was really important to them was to see what they would strike about and vice versa. It was a game of chicken to see if the other side was willing to drive off the cliff."

Was he motivated to try something new? I sensed that he was skeptical about the notion of negotiation therapy and not entirely sold on me, either. But, as he said, "the strike was a disaster," relationships were terrible, and he wanted to improve them.

I left my session impressed with Pastreich. He was sophisticated and worldly, but the Brooklyn boy in him abhorred pretension and snobbery. He thought orchestra musicians needed collective bargaining. When he stepped out of his role and analyzed a situation, he was astute and even self-critical. But I understood why many musicians saw him as the enemy: his competitive, controlling nature often caused him unintentionally to offend others. I did not think he was a bad man. He was certainly not evil.

———————

My third meeting was with Nancy Hellman Bechtle, president of the board of governors. She had invited two other trustees to join us: Dick Rosenberg, former chairman of the Bank of America, and Len Kingsley, the head of the trustees' labor-management subcommittee.

Bechtle, the scion of a pioneer California banking family, had a commitment to the San Francisco Symphony that ran in her Hellman blood. I would later learn that her great-uncle had been a founder of the symphony and that her grandmother, father, and mother had all served on the board. I found her energetic, welcoming, and quite down to earth—there was not a whiff of self-importance about her. I also sensed a certain toughness that I liked, a confidence and directness that made communication easy.

Bechtle's leadership of the board was undisputed, and her role represents the second point in the symphony's leadership triangle. There are about eighty-five governors (akin to trustees) listed in the symphony's programs. All are expected to contribute financially. A small number are actively engaged in governance. When I asked Rosenberg to tell me a bit about the board, he pointed to Bechtle and said, "She *is* the board. She raises more money than the rest of us, she works harder and puts in far more hours, and she knows more about the organization. She really is our leader."

The board's view of the strike was essentially that the musicians had behaved like spoiled children. Where did they think the money for their salaries came from? Without the board and its constant fund-raising, they'd all be out of a job. At the time, the annual operating budget of the symphony was over $40 million, and only about half came from ticket sales. The other half came from philanthropy. "We work very hard," Bechtle told me. "A city like San Francisco has scores of worthy causes—the opera, the ballet, museums, hospitals, universities—all competing for donors. We're volunteers. There are a lot of other institutions asking for *our* time and money. We don't have to do this." And yet the musicians' behavior during the strike had made the whole institution look foolish—and the board's job harder. "After this last strike, some donors just looked at me and said, 'Why should we give money to that screwed-up organization?' "

The board was most offended by two things the musicians had done during the strike. One was the Negotiating Committee's claim—reported frequently in the press—that the operating deficit was phony. That had really sent the board's finance committee through the roof. The other was the orchestra's decision, during the last European tour, to distribute leaflets to concertgoers complaining about their working conditions back home. For what purpose? Solely to embarrass the trustees. In London, Paris, Berlin, musicians in formal dress had stood outside the concert halls handing out flyers complaining about their compensation.[8] These tactics had drawn publicity all right, but not sympathy. The Europeans thought it was *nuts*. "It seems strange," scoffed a London critic, "that an orchestra should come all the way across the Atlantic and then threaten not to play." The Vienna Symphony director warned that his patrons hated such behavior, that the SFS might never be invited back, and that the Viennese saved their sympathy for the penniless Russian orchestras.[9]

Indeed, the feeling around the boardroom was that the musicians didn't appreciate how good they had it. They had great jobs that most classical musicians would kill for, they got to live in the San Francisco Bay area, and they earned full-time salaries for what amounted to part-time work, with ten weeks of paid vacation and plenty of time to teach and perform on the side. Yet the ingrates had staged three strikes in ten years.

Bechtle was a great admirer of Pastreich, whom the board had firmly supported during the strike. (As she told me later, Pastreich was "brilliant," "creative," and open-minded, but "he was always debating; he turned every discussion into a debate. And he always had to win.") The subject of Pastreich led to a revealing conversation.

I asked her, "What is the most important challenge facing the symphony?"

She answered without hesitation: "To restore relations with the musicians and improve labor-management relations."

Rosenberg turned to her and said, "I wonder if that is your top priority. If it were, Peter would no longer be here."

So the board understood that Pastreich was part of the problem, I thought. I wondered if some trustees felt that firing him might be the easiest way to get things back on a productive track.

But my stronger sense was that the trustees primarily blamed the radical wing of the orchestra for their troubles. According to Bechtle, there is a "toxic ten percent" in the orchestra. "In any other world this ten percent would quit or be fired. . . . If you are that unhappy, you shouldn't be in this job." It occurred to me that blaming a toxic 10 percent of the musicians for all the symphony's problems may have allowed the trustees to exonerate everyone else, including themselves. That's why people often find it comforting to demonize.

The trustees were eager to avoid another debacle, and Bechtle in particular saw the value-creating possibilities of a negotiation skills program. Her only concern was whether the musicians would go along.

The next morning, I met MTT at his magnificent, sprawling home in Pacific Heights. It wasn't strictly necessary for me to meet him—he had not been involved in the strike—but it was fun. The maestro was a celebrity. He was the public face of the symphony; he carried the brand. The light posts near Davies Symphony Hall were hung with large banners bearing his likeness and name.

MTT represented the third point in the leadership triangle. As the music director and principal conductor, he provided the musical vision. He was responsible for choosing the repertoire and for hiring, evaluating, and developing the musicians. Like most conductors, he was largely insulated from the business affairs of the orchestra. He lived in San Francisco for only part of the season, spending the rest of his time as artistic director and founder of the New World Symphony in Miami and traveling around the world as a guest conductor for other orchestras.

When I asked him about the strike, MTT made it clear that he had taken no sides. All he cared about was building the orchestra and making music. He had worried that the strike would affect the performances, but the players had really come through. He was pleased by that.

When I asked why he thought this particular strike had been so destructive, he saw contributions on both sides. Pastreich "delivers zingers and he's not aware of it," he said. The musicians' demands had been unrealistic: "They are living in Paradise and are unaware of it." I could almost hear him thinking, Thank God I don't have to bargain with any of these difficult people.

He speculated that American musicians were jealous of their counterparts in Europe, where orchestras enjoy government support and musicians have more institutional power. In any event, he said, he would support any initiative that would help heal the rift. He was not going to be involved, mind you, and he would not attend any workshops, but "we sure hope you can help."

⎯⎯⎯⎯▬⎯⎯⎯⎯

By the end of my two days in San Francisco, I was thinking, "These people need help. Lots of zero-sum thinking, and demonization, too. Relationships are a mess and they're in terrible pain. But they are motivated to change." I was also thinking that the project might be fun. Most people don't like being in the middle of conflict, but I rather enjoy it, especially when I think I can help the combatants. I thought, *They* don't have confidence that they can recover from this, but *I* have a lot of confidence they can. And I had the germ of a clever idea (clever at least in my own mind) about how to proceed.

But first I had more to learn. As one experienced labor arbitrator has said, symphony musicians have "the reputation . . . of being the angriest, most militant group in the whole field of entertainment and the performing arts." I wanted to understand why.

History provided part of the explanation. In the early days, before American symphony musicians were unionized, they were underpaid and often exploited. There was no job security. There was a glut of classical musicians who could be hired for "pickup orchestras," one gig at a time. Even after orchestras with full-time musicians were formed, symphony managers "did the minimum necessary, believing correctly that the musicians would continue to play, whatever they were paid," Pastreich told me. Things changed only after symphony musicians unionized (under the aegis of the American Federation of Musicians) and learned to push back hard. One of their key discoveries, said Pastreich, was that strikes were a "social embarrassment to the boards and management."

But more secure jobs and better pay did not eliminate the musicians' anxiety and resentment over being insufficiently appreciated. In Chris Gilbert's words, "Classical musicians have been struggling for recognition as hardworking, highly skilled professionals. Like a doctor or law-yer, we deserve to be highly regarded and respected. At least part of that respect must come in the form of money."

Another source of discontent had nothing to do with money. "Even the highest wage can never compensate for the inner distress which clings to the whole profession," wrote another commentator. Most gifted musicians, especially violinists, are trained to perform as solo-ists. They begin studying an instrument at an early age. Some are child prodigies. As kids, while their friends are goofing off, they devote thou-sands of hours to practice. Their grandmother tells them they are going to be the next Jascha Heifetz.[10] Then they end up sitting in the third row of the orchestra.

According to one expert, "The basic skill in orchestra section play-ing . . . lies in knowing how to suppress individual expression for the sake of the group effect."[11] This requirement is most burdensome on the string players, who are the most numerous and whose lush sound requires them to blend in—to the point where they typically cannot even hear themselves play. A musician likes to be heard! That's why string players prefer chamber music, where each musician has a unique role. The happiest musicians are those whose instruments stand out—the oboists, flutists, and trumpet players, for example, who can often be heard individually and sometimes have solo lines. Of course, by that measure the percussionists should be the happiest of all. And they aren't. Hemphill, who used to be a jazz drummer, found the adjustment to orchestra life difficult: "When you're a classical percussionist, you sit there; then all of a sudden you stand up and play something; then you sit down again."[12]

So, are these just a bunch of whiners? No. These are artists who are extremely ambitious and gifted, who have competed fiercely to get where they are, who have probably reached the peak of their careers—and who have almost *no control over what they create*. They don't choose the music they play or how to interpret it. That's the conductor's job. Musicians live in a state of "psychic bondage" to the conductor, whom they are expected to "obey blindly" while completely subordinating their own artistic preferences.[13]

All these frustrations have no regular outlet except the collective bargaining process.

Pastreich saw nothing wrong with that. Plus, hard bargaining was a game he knew and even enjoyed. He could still bargain after staying up for forty-eight hours; the musicians typically couldn't. "I was still very good at hour forty," he said. With some pride, he reported that the orchestra had once passed a resolution forbidding bargaining past midnight, lest Pastreich wear down the Negotiating Committee.

Over the years, the dynamic at the SFS became even more contentious than at most professional orchestras. Brinkmanship became a way of life. Each side would develop targets in advance and then boldly overstate opening positions. They would commit to these positions early and publicly, and channel all subsequent communication through a spokesman. They would try to keep the other side off balance by using tactics designed to divide the constituents on the other side. There was almost always a strike. "Rightly or wrongly, it was almost seen as a necessary part of negotiating in San Francisco," Gilbert explained. "We would always plot our strategy to try to pick out [the] maximum leverage [for] a strike deadline.... We would see if we had a tour coming up, or some important concert that would provide additional leverage." If ultimately the contract was accepted with great reluctance by both sides, this was taken as a sign of success. For management it was a sign that they had maintained fiscal discipline. For the musicians it showed they had extracted as much as they could.

———

But according to my view of negotiation theory, this was exactly the wrong way to go about it. I believe that effective negotiation requires the management of three discrete tensions:

1.   Between opportunities to expand the pie (by creating value) and the need to divide the pie (by distributing value);

2.   Between communicating with empathy (demonstrating that you understand the other side's perspective, even if you don't agree with it) and communicating with assertiveness;

and in some cases,

3.   Between the representatives negotiating at the table and their constituents behind the table.

At the SFS, I discovered, these tensions weren't being *managed*—they were being trampled by a herd of stampeding cattle. Indeed, the negotiations surrounding the 1996–97 strike were a textbook example of how to manage the tensions badly.

Behind the table on the orchestra's side, the Negotiating Committee majority was made up of unseasoned negotiators who "wanted to show who's boss this time," as Gilbert recalled. "There were people who felt that if we just were tough [enough], that would fix things." So they turned to I. Philip Sipser,[14] a well-established labor lawyer who had lots of experience representing the musicians' union and was known to be a hard bargainer. It was the first time the committee had looked outside San Francisco for a lawyer, and they wanted a gladiator. Sipser was as tenacious and tough as Pastreich. That signaled to management that hammering out a new contract would be contentious. But it doesn't explain why the negotiation went off the rails. Pastreich and Sipser had known each other for years and played the same game. A more significant factor, I believe, was the List of 65 Demands. Here is the story behind it.

———

The Negotiating Committee was well-intentioned and wanted to be responsive to its constituents. So, in preparing for the negotiations, it sent each musician a questionnaire with a long list of potential issues for bargaining. Next, a member of the committee interviewed each musician. "What we did," Gilbert recalled, "was go through, point by point, virtually everything in the contract and ask them, 'Do you think we should have an improvement in this?' Which of course yields a lot of yesses." The committee also asked: "What are the ten most important things that you think should be changed in the next negotiation?" Not surprisingly, they ended up with a long list of desired changes. For example, the old contract provided that each player receive $30 per radio broadcast; some musicians wanted $40. Overtime started after fifteen minutes; some wanted it to be ten minutes. Some musicians hated long rehearsals; others hated playing on Saturdays. The mushrooming list eventually included heaters and canopies at outdoor concerts, coverage for orthodontia, and a prohibition on folding beds on tours.

When Sipser, the lawyer, saw the List, he warned the committee not to use it. Gilbert wished they had listened. "He did counsel us against having a laundry list and he did assure us that what we had was a laundry list," Gilbert said. But the committee rejected the advice.

This is an excellent example of the negative traps clouding the judgment of inexperienced negotiators behind the table. Indeed, nearly all of the traps—Tribalism, Demonization, Dehumanization, Moralism, Zero-Sum Fallacy, Fight/Flight, and the Call to Battle—seemed to be at work here. The committee wanted to "bloody" Pastreich, and the List was one of their weapons. It was also the product of a terribly ineffective process behind the table. In trying to serve its membership, the committee had collected a list of fantasy benefits and provided no leadership in setting priorities. The Hard Liners on the committee then proceeded to ignore their lawyer, one of the most seasoned fighters in the business, in planning their strategy. That was inexperience *plus* the negative traps at work. How dumb is it to hire an experienced, hard-nosed labor lawyer—the attack dog you thought you wanted—and then refuse to take his advice? I doubt the committee intended to blow off their own fingers while setting a bomb for Pastreich. I think they were just in a vengeful frame of mind and not thinking clearly. Spock would have strongly disapproved.

The List also demonstrates how an opening move can influence much that follows. Putting that List on the table was a disastrous move, largely because Pastreich didn't understand the flawed process that produced it. He was not only shocked, but alarmed. When he asked the committee, "Which of these things really matter?" and they said, "All of them matter," he heard a declaration of war. Which it partly was. But what he couldn't have known, because the committee wasn't about to admit it, was that the committee *didn't know the answer to his question.*

As might be expected, the negotiation across the table was zero-sum all the way. Pastreich responded in kind with his own set of extreme demands. The tension between assertiveness and empathy wasn't managed at all: the discussion was all assertion and no empathy. According to Pastreich, the negotiation went as follows:

> We [management] said, "We have a serious deficit so we are not going to be able to give you a really good contract. We're not going to be able to give you anything special this time because we have a financial problem." And they said, "We don't believe you. We

don't think you have a deficit. We don't think you have a problem." And they came in and said, "We are working harder than any other orchestra in the country and we are getting sick and injured as a result of all that, so we need some serious relief." And we said, "We don't believe you. We don't think that injuries have anything to do with overwork, we don't think you work harder than anyone else." So with respect to the two most contentious issues we didn't believe one another. . . . Each side knew that the other side didn't really believe them. . . . A kind of desperation set in on both sides where each of us said to ourselves, "We're not going to get anywhere with these people. They don't even hear what we are saying." And that turned into great anger.

A similar exchange took place during a heated argument about auditions. One issue was the musicians' demand for equal power in hiring decisions.

Committee member: In my opinion, the power divided [should be] precisely equal. Each side must agree on a candidate for them to be hired.

Pastreich: We do not feel they should be equal. The board feels that the music director should have more power in making the decision than the orchestra.

Another committee member: I hope that this issue would be [discussed] under an umbrella of greater respect.

Pastreich: This is not a matter of respect.

But what were they arguing about, if not respect? Pastreich was focusing on the committee's demands without fully understanding what was motivating them. Pastreich later came to think, "It was a strike looking for issues. It wasn't about any real issue, it was about the *relationship.*"

I would agree with that, with one qualification: negotiations are almost always about both the substantive issues *and* the relationship.

———

Now I understood the territory and had a plan. Within six weeks of my first visit, I agreed to undertake a negotiation program on two conditions. First, the symphony people would have to be in control. I didn't want the Hewlett Foundation grant coming directly to me. I wanted it to go to the symphony. Control of the process would be shared by all three groups—the musicians, management, and the trustees. They would have the power to hire and fire me. They would share ultimate responsibility for the project's success or failure. And as their first therapeutic exercise, I decided, they would jointly prepare the grant application to Hewlett, with my help. This would encourage "buy-in" and show them that they could start working together.

My second condition was that I would build a team to help me with the project. It would include Joel Cutcher-Gershenfeld, a labor-management expert who was then a faculty member at MIT and part of Harvard's Program on Negotiation. The third member would be Gary Friedman, an experienced Bay Area mediator who had worked with me for many years both at Stanford and at Harvard. Gary would serve as our West Coast anchor and be more readily available than I could possibly be, given my obligations in Cambridge.

My proposal won immediate support from everyone I had met at the symphony: Bechtle, Pastreich, and the Players' Committee. But there was still one group that needed to be persuaded: the musicians themselves. The committee was still in a state of high anxiety about this task and I soon understood why.[15] Moving the orchestra was like pushing an elephant uphill. It took three long meetings, including one at which Gary Friedman and I answered questions for several hours, to persuade the musicians that interest-based bargaining was not a tool of the Devil and that this proposal was not a management initiative. There were some dissents, and a handful of musicians viewed the committee's endorsement of the program as a "betrayal," but ultimately the orchestra approved the program by a substantial majority.

On November 24, 1997, as I had hoped, the key stakeholders jointly submitted their grant application to the Hewlett Foundation. It was signed by all five members of the Players' Committee; by Pastreich as executive director; and by two board members, including Bechtle.

A Hewlett grant was forthcoming.

———————

We began our project by tending to the people who were suffering the most: the musicians. I knew that until the orchestra began to heal its internal conflicts, we would make no progress elsewhere. In January 1998, Gary Friedman facilitated three open meetings, during which musicians discussed their feelings about the strike and why they thought it had happened.

It was tough going at first. People were reticent. In the second session, Gary taught the musicians a method of "active listening" that we call "looping." He conducted a practice exercise in which the musicians paired up. One member of the pair was asked to give her perspective on a particular topic, such as the strike. The other person was asked not to agree or disagree but instead simply to reflect back what he heard as accurately as possible, in his own words. The listener would then ask the speaker whether he had understood what had been said. The loop was complete only when the speaker confirmed that the listener had "gotten it." After a few minutes, the pair would reverse roles so everyone could try their hand.

This exercise was remarkably effective in helping some musicians open up, first in pairs and then to the entire group. Several people broke down in tears. Some were able to communicate directly with colleagues they hadn't spoken to in almost two years. In the group discussion, one member of the 1996–97 Negotiating Committee said she was afraid to express any views to the group because she felt she had made so many enemies during the strike. Another committee member said he had felt "confused" during the negotiations and had adopted the "safe route" of an extreme position, which he now recognized had escalated the conflict. He added that he felt he lacked the skills to negotiate effectively. Other musicians not only described their experiences of the strike, but their love of making music. Musicians who had previously seen each other simply as political opponents rediscovered their shared passion, and this helped them better tolerate their differences.

Another aspect of our early work was a two-day workshop at a retreat center in Marin County. We chose the participants carefully: there were sixteen musicians, including all the members of the Players' Committee; nine trustees, including Bechtle; and seven managers, including Pastreich. We wanted to introduce them to interest-based bargaining, but above all we wanted them to have fun—to see each other as individuals and to begin the process of de-demonization.

Our negotiation simulations elicited the laughter we hoped for. These exercises had nothing to do with collective bargaining, which made the participants feel safer. In one exercise, Hemphill found himself in the same group as board member Len Kingsley and whispered playfully, "Hey, Len, let's slime these guys." And they did.

We also did a series of exercises on active listening and effective assertion. Through a simple pencil-and-paper exercise, we helped each participant learn more about his or her own tendencies when faced with conflict. Some people tend to be *competitive*—they do a whole lot of asserting without expressing much understanding of the other side. Others tend to be *accommodating*—they understand the other side's interests so well that they have difficulty asserting their own interests. Still others tend to be conflict *avoiders*—they neither assert nor demonstrate understanding; they just withdraw. Competitors are often easy targets for demonization, especially by avoiders or accommodators who are not very assertive themselves. (I and everyone else could predict where Pastreich would come out: he scored as a competitor. So did Hemphill. Chris Gilbert was an avoider.) Our goal, however, was not to typecast anyone, but instead to help participants think about their default tendencies and how they might broaden their negotiation repertoire by becoming better listeners and more effective advocates.

Pastreich later reported: "I came to understand how important it was for me to listen to the other side. . . . It became clear to me that one of the things that the musicians were angry with me about was they felt . . . I wasn't even listening to what they were saying. And I think it is true. Nor do I think they were listening to us."

The next part of the workshop brought things a bit closer to home: a simulated negotiation between a school district and its teachers' union.[16] Each team included agents and principals. The union representatives had to deal with their constituents; management had to deal with the school board; and the two sides had to negotiate with each other. In making the role assignments, we mixed things up. Some musicians were assigned to management roles and some board members were assigned to the union. The idea was to increase everyone's sensitivity to the perspectives of the other side, a key piece of any negotiation training. The board members, in particular, seemed delighted (and rather starstruck) to be working with the musicians. This generally worked, although one musician assigned to a management role dropped out of the exercise, saying she simply "couldn't think that way." I suspect at some level she thought she would jeopardize her own values or even soil her soul by trying to see the world through manage-ment's eyes.

When we returned from the workshop, our next task was to help the Players' Committee redesign the process by which the musicians would elect the next Negotiating Committee. These elections had typically been held in a perfunctory way, with no real opportunity for candi-dates to explain how they intended to approach the negotiations and what they saw as their role. The new process required candidates to explain, at a meeting of the orchestra as a whole, how they would ap-proach the next negotiation. None of the Hard Liners from the old committee were nominated, and most of the candidates had attended our first workshop. Several made a point of expressing their commit-ment to interest-based bargaining—a broad term that puts the empha-sis on a more collaborative, less adversarial process that focuses on the parties' underlying interests, not simply their stated demands or positions.

In May 1998, the musicians elected a new Negotiating Committee. Chris Gilbert was elected chairman, and all members expressed inter-est in further negotiation training. Pastreich said he thought it was the most positive committee in twenty years.

———

That same spring, Pastreich dropped a bombshell by announcing that he planned to retire in 1999, after the next round of contract negotia-tions. I wondered: Had Bechtle and the trustees eased him out, or had Pastreich simply decided that after twenty-some years it was time to move on? I have never learned. For my purposes, what I found most significant was that Bechtle and the board were giving him one more chance to negotiate. I was glad they did, because by this time I was per-suaded that Pastreich was going to be part of the solution: he had thrown himself into the training, was a quick study, and seemed eager to demonstrate he could be an effective problem solver. (My only con-cern now was that in trying to shake his reputation as a devil, he might make *too* many concessions, because he wouldn't have to live with the financial consequences.)

Our second two-day workshop focused on the special features of collective bargaining and was designed for a smaller group: the sixteen people who would play the most active roles in the next round of negotiations. Half were musicians, including all the members of the new Negotiating Committee. Management included Pastreich, five of his key managers, and two trustees: Bechtle and Len Kingsley, who chaired the Labor-Management Committee. Again we conducted a labor-management simulation in which each side included constituents as well as negotiators.

At the end of the workshop, we told the participants it was time to put their new skills to use on symphony business. Although the existing contract would not expire until November 1999, both management and the Negotiating Committee wanted to negotiate the new contract well before the deadline, perhaps by the end of 1998. What preparation must be done separately by each side? What preparation might best be done jointly?

The group decided to use joint task forces, composed of labor and management, to develop basic factual information, define issues, and generate options. The use of joint task forces to prepare for negotiations isn't typical in collective bargaining, but recent surveys suggest that about one in five labor negotiations use them.[17] Our group created several joint task forces by the end of the summer of 1998.

One group was charged with gathering factual information about the latest contract terms of other major American orchestras. This information was critical to both sides. Some issues, such as minimum weekly salary, are negotiated by reference to other orchestras. Having common information would avoid needless arguments about basic facts.

A second task force was created to conduct preliminary research on pension and retirement issues. This was a long-simmering issue at the SFS. Some musicians liked the current pension plan. Others preferred the one sponsored by the AFM. Which was better? Should musicians be given a choice? These seemingly simple questions raised financial, accounting, and legal questions that were too complicated for laymen to answer, and the negotiators had not made much progress in the past. This time the workshop participants decided that each side would retain its own pension consultant to assist the task force.

A third task force was created to investigate the possibilities of "string relief." This had been a difficult issue in every previous negotiation. String players spend more time onstage playing their instruments than other orchestra members. As a result, many string players claimed, they were much more prone to developing serious stress-related injuries. The issue had been a priority for the string players, of course, but not for some other musicians. The issue had not advanced very far in the past. The task force would try to lay a foundation for approaching this problem in more creative ways.

In the next phase of our project we worked behind the table with the Negotiating Committee. With our help and support, the committee set about designing a process to identify the orchestra's most important priorities. There would be no laundry list this time. The committee wanted to involve the orchestra in the process of preparation, but they now understood the importance of exercising leadership. As representatives, how could the committee guide the musicians as well as being responsive to them? Although it was no easy task, the committee did a superb job.

First, the members spent many hours together discussing their own sense of the orchestra's interests and priorities. In the process, they learned how to solve problems *within* the committee—to negotiate effectively with one another. Gilbert, the chairman, came to understand that it was essential for the committee to work by consensus and not simply decide by majority rule. Operating by consensus means that everyone makes a good-faith effort to meet the interests of all the committee members. Consensus is ordinarily reached when everyone agrees they can live with whatever is proposed, after every effort has been made to meet the interests of the parties. While consensus-building aims at seeking unanimous agreement, it does not necessarily require unanimity. Unanimity would allow an individual member to hold out and veto a course of action. Instead, consensus-building requires that everyone's viewpoint be taken seriously and that every effort be made to meet everyone's interests.

Once the committee reached some preliminary conclusions about what the issues should be and what interests lay under those issues, they sent a survey to the orchestra. But unlike their approach in 1996, when they had essentially gone around inviting demands indiscriminately, this survey laid out the committee's recommendations and asked for specific feedback. Because this was so well done, it bears quoting it at length. The preamble stated:

After many hours of active discussion, we have come up with a list of areas/issues, which we believe are the most important to the orchestra. We then divided this list into categories: Class I, issues that are of primary importance to this negotiation; and Class II, issues that we will address vigorously, but are of somewhat lesser importance. . . . Also, in keeping with our commitment to an "interest-based" bargaining process, we have identified what we believe are the orchestra's underlying interests for each area/issue.

For example, under "Compensation" two interests were identified:

- Compensation commensurate with industry standards in light of our artistic achievement; and

- Ability to attract and retain the best players.

The survey asked each musician to indicate whether he or she agreed or disagreed that compensation, pension, string relief, and health benefits should be the Class I issues, and whether they agreed or disagreed with the committee's characterization of the underlying interests. The survey also listed the Class II issues and asked whether the respondent

- agreed with the Class II characterization;

- thought the issue should instead be Class I; or

- thought this was an issue that need not be included in the bargaining.

Respondents were also asked to add other issues to the list, along with an explanation of underlying interests.

The survey results showed—and a subsequent orchestra meeting confirmed—that a substantial majority agreed with the committee's priorities. The committee concluded that compensation, pension, and string relief would be Class I issues. The players were satisfied with their existing health plan, so the committee decided not to bring this issue to the table but agreed that if management raised it, it would be a Class I issue. The Class II issues were scheduling, auditions, the treatment of past retirees, the possibility of personal leave, and the public use of the

San Francisco Symphony's name in a way that included the musicians and not simply the corporate body. Management accepted this classification of issues and asked that health insurance be discussed because of management's concerns about costs.

In addition to setting priorities and building a mandate, the Negotiating Committee also carefully considered what role it wanted its lawyer to play. In the 1996 negotiations, the musicians had used their attorney as their primary spokesman and negotiator. This time, the committee preferred that labor and management deal directly with one another instead of acting through counsel. After confirming that management found this approach acceptable, the committee decided to retain a lawyer who supported the concept of interest-based bargaining. In a highly unusual move, the committee also decided to look for a lawyer who would find it acceptable not to be at the table. After interviewing candidates, the committee retained an experienced labor lawyer who later comfortably played just that role. This proved to be a significant decision for the committee—a signal to both sides that the Negotiating Committee would be in control of the bargaining process for the musicians.[18]

By November 1998, the parties had been in negotiation training, on and off, for fourteen months. Now they were ready to negotiate across the table. This negotiation took place in two stages and required *only six days in total*. Note the ratio. We and the parties had spent over 90 percent of our time on preparation behind the table and in joint committees. For a complex negotiation, with critical conflicts behind the table, this is an appropriate ratio.

In November, during this first phase of the actual negotiations, Gary and I met with the parties for two days—to clear out the underbrush, so to speak, and to identify the precise issues that needed to be resolved. One important issue the parties identified was whether the contract term should be longer than the usual three years, to provide more stability. They preliminarily agreed that they would aim for a contract that would not expire until November 2005—nearly six years later. They also developed a detailed schedule for the negotiations and agreed on basic ground rules concerning confidentiality and statements to the press. They even reached substantive agreement concerning two

Class II issues relating to "past retirees" and the use of the symphony's name.[19]

The parties also laid a foundation for addressing the nettlesome issue of string relief. At our suggestion, everyone present was arbitrarily assigned to one of three groups, each containing both musicians and managers. The groups were charged with an identical task: to create a statement of the goals of string relief. The groups then pooled their results and agreed on the following joint statement:

> The goals of string relief are to raise morale, promote a sense of physical and mental well being, and improve the already high level of performance of the San Francisco Symphony's string players. Solutions will be sought to reduce the time on stage and physical demands on string players and to make stage time more rewarding. All elements of the symphony, including the music director, musicians, staff, and board will work together to accomplish these goals.

The entire group then engaged in brainstorming to generate options that might contribute to string relief. We set two ground rules for brainstorming: no evaluation (that is, no judging ideas as good or bad) and no ownership of ideas. Crazy ideas were welcome! They stimulated creativity. Among the ideas generated: a smaller string section, more substitutes, more comfortable clothing, and on-site tai chi or physical therapy. Based on this work, the group decided to develop concrete proposals for the final negotiating session in December.

The effect of this work on the string players was profound. For the first time, *everyone* was focusing on their problem—not just the entire orchestra, but management as well. On this issue, at least, the string players were finally being heard. (The contract would ultimately include innovative provisions for string relief. Said Gilbert: "We might never have to talk about string relief again.")

The parties set aside five full days in December to address the core issues. During this period, they successfully negotiated all the terms of a new agreement, including a six-year term. Gary and I facilitated these meetings and acted as mediators. The following anecdote illustrates the problem-solving spirit in which both sides approached these negotiations.

Pastreich wanted to keep the existing pension plan, but for the first time he was open to other options. The pension experts went to work and ultimately agreed that the costs of funding two separate plans were too high. "It was a very tense moment," Gilbert said. "It was not what we wanted to hear, obviously, and it speaks well of where we were at that point that the committee could accept it." When one committee member expressed concern that some members of the orchestra would be disappointed, another member declared, "We'll have to explain our thinking and show some leadership." It is moments like this that a teacher lives for.

The final stages of the negotiation came down to salary and pension benefits.[20] Management presented three different packages: alternative combinations of salary and pension. After a brief caucus, the committee chose the option that it believed best served the interests of the musicians. A great cheer went up in the room and a cork was popped. Everyone in the room knew the deal was done.

The proposed contract was presented to the orchestra on January 9. Three days later, the musicians overwhelmingly ratified it. At the time, the salary terms placed the SFS among the half-dozen best-paid orchestras in the United States.

The deal was announced at a euphoric press conference at which the key negotiators toasted each other with champagne. The *San Francisco Chronicle* hailed the new contract as "an astonishing turnaround" and credited our intensive seventeen-month project and the Hewlett Foundation's support.[21] At the press conference, Pastreich saluted the musicians on the Negotiating Committee by name and said how pleased and proud he was that this negotiation, his last on behalf of symphony management, had provided a foundation for the years to come.

But what did we really accomplish? Now, ten years later, I can better assess the results. We certainly demonstrated that individuals can change the way they manage conflict. No one illustrates this better than Pastreich. Since his retirement in 2000, he has created a new career as a consultant and mediator to orchestras throughout the country. His favorite work is to help rescue a symphony in deep financial trouble, where the musicians are being asked to make concessions. What I find most impressive is that it is not just the trustees and managers who want his help; the musicians, too, want him on board because they trust him as a straight shooter. He tells management and trustees that the musicians should not be asked to make concessions unless management has a plan to turn things around and the capacity to implement it. As he told me, "It's not rocket science. I ask: How well has management mobilized community support for an orchestra? How well is the development work organized? What resources can be generated? I think it is wrong to ask musicians to make concessions unless the management and trustees have a thoughtful plan."

As for the San Francisco Symphony, the results have been mixed. The good news is that there have been two further rounds of contract negotiation with no strikes. This is not trivial. With one exception, the twenty-year period before our intervention had featured a work stoppage every three years. Moreover, the most creative aspect of the 1999 contract—the string relief provisions—has remained. And Gilbert was right. They never had to talk about string relief again.

The bad news is that the parties have essentially reverted to their old pattern: a deadline-driven, hard-bargaining style that is nearly as adversarial as it was before. In both 2005 and 2008, the old contract expired without a deal. In both cases, the union voted to authorize a strike shortly before an upcoming tour. Both times, after protracted arm wrestling, traditional haggling led to a deal.

Why did they revert?

The simplest reason: too much turnover with no additional training. In the summer of 2004, I received a letter from the symphony inviting me to offer another negotiation program. (By this time Bechtle and Pastreich had moved on, but Chris Gilbert was chairman of the Players' Committee.) I responded that I would be glad to do so on one condition: that those who would play leadership roles in the next round, including all members of the new Negotiating Committee, be "willing to participate in an initial joint workshop to learn more about negotiation and our approach." The Negotiating Committee had not been elected yet, and I needed to know whether those musicians were interested in learning more.

I received no formal response, but word got back to me that a majority of the new Negotiating Committee did not want such training. In fact, they had become suspicious of interest-based bargaining.[22]

Why? In the aftermath of our program, the national union and its lawyers fiercely criticized interest-based bargaining. Attorney Leonard Leibowitz, Sipser's successor and son-in-law, led the charge with an article in *Senza Sordino*, the newsletter sent nationally to all unionized symphony musicians, claiming that collective bargaining was "by its very nature" adversarial. His goal as an agent was to reach the "best agreement possible" for his client, he wrote, and such a deal could usually be made only at "crunch time," when everyone was facing disaster.[23]

In response to that article, Pastreich wrote Leibowitz that he'd initially had the same emotional reaction to interest-based bargaining—or "IBB," as some call it—but now believed that if you counted the financial impact of strikes on the musicians, they did *worse* with the traditional hard-bargaining approach. He concluded:

> The greatest value of adversarial negotiation might be the opportunity it gives musicians to express anger and frustration accumulated during 3 years of doing a job that, by its very nature, allows them relatively little control over their working lives, while the greatest value of IBB might be the opportunity it gives musicians to work with managers and board members at solving problems in an atmosphere of teamwork and cooperation. I've changed my mind about which matters most, and perhaps you will too.[24]

Leibowitz didn't come around.

The national union followed with a public broadside claiming that IBB "eliminates the union," its members' "sense of solidarity," and their "ability to confer privately."[25] These claims were, of course, preposterous. Eliminates the union? Interferes with solidarity? I believe the sense of solidarity among the unionized musicians at the SFS was greater in the 1998–99 negotiations than ever before. But it's true that the national union—the AFM—and its lawyers were not involved in the SFS negotiations, so their complaint was real, if not accurately stated. Leibowitz and the union further contended that IBB can lead to long-term agreements that are "dangerous" for musicians.

By 2004, this last argument fell on receptive ears at the SFS, which was nearing the end of its unusual five-year contract that had been negotiated long before. As it happened, the salaries provided in the last two years now fell somewhat behind those at some other major symphonies, which had recently renewed three-year contracts. If the economy had been weaker this might not have been the case, but the SFS musicians bought Leibowitz's argument that this salary discrepancy was the fault of IBB and its proponents. It is always easier to blame someone else than to acknowledge that your own group participated in a decision that, although reasonable at the time, may not turn out to be optimal with the benefit of hindsight.

So what do I take away from the experience? First, an appreciation of how difficult it is for a musician, and perhaps any union employee, to play a leadership role in building a mandate for IBB. It's hard enough to be an effective leader when IBB *isn't* involved—to be responsive to one's constituency while not being dominated by the most militant factions. IBB is counterintuitive and can be emotionally threatening. The concept of empathy—respecting the interests of the other side, even if you don't agree—is hard for many people to accept. There is a natural "fear of empathizing," as Gilbert put it. "Fear of hearing somebody else's side. Fear that it is going to make it harder for them to disagree." This puts negotiators on both sides at risk of appearing "too nice," but the risk is far greater on the labor side, where the constituency is large and dispersed. Labor leaders are under constant pressure to show the rank and file that they're being "tough." With IBB, the constituency doesn't see you being tough—it sees you cozying up to management and giving away the store. (Or so it may appear.) It's far easier to build solidarity by demonizing management and leading the troops into battle.

Second, I have a much deeper understanding of how difficult it is to change the negotiation culture of an organization. It requires not simply initial "buy-in" but constant reinforcement. There must be ongoing training for the negotiators, who change from year to year, and education for the rank and file, who, like everyone else, have to understand the approach in order to trust it. Without this reinforcement, their natural fears—the negative traps—may reappear.[26]

Change also requires motivation, which can't be faked. In San Francisco the initial motivation was provided by trauma and crisis, as is often the case. But this kind of trauma is in no sense required. Organizations with less adversarial cultures may be able to improve the way they deal with conflict, as long as the key stakeholders are committed to the process. But there is no permanent fix. The motivation must be real, and it must be shared by those who come later.

PART IV

Family Devils

NINE

A Devilish Divorce

"Frankly," Brenda Thomkins said, "it's a relief to have Thomas out of the house."[1]

Brenda was a slight, casually dressed woman of about forty who had come to see me about her divorce. Thomas was her soon-to-be-ex husband. I was surprised by her composure—she seemed more determined than worried, and not at all depressed.

But I had seen the case file. Brenda alleged that Thomas had struck her and she feared for her safety. A court had ordered Thomas to stay away from the family home. Thomas had responded by emptying the joint savings account and moving the money elsewhere. Although Brenda had filed on the no-fault ground of "irretrievable breakdown," Thomas's cross-complaint alleged adultery.

Naturally I wondered how many of these allegations were true and to what extent they were being used as bargaining chips, but that was none of my business. She had come to see me because she needed a new lawyer. Her attorney, a solo practitioner, had been seriously injured in a car accident and was out of commission. At a friend's recommendation, Brenda had come to me for a referral. She'd been told I didn't practice family law but could put her in the hands of a good lawyer who did.

"Tell me more," I suggested, wondering if she would raise the sensitive issues on her own. Privately I was thinking that this case was off to a terrible start.

Brenda said she had been the one to end the marriage. Thomas, a vice president of a small high-tech start-up, was a "workaholic" engineer who traveled all the time. They had been married for twelve years, and she had been unhappy in the relationship for at least five. She described Thomas as a "clueless" and "insensitive" husband who had taken her for granted. Although she didn't go into any details, she said the final breakup had been "explosive." After a bitter fight over who should move out, Brenda had "won that round," she said with apparent satisfaction.

What had happened since Thomas moved out?

Brenda's smile vanished. "He's trying to punish me," she said. Thomas was providing no financial support except to pay the monthly mortgage on the house. Brenda had been surviving on their joint checking account, which was now nearly depleted. "He told me I should rent an apartment and get a job! I haven't worked since the kids were born," she said with indignation.

There were two children, now ages eleven and eight.

"And to top it all off, he's asking for shared physical custody of the children." She pursed her lips in apparent scorn. "Who's he kidding? Until now he's always been too busy to make it to a single one of Gabriel's soccer games! He's just trying to pressure me to take as little money as possible."

Every divorce involving children raises four central legal issues: (1) child custody and visitation; (2) child support payments; (3) spousal support payments; and (4) property division. These are closely related and involve genuinely hard distributive problems. But they can also be used as strategic weapons, and spouses who don't trust each other often suspect each other of evil motives.

As the financially dependent spouse, Brenda was understandably worried about the support she would get from Thomas, and I wondered if her bravado was partly a cover for fear. "His last offer was deliberately insulting," she reported. "Only child support. No alimony." His offer with regard to property division was equally parsimonious, she felt. "Half the proceeds of the house when it's sold. None of the stock in the company he works for, and nothing from the million-dollar investment portfolio he inherited from his mother."

I nodded, still trying to get a read on Brenda. I asked what she thought was a fair arrangement.

"Eleven years ago I gave up my job to stay home and care for the children," she said. "*Both* of us wanted that for the kids." Given how demanding Thomas's career had become since then, she thought he should have reasonable visiting rights but doubted he could handle more than that. She expected sufficient alimony and child support to allow her and the children to maintain their standard of living. And she wanted half the value of all their combined assets—including Thomas's inherited stock portfolio. As part of her half, she wanted ownership of the house free and clear. "I deserve nothing less," she declared. "I'm not going to stand for this. Custody is not negotiable and I insist on financial terms that are fair to me and the children. Anything less would be giving in to extortion!"

When I hear words like *extortion* in a divorce case, I start to worry. Brenda and Thomas probably did not view one another as inherently evil people—few divorcing couples do. But their hostility toward each other bordered on demonization and could lead to all-out legal warfare.

Worse yet, their lawyers seemed to be egging them on. The lawyers had exchanged half a dozen venomous letters without managing to resolve the most urgent and basic issues of this early phase: interim custody and support while the divorce was pending. A court hearing to resolve such matters had been postponed because of the hospitalization of Brenda's lawyer. No wonder Brenda seemed so brittle.

"How are the children handling all this?" I asked.

Brenda fell silent and looked away. When she spoke again, she sounded less sure of herself. "Thomas has the kids on weekends," she said. "When they came back home last Sunday night, Amanda said to me, 'Daddy says *you're* the one who wants a divorce. Daddy wants the family to stay together. He says Mommy is the bad one.' "

Her eyes filled with tears of rage. "I want a lawyer who is really tough. What names can you give me?"

THE FOUR DIVORCES

The Spock in me was on red alert. I wanted to warn Brenda about the negative traps. I wanted to give her my standard pitch: that it's almost always wiser to negotiate a divorce settlement than to fight it out in court. I wanted to remind her, although she surely knew this, that legal warfare is terribly costly—both financially and emotionally—and usually hurts everyone, especially the children.

But I resisted the temptation. I wasn't her lawyer and she hadn't asked me for that kind of advice. Instead I nodded as empathetically as I could and offered a platitude: "The process of divorce is very tough for most families."

"But why does it have to be so hard?" Brenda demanded. "Thomas knows the marriage is over. We separated three months ago! Why doesn't he move on? I don't even recognize him anymore. He used to be so logical. He used to call *me* the irrational one. Now he's acting like a spiteful child. Why can't we work out the logistics without all this melodrama?"

"That's a great question," I said. "It's one I've thought and written about quite a bit. Why do otherwise sensible people seem to go half crazy—especially from the perspective of their spouses—when they're going through a divorce?"

She nodded eagerly.

"I may be able to help you there," I said.

Some years ago, I explained, I teamed up with Eleanor Maccoby, a world-renowned developmental psychologist, to conduct a long-term study of divorcing couples. For four years, we followed about eleven hundred divorcing couples with children. The result was a book called *Dividing the Child.*[2]

"You followed them for four years? Don't tell me getting a divorce takes that long!" Brenda said half jokingly.

It doesn't take nearly that long to get a divorce decree, I reassured her. But Eleanor and I believe that divorce can be best understood not as a single event (like the issuance of a court decree) but as a continuing process that can begin long before a spouse files for divorce and continue long after the decree is issued.

The process of disengagement can be confusing—even profoundly disorienting—to divorcing spouses because divorce requires the transformation of not just one relationship, but several. Indeed, every divorce with children involves *four different divorces:*

The Spousal Divorce: The end of intimacy—sexual, psychological, and social—between husband and wife.

The Economic Divorce: The end of an economic relationship based on a single household.

The Parental Divorce: The end of one arrangement for raising children and the beginning of another, along with a redefinition of parental roles.

The Legal Divorce: The formalization of custodial and financial arrangements that will govern after the marriage is dissolved.[3]

Each of these dimensions affects the others.

Because Brenda had told me that she initiated the breakup, I began by explaining the "spousal divorce." The end of intimacy and the process of spousal disengagement require psychological and social adjustments that take time—and the two spouses may be out of sync. One spouse may have been thinking about ending the marriage for months or years, perhaps without discussing it with the other. When the "initiator" finally announces a desire to leave, the other spouse may be blindsided.

"That sure describes our situation," Brenda said. "I've been thinking about divorce for at least three years." She had hoped that as Thomas's start-up company became more established, he would have more time for family life. But instead Thomas became busier, and Brenda grew lonelier. Now that she had survived the "blowup," she said, she was elated to be freed from the marriage. "I'm eager to get on with my life. I just want the legal stuff to be over."

"And Thomas?" I asked.

"He was shocked," she said. "Devastated. I think he still is. He's angry and he blames me."

"The person who is left behind is often very angry," I said. "Thomas may not yet be ready to let go." I added that although the law may characterize a divorce as "no-fault," emotional logic doesn't work in no-fault terms. When a marriage fails, spouses often feel the need to assign blame. Sometimes they blame themselves, but more often they blame each other. And even judges aren't immune to the temptation to blame one spouse or the other.

As we talked further, Brenda said a big source of anxiety for her was the economic divorce. She had worked before having children, earning $75,000 a year as a marketing executive for a Boston department store. But even then, Thomas had out-earned her, making $120,000 a year and establishing himself as a rising star in the company. So it had made sense for him to be the primary earner. He now earned $225,000. "Once Amanda was born, our 'deal' was that Thomas would bring in the money and I would raise the children and run the household, at least until they were in high school. Thomas should continue to honor that deal."

Brenda had loved being a full-time mother but hadn't realized how financially vulnerable it would make her. She had no income of her own. Someday she wanted to resume a career in marketing, but only when the children were older—not now. It would be five years before her younger child was in high school. Besides, her earning potential now was not what it used to be. The last ten years of her résumé would now read "homemaker." She had done nothing to maintain her skills, other than attend an occasional seminar. While she hated the thought of being financially dependent on Thomas, especially now that their relationship had become so hostile, she strongly believed it was best for the children if she stayed home until the youngest entered high school. Maybe then she would go back to school to get an MBA, she said, if she could afford it.

"Thomas holds all the high cards financially," she said. "I'm thinking about the children. I don't want them to suffer from the divorce, and that means maintaining a certain standard of living." Her voice rose. "Doesn't he realize that being stingy with me leaves the kids worse off, too?"

"It's a very difficult situation," I agreed. Privately I doubted that Brenda had accepted the full significance of the economic divorce, which can be a disaster for all but the richest and poorest couples. When two households must be supported instead of one, both spouses typically suffer a marked drop in their standard of living. That would be true of the Thomkinses, despite Thomas's salary. If Brenda truly wanted to maintain her standard of living, she would probably have to return to work sooner rather than later. But it wasn't my job to tell her that; her lawyer would have to address that with her.

On the other hand, Thomas *didn't* hold all the high cards, and I thought it was appropriate to point that out.

"Even if you and Thomas can't agree on these financial issues, he doesn't get to do whatever he wants," I told her. "There are laws that protect you to some degree. Your new lawyer can help you assess what a court would be likely to do in this state if you and Thomas can't agree. These predictions of what would happen in court obviously influence the divorce negotiations. I call this 'bargaining in the shadow of the law.' "[4]

As we talked, Brenda quickly grasped how the four divorces were interrelated. Thomas's strong emotional response to the spousal divorce seemed to be driving much of his behavior, just as Brenda's anxieties in the financial realm were driving hers. Thomas's outrage seemed to be affecting the economic divorce, in which he was withholding financial support from Brenda, and perhaps also the parental divorce, in which he was demanding an equal parenting role for the first time in their marriage. All three of these dimensions were affecting the legal divorce, in which each side was making aggressive and unrealistic demands.

I told Brenda that the right lawyers can be indispensable in a divorce and the wrong lawyers can make it a lot worse. Even if the spouses are not on speaking terms, two lawyers with problem-solving attitudes can work out arrangements that serve both spouses' long-term interests and increase the likelihood that the parents can "do business" together afterward.

Brenda wasn't buying it. "Look," she said, "we're fighting over money and time with the children. Those are finite. More money for Thomas means less for me. The more time the kids spend with Thomas, the less they spend with me. Thomas's lawyer, Glen Palmieri, is a shark. I need a lawyer who can outmaneuver him or I'll end up with nothing."

She was right, of course, that money and time raise distributive issues. That's what makes it so easy for the zero-sum gremlin to creep in and sandbag these discussions. But I told her I didn't view the situation in such zero-sum terms. She and Thomas had some common interests: keeping the children healthy and happy, minimizing lawyers' fees, and even encouraging Brenda's financial independence. "There may be more ways to create value than you or Thomas realize at the moment. Your lawyer may be able to come up with creative arrangements that take advantage of tax benefits, for example, or create a visitation schedule that's better for both of you."

Brenda still looked skeptical.

"I'm not asking you to compromise what is most important to you," I persisted. "The two lawyers I'm recommending to you, Diana Cooper and Thomas Lee, can fight for you in court if necessary. But they'll also be able to negotiate effectively with the other side for a solution that serves your interests better than going to court." I spent a few minutes telling her a bit more about Cooper and Lee.

"I really appreciate this," Brenda said quietly. "You've been enormously helpful."

"Keep an open mind," I urged her. "The overwhelming majority of divorce conflicts are ultimately settled through negotiation."

I tell the rest of this story through the eyes of Diana Cooper. I didn't see Brenda again, but she immediately hired Diana and asked her to consult informally with me periodically. I welcomed my talks with Diana because they gave me a chance to follow the case, commiserate with Diana, and help her think strategically about her next move. The case turned out to be more challenging than either of us expected.

Diana's first call came within two weeks of my meeting Brenda. She thanked me for the referral and, after the usual pleasantries, brought me up to date.

"I like Brenda, but this case has the potential to be a real mess," she said. "Thomas's lawyer is playing hardball, and Brenda and her husband are at each other's throats."

Diana reported that her first meeting with Brenda had gone well. Diana found Brenda to be intelligent and determined. The catalyst for ending the marriage, Diana learned, was Thomas's discovery that Brenda was having an affair with a neighbor, also recently divorced. When Thomas confronted her about his suspicions, Brenda first denied the relationship, then admitted it, then told him she no longer loved him and wanted a divorce. For the first time in their marriage, Thomas slapped her. She told him to get out of the house. He moved out that night, and Brenda filed for divorce shortly thereafter.

Diana, of course, probed as to whether physical abuse had been an issue in the marriage. "Not at all," Brenda said, rather breezily. The slap had really been more of a push; nothing like it had never happened before or since, and Brenda really didn't think Thomas posed a physical threat.

"Frankly," Diana told me, "Brenda's big concern was money. Her first lawyer had added the abuse claim because Thomas had taken the money from their joint savings account. I told her that I thought I could do something about that, but I also suggested that a court wasn't likely to give her as generous a financial package as she was hoping for. I'm not sure I got through to her, but we have plenty of time yet."

Soon after that meeting, Diana said, she called Thomas's lawyer and started to negotiate terms. The discussion was cordial and the two quickly made their first deal: if Thomas would account for the money

he took out of the joint savings account, Brenda would drop the restraining order.

Diana then tried to negotiate an agreement on interim custody and
support so the clients wouldn't have to wait for a hearing. She proposed
to maintain the status quo with respect to custody and give Brenda
$7,500 a month for interim family support—"enough to allow her to
keep things together."[5]

I thought to myself, Diana is on target—she's signaling to the other
side that Brenda has a new lawyer who's prepared to take a more collaborative tack.

Thomas's lawyer had been noncommittal on the phone. Diana went
on, "He promised he'd speak to Thomas and get back to me. But he never
did. Instead, he served me with a seven-day notice of a court hearing on
the interim custody and support issues." Thomas was still demanding
shared physical custody. Diana had promptly filed a counter-motion.[6]

A week later, the parties had appeared before Judge Goldstein.

"The good news," Diana told me, "is that with regard to interim support, the judge gave us nearly as much as we asked for. That will give us
some breathing room."[7]

The custody issue, however, was more complicated.

In court, Diana made the standard argument in favor of awarding
physical custody to Brenda. Brenda had always been the primary parent and the kids were doing well. Why disrupt their lives with such a
radical change? Diana also pointed out that unless Thomas changed
jobs he was going to have a hard time being a full-time parent two
weeks a month.

But Thomas's lawyer had a few surprises for her. First, he made a
plausible argument in favor of shared physical custody. Thomas's new
apartment had room for the kids and wasn't far from their school.
Thomas had arranged for a nanny to be home when the kids got home
from school. He was cutting down on business travel. Although he
hadn't spent much time with the children before the separation, he was
very committed to them and deserved a chance now to play an equal
role in their lives. He wanted the kids to live with him every other
week.

At the last moment, Thomas's lawyer also submitted an affidavit
from Thomas that "really hurt us," Diana said. Thomas alleged that the

children had told him that Brenda's new "love interest" had once spent the night at the house. Thomas further stated that this was confusing to the children and that he was concerned for their welfare.

Lawyers hate to learn things from the other side that they should have learned from their client. The news of the "overnight" had caught Diana off guard, and I could hear the frustration in her voice. "Of course I had told Brenda not to have any romantic partners in the house while the kids were home—not even for dinner, much less to spend the night! But she didn't mention that she'd already had a sleepover. The judge asked her whether this was true and Brenda admitted it was so."

Under Massachusetts law, the sexual morality of a spouse has no bearing on custody arrangements unless it can harm the children. Officially, the sole criterion for custody is the best interests of the children. But a lawyer can get the issue of new sexual relationships in "through the back door," so to speak, by arguing that the other parent's new partner is creating adjustment problems for the children, or that the parent is too distracted by the presence of the new love interest to give the children the attention they deserve. For that reason, courts often order both parents, on an interim basis, to keep new lovers out of the house (at least overnight) when the children are in residence. Judge Goldstein had issued such an order.

Part of me wondered whether Brenda wanted to have her cake and eat it, too—significant financial support from Thomas and the freedom to enjoy her new partner.

What did the judge decide on interim custody?

Diana sighed. "He didn't decide. For now, Brenda still has the kids most of the time. But Thomas's request for shared custody is still alive. The judge ordered that a guardian ad litem be appointed to investigate how the kids are doing and to report to the judge in ninety days."

In court proceedings that affect the interests of children, a court can appoint a guardian ad litem ("GAL") to advise the court on what arrangements best serve the children's interests. In custody disputes, the GAL is a court-approved mental health professional or lawyer who meets with the children, interviews both parents (and sometimes teachers and neighbors), writes a report, and makes a recommendation to the judge. These reports are taken very seriously by the judge and can significantly influence the outcome.

"I told Brenda," Diana went on, "that the odds are still good that she will ultimately get sole physical custody, but there's no guarantee. What she has in her favor is that she has been and continues to be the primary parent. The kids are still spending over eighty percent of their time with her. The status quo counts for a lot."

"What do you make of Thomas's demand for shared custody?" I asked. "Do you think he's serious?"

"At first I thought they were using the custody demands purely as bargaining leverage," she responded. "But I'm no longer sure that's all there is to it. I think it also has to do with Brenda's affair. My guess is that Thomas is humiliated by these events and afraid that this new man might jeopardize his relationship with his children. When Thomas testified at the hearing, he came across as a man who genuinely loved his kids and was afraid of losing them in the divorce. He was totally believable."

"And Brenda? How is she handling all of this?" I asked.

"She's immovable," Diana said. "She won't give an inch on the money issues, and she insists on sole physical custody. She thinks it's best for the kids, and, frankly, I think her identity is a bit at stake as well."

As I listened to Diana, I thought about how much the legal and social framework for divorce has changed in the last thirty-five years. Divorce used to be comparatively rare, and married women with children typically stayed at home. But since the 1950s, married women with children have entered the workforce in unprecedented numbers. At the same time, the divorce rate has risen and divorce law has been transformed. Between 1969 and 1985, the "no-fault" revolution swept all fifty states. Now in nearly every state, either spouse can unilaterally dissolve a marriage. I reflected that Brenda's situation seemed to straddle all of these eras: she and Thomas had a very traditional economic and parenting arrangement, but with regard to her personal relationships, she was a liberated woman.

A second set of revolutionary changes has been the removal of gender role stereotypes from divorce law. In the old days, Thomas would not have had a chance at getting any sort of custody. Before 1970, family law reflected and reinforced a traditional division of labor between husbands and wives: the custody standards explicitly favored mothers, and child support and alimony standards reflected the assumption that fathers were the primary wage earners.

Those assumptions are now gone. Custody of children is no longer awarded reflexively to the mother. Instead the judge has to decide, on a case-by-case basis, what is in the child's best interest. In the last twenty years, there have also been radical departures from the traditional notion that one parent should have custody and the other visiting rights. Many states now authorize—and some encourage—shared custody arrangements in which both parents retain responsibility for the children after the divorce.

There are two aspects to this. One is shared *legal* custody, in which both parents have identical rights to make decisions about the child's medical care, education, and religious upbringing—even if the child lives with only parent. Shared *physical* custody, by contrast, empowers both parents to have some day-to-day responsibility for the child's care. This approach is based on the notion that, even after divorce, the parents should have roughly equivalent roles—or at least that the child should be spending a significant amount of time residing with each parent.

"What's the story in Massachusetts? How do courts actually handle shared custody?" I asked Diana.

In nearly every case, Diana said, the courts grant shared *legal* custody unless one parent is somehow found to be "unfit." Diana thought Brenda's first lawyer had been unnecessarily provocative in asking for sole legal custody—not to mention seeking a restraining order against Thomas.

A significant minority of cases involve shared physical custody as well,[8] and Massachusetts law generally encourages continuing contact with *both* divorcing parents. I said that a shared physical custody arrangement—at least one with the children alternating weeks with Mom and Dad—sounded like a terrible idea in a case like this, where the parents were fighting. Shared physical custody requires a good deal of coordination. It makes sense only when parents can do business together, at least with regard to the kids.

"That's one of my best arguments for Brenda having primary physical custody!" Diana exclaimed. In fact, she said, when parents are locked in serious conflict, some judges refuse to award shared physical custody and guardians ad litem typically recommend against it.

Nonetheless, given all these conflicting policy goals, and broad judicial discretion, it was hard to predict with certainty what a court would do in the Thomkins case. What seemed clear to both Diana and me was that Brenda and Thomas were better off making their own custodial arrangements than leaving it up to a judge.

Could they do this? Not, I thought, without squarely addressing the parental divorce.

Divorce forces most couples to redefine their parental roles. When both parents want to remain involved in the children's lives, and when the children will be spending some time in both households, the parents have to continue to deal with each other as co-parents. Their spousal and co-parental relationships were previously interwoven. Terminating one relationship while maintaining the other can be very difficult.

Thomas and Brenda really hadn't worked through this process. The old family system, with its informal exchanges within a single household, was ending, but what would take its place? Thomas would have to learn to be a primary parent—responsible for feeding the kids, putting them to bed, etc. This would be a new experience for him. Brenda too, would see some changes in her parenting role. She might have to return to work, at least part-time. She wouldn't have Thomas's help with chores. She would no longer have a "backup" parent—in person or in name—to support her authority. Instead of telling the kids to clean their rooms "so your father won't be disappointed," she would have to assume full responsibility for discipline and order while the kids were with her.

In effect, Brenda and Thomas were becoming single parents in separate households. That would take some getting used to, for themselves and for the children.

About three months later, Diana called me to report that she and Brenda had received a copy of the guardian ad litem's report. Under court rules she could not send me a copy, but Brenda had authorized her to discuss its contents with me.

Dr. Frances Dorfman, a family therapist, had met individually with each of the children, Gabriel, eleven, and Amanda, eight. She found that both children were distressed by their parents' separation and ongoing conflict. Each child told Dr. Dorfman that they wanted their parents to get back together. Gabriel showed his emotions more openly and expressed some hostility toward Brenda; he blamed her for the separation. Amanda, on the other hand, seemed to be blaming herself, worrying that she hadn't been "nice enough to mommy and daddy." Dr. Dorfman suggested that Brenda and Thomas reassure Amanda that she had not done anything to cause the breakup.

Both children expressed a strong preference for staying in the family home and continuing to attend their current school. Gabriel, however, made a point of saying that he "loved his parents equally" and that, "to be fair," he wanted to spend exactly half his time with each parent.

After interviewing both Brenda and Thomas, Dr. Dorfman found that both were committed to the children's well-being and fully capable of being custodial parents. The report noted, however, that Thomas expressed intense hostility toward Brenda and was finding the transition required by divorce very difficult.

Dr. Dorfman strongly endorsed shared legal custody, finding both parents eager and able to participate in major decisions about the children's medical care, education, and religious upbringing.

To my relief, Dr. Dorfman recommended that the children should continue to live primarily with Brenda because a 50/50 split would be too disruptive. But Dr. Dorfman recommended that Thomas get substantially more time with the children: three weekends out of four, at least one dinner during the week, and equal time during holidays.

So far so good, I thought. I predicted the judge would give Brenda primary physical custody.

I was right. In her next call, Diana said that the judge essentially accepted Dr. Dorfman's recommendations. The judge left Thomas's support obligations unchanged.[9]

"Okay," I said to Diana. "What comes next?"

"The case should settle," Diana said, with a slight laugh, "but it's anybody's guess whether it will."

The problem was that the economic, emotional, and custody issues were so tightly interwoven. Without significant movement in at least one of those dimensions, she said, she couldn't see how this Gordian knot was going to be untied. Brenda's demand for sole physical custody wasn't just an issue of personal identity or parenting preferences; it directly affected her income. Under Massachusetts law, as long as Brenda retained custody most of the time—two-thirds or more—Thomas had to pay the maximum amount of child support for his income bracket: about $4,800 a month. Right now, under the judge's recent order, the kids were spending slightly more than two-thirds of their time with Brenda. But if the custody balance tipped further in Thomas's favor, the amount of child support might be reduced under the new Massachusetts child support guidelines. So Thomas had a powerful economic incentive to seek more time with the children.

The final hearing was scheduled to take place ten months later.[10] If the Thomkinses couldn't agree on custody by then, the judge would make that decision for them.

And Brenda? Any new thoughts on the money issues?

"She won't move," Diana said. "She isn't being realistic."

With regard to the house and Bill's company stock, an even split was very likely. But, as Diana had explained to Brenda, the stock was not publicly traded and Thomas had only a minority interest and no control. A court would not place a high market value on it. If the Thomkinses persisted in fighting over this issue of valuation, they would each have to hire dueling experts to value it. And that, Diana thought, was just a dumb way to spend their money.

The inherited property was a much bigger problem. Thomas's portfolio consisted of publicly traded stocks and bonds, now worth about $1,050,000. When courts decide how to divide inherited property, they take many factors into account—but none of them favored Brenda. One was how long ago the property was inherited. Thomas's mother had died only five years ago. Another was how the inherited property had been used during the marriage. Thomas had used only the income from the securities (about $25,000 annually) for family expenses but hadn't touched the principal, so the inheritance had not affected the family's living standard for most of the marriage. In Diana's experience, on these facts, a court was not likely to give Brenda half of that portfolio.

"But Brenda insists that I continue to demand exactly half of everything. She's not negotiating!" Diana said. "Her intransigence is really not helping the situation. On the other hand, judges have a lot of discretion. A court might give her what she's asking for. We can certainly show that even if she gets half of all the property, her standard of living is probably going to drop."

I was feeling a bit sorry for Diana. Brenda was not an easy client. In fact, I had to admit to myself that Brenda's behavior was starting to annoy me. I thought she sounded reckless and narcissistic. A mom with two kids has an affair, dumps her husband, and now thinks her soon-to-be-ex should support her so she doesn't have to go back to work? Meanwhile, what was happening to the kids? Nothing good, that was for sure. As far as I could see, Brenda had never accepted responsibility for her own contribution to the conflict. I had to remind myself that divorce doesn't always bring out the best in people.

I heard nothing further about Brenda and Thomas for nearly ten months. Shortly before the trial date, Diana called to say that Brenda was still refusing to negotiate and the case was going to court.

I was very surprised. Divorce cases rarely go to trial. Most cases are settled with the help of lawyers, mediation, or both.[11]

Diana explained, "Thomas made an aggressive final settlement offer that offended Brenda."

Privately I thought, Brenda was offended? That's not a basis for making a wise decision. But I told myself to listen to Diana's account before jumping to conclusions.

The latest skirmish, according to Diana, had started a few days before when Diana got a call from Thomas's attorney, Glen Palmieri. He was a bit vague but said he was prepared to offer something that would give Brenda "most" of what she wanted, including the house and primary custody. But the inherited property was not negotiable, Palmieri said. That was "sacred" to Thomas. "It drives Thomas crazy to think that *one cent* of his parents' money might go to Brenda and her new boyfriend."

Diana chose not to argue the point. They both knew each other's arguments. She told him to put his offer down on paper.

A few days later, a written offer arrived: Child support at the current level, as required by the schedule. A parenting plan that maintained the status quo—about a 70/30 split of the kids' time—but called it "shared physical custody." ("Interesting," Diana thought. "Labels are important to Thomas.") Full title to the house, subject to the mortgage (a net value of $400,000). No other property and no spousal support. All in all, Diana considered the offer very one-sided but not outrageous—far better than anything Palmieri had suggested before.

Then she read the cover letter, which contained a threat. "This is a final offer," it said. If Brenda didn't accept it, Thomas would go to court and ask for a fifty-fifty physical custody split.

Diana thought to herself, Making that kind of threat is the wrong way to deal with Brenda. My job has just gotten a lot harder.

As Diana predicted, Brenda bristled when she saw the cover letter. "Final offer?" she said contemptuously. "It's an empty threat. I don't believe for a minute that he really wants a fifty-fifty custody split. He's prepared to accept the status quo if we give it a nice label. And I think a seventy-thirty split is actually what he'd prefer. Fifty-fifty would be a disaster for the kids—and for him! In a week he'd be begging me to take the kids off his hands. Surely the judge would see that. Besides, I don't like the idea of calling the status quo 'shared physical custody.' Not when he's threatening a fifty-fifty split to get me to accept less money."

Diana thought Brenda was probably right about Thomas's true preferences, but she didn't want to get sidetracked into speculation about his motives. She wanted to focus on the proposal, help Brenda evaluate it, and decide how to respond.

She explained the terms one by one.

The parenting plan was good for Brenda, Diana said. "If you can look beyond the label, it really is what you want."

The support figures were not unexpected. Brenda would get full child support but no spousal support—and she would probably get about the same in court, although she might do somewhat better.

As for the property, "In essence, he's offering you four hundred thousand dollars out of a total property value of about $1.8 million, depending how you value the company stock," Diana said. "If you put the inherited property aside, he's offering you exactly half of the undisputed marital property. And you're getting the better half. You're getting the house, while he's getting stock that isn't marketable. That's a good trade for you."[12]

"Well, I'm not putting the inherited property aside," Brenda said. "How am I supposed to pay the mortgage and taxes?"

Diana nodded. They had discussed this several times. "You might have to go back to work, at least part-time."

Brenda shook her head. "It's too soon. The kids need me at home. This is what makes me so mad. Thomas is punishing them because he's mad at me."

"That may be," Diana said. "But the immediate task is to decide whether this offer is better or worse than what you could probably get in court."

She then spelled out the opportunities and risks of going to trial. "Let's talk about custody first. If you go to court, let's assume the worst: Thomas makes good on his threat and asks for a fifty-fifty split. What happens next? The judge will interview the kids. That's something to think about. How do you think they'd react to another set of interviews?"

Brenda looked thoughtful but didn't say anything.

Diana went on: "If the judge interviews the kids, Gabriel might say he prefers a fifty-fifty split. That's another risk." Although Gabriel was not yet fourteen and didn't officially have a vote, his preference could influence the judge. "Now, is the judge going to give Thomas fifty-fifty? Probably not—I agree with you there," Diana continued. "But there's a significant risk, I'd say one in three, that he'll give Thomas more than one-third of the time with the kids—which could mean less child support for you. So there are some real risks here." On the other hand, Diana said, Brenda might find it easier to manage part-time work if the children were spending more time with Thomas.

Brenda's face was impassive, but it was clear she was listening.

As for spousal support, Thomas was offering nothing, but Diana thought it unlikely that Brenda would do better in court. The judge would consider her age and work experience and might well conclude she had the capacity to earn $40,000 or $50,000 a year. So she should not expect much, if any, alimony.

Diana moved on to the property issues. Thomas was offering Brenda about 22 percent of the total property value. "I know you want *half* of the total," Diana said, "but I can tell you that the odds are ten to one against it," mainly because the inherited property hadn't greatly affected the family's standard of living. Palmieri had also threatened to bring up the adultery issue in connection with the inheritance, Diana warned. "He'll probably say something dramatic like, 'Thomas's mother would turn over in her *grave* at the thought of her money subsidizing Brenda's life with a new man!' And who knows? The judge might be influenced by that."[13]

But there was some good news: Diana was very confident that a judge would give Brenda more than 22 percent of the total asset value.

Brenda brightened at this. "How much more?"

Probably something in the range of 30 percent to 40 percent, Diana said. That could add a significant cushion to Brenda's financial life—as long as it wasn't in the form of company stock.

Brenda was looking more animated now. She asked whether Diana thought she should accept the offer.

"No, I don't," Diana said. "At least not yet. I suggest we make a counteroffer asking for forty or forty-five percent of the total property. If we can get Thomas up to thirty percent or so, I think you should definitely take it. Even if they offer less, I think you should very seriously consider it. The costs of litigating aren't trivial. Frankly, I think you and Thomas need your money for other things. You need every cent for other things. And a trial will take a tremendous emotional toll on you and the children."

Brenda looked down at the table, then shook her head. "That's just what Thomas is banking on. I know him. He's dug in. He won't change his mind. This really is his final offer. He expects me to take his stingy offer instead of going to trial because I'm the one who's supposed to be 'thinking about the children.' Why doesn't he think about the children? He's using them as hostages. I don't respect that and I won't give in. On principle, I think what he's doing is wrong and I don't want to bargain with someone who behaves this way. Enough! Let's just go to court."

Diana spent nearly an hour trying to persuade Brenda she was making a mistake. But Brenda would not be swayed.[14]

———

The case went to trial and the outcome was very close to what Diana predicted. Brenda did receive a better package from the judge than what Thomas had offered. She got sole physical custody with a 70/30 split.[15] She kept the maximum scheduled amount in child support and even got some spousal support—$750 a month. The court awarded her the entire house, subject to the mortgage, and $170,000 in cash—a package that represented almost exactly one-third of the judge's valuation of all the property.

But there was no winner here. I ended up thinking, what a terrible waste.[16] Brenda and Thomas spent about $150,000 on lawyers, experts, and the guardian ad litem—nearly 10 percent of their combined family assets.[17] Sadder still, Thomas and Brenda put themselves and their children through a bruising fourteen months.

Could this outcome have been avoided? The mediator in me thinks that if the court had required mediation before trial, the Thomkins case might very well have settled. I also wondered about Palmieri. These were difficult clients in the grip of very powerful emotions. I thought Diana did an excellent job of representing Brenda, but I had no way of knowing how Palmieri handled the counseling function, which is so critical to thinking through whether settlement makes sense.

ASSESSMENT

Now for the core question. Was Brenda's refusal to negotiate with Thomas wise?

In my opinion, it was not.

There's no doubt she thought his motives were evil: threatening a custody fight to force her to accept less than what she saw as her fair share of the family's assets. If her reading of Thomas's motives was right, I would have to agree that it was an evil thing to do.

But so what? No matter what Thomas's motives were, I think it was very unwise for Brenda not to follow Diana's advice and make a counteroffer. In fact, she didn't negotiate at all. She made one offer through her first lawyer and didn't move—even when Diana advised it.

I think there was a good chance that Thomas would have agreed to a counteroffer, especially if it were framed in a way that spoke to his emotional and identity concerns. For example, Diana might have presented the offer this way:

"Let's agree on a parenting plan that uses no label at all. It will simply specify that the children spend three weekends out of four with Thomas. We won't call it shared physical custody or sole physical custody.[18] We accept the scheduled child support, and we are not asking for spousal support at all. If Thomas pays off the mortgage and transfers the house to Brenda free and clear, she'll drop all her claims to the company stock or the inherited property."

This deal would have served Brenda's interests far better than going to court. It would have given her about 40 percent of the total property and a custody arrangement that maintained the status quo. Thomas might have accepted. His time with the children wouldn't be disparaged by the word *visitation*. And he could tell himself, "Brenda's only getting the house," although in reality he'd probably have to sell or use part of his inheritance to pay off the mortgage.

It will never be known, of course, whether Thomas would have accepted this offer. But framing it as I have suggested would probably have made it more palatable to someone as sensitive to labels as Thomas. He might have said yes, especially if his lawyer recommended it. Or he might have made another counteroffer, which Brenda was still free to reject.

From Brenda's standpoint, I don't think she had anything to lose by negotiating. To negotiate didn't mean she had to agree, or to compromise her vital interests if her alternative was better.

The hardest question would be: What if Thomas's last offer really *was* his final offer? Should Brenda negotiate or resist? Should she accept the offer (to spare the children from the stress of a trial) or go to court? I think it's a close question. If I consider Brenda's interests alone, I wouldn't criticize her for fighting on, because she would probably get a better financial deal in court, as indeed she did. But how about the kids? For them, would the chance of shifting more money from Dad's household to Mom's be worth the anguish of another battle in court? I think the answer is no. My bet is that they would rather have the war end without the trial and have Brenda go back to work a little sooner.

In the end, what troubles me about this case is how hard it is to discern the true basis of Brenda's decision. I'm sure that in her own mind, she believed she was acting for the children's benefit as well as her own. But if her decision was based on demonizing Thomas or some reflexive notion of her "integrity," as I suspect it was, I could not call her decision wise.

TEN

Sibling Warfare

Audrey spoke first. She was the oldest of the three Harding siblings and I sensed she was used to being in charge. The siblings had come to me for possible mediation of a family fight related to their father's estate. All I knew was that it concerned the inheritance of a valuable Cape Cod family vacation home. Although this may sound like a nice problem to have, I knew it could tear a family apart.[1]

Audrey was an attractive woman in her midfifties whose style I would describe as bohemian. She wore jeans, a shapeless sweater, and scuffed Frye boots that could have been originals from 1969. No makeup. Long dark hair, streaked with gray, pulled back in a ponytail, and a chunky necklace.

"Daddy died eighteen months ago," she began matter-of-factly. "He left us Swann's Way, the family summer place on Cape Cod. We can't seem to agree on how to deal with it. An old family friend said we should try mediation before spending more money on lawyers."

Audrey explained that Swann's Way had nine acres, a private sand beach, a five-bedroom main house with water views, and a two-bedroom guest cottage. A broker had told her it would sell for at least $6 million.

"I live in Oakland, California, and I don't make a lot of money," she said. "The last thing in the world I need is a one-third interest in a waterfront estate three thousand miles away. I can't afford to pay my share of the annual upkeep and taxes, and now that both of our parents are gone, I'd never use the place."

For readers not familiar with mediation, I will use the Harding story to give you an idea of how a family mediation might unfold. In an initial session, one of my goals is to develop a rapport with each party by demonstrating that I'm listening closely to them. I do this by reflecting back in my own words what I have just heard them say. My comments may sound obvious or repetitive to a neutral observer, but the parties find them very reassuring.

I did that now. "As I understand you, Audrey, the three of you have inherited a very valuable vacation property. Because you live in California, you feel you will rarely use the property; you can't afford to maintain it, and you need to sell your one-third interest, which you think is worth at least two million dollars."

"That's right," Audrey said. "You should also know that we're tenants in common—equal one-third owners—so I can't sell my share on the open market. No one would buy it. I've repeatedly explained to my sister Stephanie that she and my brother Matt have a very simple decision to make: either I sell my share to her and Matt for two million, or we sell the whole property and divide the proceeds."

"You left one thing out," Stephanie interjected coldly. "When I turned down your ultimatum, you sued me."

That got my attention. If there was a lawsuit pending, this conflict was worse than I thought. Bringing a lawsuit against a family member is an extreme act, usually signaling a total breakdown in a relationship.

Stephanie was the middle child, a few years younger than Audrey. Her hair was short, blond, and topped by a headband. She wore a pale yellow cashmere sweater and a pair of tailored khaki pants. Her arms were crossed and her lips set grimly. "This is a private matter," she told me. "I find it humiliating to have it aired in public. I can't believe Audrey is being so selfish and hurtful."

"I sued in desperation!" Audrey broke in. "You refused to respond to my calls or letters. I was at my wits' end. You left me no choice."

By this point I realized that Audrey must have filed a partition suit in state court. When joint owners can't agree about whether to sell a property, a court can be asked to resolve the matter by either dividing the property or having it sold and dividing the proceeds.

Stephanie ignored her sister's outburst and turned to me. "Audrey and Matt know I will never allow Swann's Way to pass out of the family. I told her I was willing to *discuss* buying her out, but only on the basis of the estate tax appraisal, which was $4.5 million. Even at that number, I doubt Matt can afford to participate, and my husband and I can't raise $1.5 million on our own. Audrey knows how I feel about

Swann's Way, and she's trying to extort as much money as she can out of me. I haven't spoken to her for months and I won't haggle."

Was that a whiff of sulfur I smelled in the air? Was Stephanie demonizing her sister? I reflected back to Stephanie what she had said, adding, "It sounds like you are afraid that your attachment to Swann's Way makes you vulnerable to exploitation by your sister."

She nodded and her expression softened a bit. "Swann's Way has been in the family for more than forty years. We spent every summer there growing up. Daddy said he hoped it would stay in the family, not just for our generation but for our children and grandchildren. But as you see," she said, flipping a hand in Audrey's direction, "Audrey could care less what Daddy wanted."

"Steph, get real!" Audrey interrupted. "Daddy's will doesn't say anything about keeping Swann's Way in the family." She turned to me. "Don't let her take you in with all this sanctimonious crap. Stephanie wants you to think that all she cares about is making Swann's Way into some kind of shrine to the Harding family. But make no mistake: this fight is really about money. She knows damn well that the current market value is far more than $4.5 million. She just wants to buy it at a fire-sale price because that's all she can afford."

Stephanie shot back, "You're the one who's making this all about money! You're the one who is suing to force a sale. That's *not* the way we were raised. It's a disgusting way to behave." She glared at her sister and then said to me, "Audrey thinks the world should revolve around her, and she always has. She bullied me when we were kids and she's trying to bully me now. I won't allow it."

"Stop!" Audrey exploded. "Why do you hate me so much? Why did you write me that letter saying I should stay away from your children because I was 'immoral and evil'?"

I was taken aback by these words. If Stephanie had really accused her sister of being immoral and evil, more than one negative trap might be at work. And Stephanie had just told us that in her eyes this conflict was about a great deal more than money. Stephanie felt that Audrey had always pushed her around and now she was determined—heroically, in her view—to resist and counterattack.

My usual move at such moments is to reframe the dilemma in neutral terms that can encompass the stories on both sides. I said, "My guess is that this conflict is causing you both a great deal of pain."

Stephanie said nothing. Neither did Audrey.

After a few moments of silence, I turned to Matt Harding, who looked frozen. He hadn't said a word. "What are your thoughts about all this?" I asked.

Matt, the youngest of the three, was the headmaster of a country day school outside Philadelphia, and he dressed the part: blue blazer, seersucker pants, and a bow tie with whales on it. At the start of the session he had given me a friendly smile. Now he looked like someone with a migraine headache coming on.

"I love Swann's Way, and so do my wife and kids," he said with a bit of sadness. "I get two months off during the summer, so we really use the place. But for me the problem really is the money. I can't afford to buy half of Audrey's share, no matter what the price. I know it would be a stretch for Stephie and Don to do it on their own, but I also understand why Audrey wants to cash out. This thing has gotten to be a nightmare. My sisters have been at each other's throats for a year. They are never going to be able to work this out. And I'm stuck in the middle."

I looked at Matt and reflected back what he had said, adding, "I bet you feel that to take one sister's side will damage your relationship with the other."

"Exactly," Matt exclaimed. "You've got the picture. We've heard you are a smart guy. Tell us what to do to get out of this mess."

Almost every family has at least one story of a bitter fight over property that got out of hand. These stories often end with "Our relationship has never been the same since." I have seen bitter disputes over family portraits, jewelry (especially engagement rings), pieces of antique furniture, and in one case a fishing camp that no family member had ever bothered to visit. I've heard of a case where two brothers spent years—and substantial amounts on lawyer's fees—fighting over the family photo album.

What triggers these disputes? For one thing, these are sometimes genuinely hard distributive problems.[2] When it comes to dividing family property, the greatest challenges arise when the property has certain characteristics: (1) it can't be neatly carved up into shares; (2) its market value is uncertain; (3) it is unique; and (4) it holds sentimental or symbolic value for at least one family member.[3]

Suppose, for example, that you and your siblings inherit a grandfather clock that has been in the family for a hundred years. No problem if everyone is prepared to sell it. But suppose one or more of you want to keep it for its sentimental value. Who gets the clock, and how should the other siblings be compensated? How should the value be established? By appraisal? The price an antique store would charge? The amount an antique dealer would pay? Should there be an auction? A public auction or only among family members? There are many different ways to structure an auction, and the structure can affect how much the highest bidder will have to pay and how much will be in the pot for the other heirs to divide.[4]

Many families muddle through such quandaries without too much strife. But others find that the challenge of dividing inherited property triggers such strong emotions that the relationships—often troubled for years—cannot withstand the strain. These relationships may have been limping along for years, even decades, without a blowup, but the intensity of this crisis finally does them in. Family members may find themselves reverting to old patterns and raising old resentments, and the emotional damage can be wildly disproportionate to what Spock would see as the practical stakes.

What sets off these potentially destructive emotions? Sometimes it's a deep emotional attachment to the property itself. Sometimes it is grief over the death of the loved one.[5] Sometimes it is "unfinished business" relating to old conflicts that were never fully resolved. When a parent dies, the conflict is often related to parental favoritism.[6] And sometimes family members may begin to feel that their very identities are at stake. For the Harding sisters, I would come to realize that all of these factors were at play.

———

In my first session, one of my goals was to connect with each sibling through active listening. A second goal related to process: I wanted each sibling to understand my approach to mediation so that each could make an informed decision about whether to participate in mediation with me. Matt gave me the perfect opening when he said, "Tell us what to do."

I asked Matt, "What role do you see me playing as a mediator?" His answer revealed that he thought my role would be akin to that of a judge or arbitrator: a neutral who would listen to everyone's arguments and then provide a solution. He understood, of course, that I would have no power to enforce my recommendation. But he thought of the mediation process as something like nonbinding arbitration, where I would announce the right result and recommend that the parties adopt my solution. In a sense, he was innocently asking *me* to assume responsibility for solving the problem.

I explained to Matt and his sisters that I wasn't going to tell them what to do. If that's what they wanted, they could go to court or hire an arbitrator. When I mediate family disputes, I am committed to a process in which the disputants accept full responsibility for deciding whether the conflict will be resolved. This model requires that the parties' participation be entirely voluntary and the neutral's role entirely noncoercive.[7]

A common occupational hazard for mediators is getting hooked into taking responsibility for finding a solution. It's all too easy for the mediator to believe that his value as a mediator depends on whether a deal is made. And many parties are all too eager to dump this burden in the mediator's lap. "Aren't we paying you to come up with a solution?" they often say—or at least imply.

I have to constantly remind myself that this is the parties' dispute, not mine. My responsibility is to help the parties better understand each other and their predicament, and then fashion their own solution. Parties seeking mediation are often in situations that put them under a lot of pressure, and the mediator shouldn't add to that pressure by pushing them toward settlement. You will note that the role I'm describing here is much narrower than the one that Jack Jones and I played in the IBM-Fujitsu arbitration. In that case, we played many different neutral roles—some facilitative and some coercive—and we assumed full responsibility for implementing the Secured Facility Regime. But in family conflicts I am reluctant to do that, because I think it's so important for the parties to learn to do business together. If a neutral makes the decision, they have no opportunity to learn.

"Does this type of mediation have any appeal?" I asked the siblings. "Do you have any concerns?"

Audrey asked, "What if Stephanie won't cooperate? Can you assure me she will participate in good faith?"

"That will be entirely up to Stephanie," I said. If the Hardings chose to mediate with me, I explained, the exit door would always be unlocked. If any of them concluded that the mediation was no longer serving his or her interests, that person was perfectly free to walk out and pursue the litigation alternative. I think Audrey was rather shocked to hear this. She probably thought I would try to sell all three of them on the virtues of mediation and settlement. Instead I suggested that mediation would give them an opportunity to better understand the opportunities and risks of litigation and to explore whether we could come up with some options that better served each of their interests.

The Hardings had other concerns about the process. Stephanie indicated that she felt uncomfortable even being in the same room with Audrey. She was willing to work with me and didn't mind Matt being present, but she had things she wanted to say without Audrey there. Matt expressed the concern that his two sisters wouldn't be able to manage a civil conversation at all. "Wouldn't it be better if you met separately with each of us and then did some shuttle diplomacy?" he asked.

Many mediators operate this way, even in family disputes. But as you may recall from the IBM-Fujitsu case, I believe that the best way for parties to better understand each other's perspectives is to meet face-to-face. This isn't easy for the participants, especially in an intense family conflict. It can be very difficult for parties to hear what the others have to say. Their usual patterns of direct communication are often very ineffective. They push each other's buttons and don't listen. But a skilled mediator can help them learn how to listen to each other—even if they strongly disagree—and to express themselves in a way that makes it more likely that they will be heard. A mediator may also be able to accomplish some of this even when meeting with parties in separate sessions, but it's far less likely. There is simply no substitute for *seeing* that your adversary understands your point of view, rather than having the mediator *tell* you it's so. Because of the increased possibilities for promoting mutual understanding, I've found that working together offers the greatest hope for finding lasting solutions and even for repairing damaged relationships.

Another reason I don't like shuttle diplomacy is that it gives the mediator too much power. Parties often want to meet privately with the mediator so they can tell him secrets that he is then obligated not to share. The result is that the mediator alone knows the whole story. That makes it all too easy for the parties to expect the mediator to tell them what to do—and for the mediator to fall into the trap of manipulating both sides to get a deal.

In addition to helping parties better understand what mediation is all about, my third goal for the initial session is to try to assess whether each party is motivated to engage in the sort of process I prefer. I explained that it would be hard work and would require their active participation. Audrey and Matt both quickly confirmed that they were ready for this. Audrey said she wanted to mediate because she hoped to find a solution without destroying family relationships she valued. Matt wanted to find a solution that would satisfy both of his sisters and allow Swann's Way to remain in the family. Stephanie remained silent.

"Stephanie, I get the feeling you're more skeptical about this process. What about it has some appeal to you?" I continued.

"Look, I'm here because Audrey sued me," she said. "Obviously I want to solve the problem. I hate the thought of airing dirty family laundry in court, so I guess mediation is the lesser of two evils."

"In other words," I said, "you would prefer mediation to having a judge resolve your conflict in open court." I began to pontificate about other options. "Arbitration is another process of dispute resolution—"

Stephanie cut me off. "I know about arbitration," she said impatiently. "I prefer mediation. I don't want some neutral imposing an outcome. It's just that I don't want to be here. It's very painful."

"Sounds like you're angry that this dispute even exists. Is that a fair statement?"

She nodded.

Privately I thought, "Well, you can probably blame your father for that. A better estate plan could have avoided this conflict." In another mediation involving an inheritance conflict among three siblings, I actually said something to that effect. More often I frame the message as "This conflict is not your fault. Your parent's estate plan created very difficult problems that might have been avoided." But in the Hardings' case, I decided now wasn't the time for such a discussion.

Instead, I asked them to think about whether they would feel comfortable mediating with me. If they wanted to explore a different approach to mediation, I would provide them with other names. If they wanted to work with me, the next step would be for their lawyers to contact me.[8] Because litigation was pending, I said, I thought it essential that each sibling have a lawyer, at least to consult with.

Within a week of our meeting, each sibling confirmed by email that they wanted to work with me. I then had a conference call with their lawyers and asked them to help educate me about the conflict. I requested that they and their clients prepare written submissions to fill me in on the background.[9]

When I received these materials, I noted with pleasure that the individual letters from Audrey, Stephanie, and Matt were very personal and well-written.

The siblings agreed on the basic facts. Their father, Joseph Harding, had been born in Cincinnati in 1921. He graduated from Dartmouth College at the start of World War II, enlisted in the Navy, served in the Pacific with distinction, and was discharged with the rank of lieutenant commander. He moved to Boston, where many of his college friends had been raised and still lived. One of those friends introduced him to the brokerage firm where he built his career.

Linda Adams, his future wife, was the daughter of a prominent Boston lawyer. They met at a Christmas party in 1947 and married a year later. With financial help from Linda's parents, the young couple bought a house in Wellesley and joined the local country club. All three children were born in Wellesley: Audrey in 1950, Stephanie in 1953, and Matt in 1956.

Joe Harding's charm and ambition made him a highly successful investment advisor. Linda Harding devoted herself to raising the children and supporting charitable causes. They bought Swann's Way in 1960 when properties were dirt cheap in Truro, at least in comparison to today, and spent every summer there. As soon as the school year was out, Linda would move the children down to the Cape and remain there until Labor Day. Joe came down every weekend.

In their letters, Stephanie and Matt described their summers with great fondness. "Swann's Way was where my father spent the most time with us," Stephanie wrote. "He taught me how to sail, play tennis, and swim." She also recalled her mother's tradition of keeping a "House Log" in which family members and guests recorded the highlights of each stay. Stephanie wrote that her own children loved to read the early entries, especially those with misspelled words and grammatical errors that she and Matt had written when they were very young.

Audrey's letter was less nostalgic. By the time she was a teenager, she found Swann's Way pretty boring. Her best memories revolved around the father-daughter tennis tournament at the local club. "Dad and I made a great team," she wrote. Apparently that was an understatement: Matt's letter revealed that by the time Audrey was twelve, she was a ranked tennis player. Joe had taken great pride in her athletic prowess, and for four years in a row they won the club's mixed doubles tournaments.

All three children went to single-sex private schools near Boston. In her sophomore year, Audrey began to veer off the course her parents had set for her. She began experimenting with drugs and became, in her own words, "very rebellious." One paragraph from her letter is worth quoting at length:

When my grades dropped and I was no longer on the honor roll, my father responded by putting more pressure on me. He said, "If you don't watch out, you'll never get into a top school like Smith or Radcliffe." I told him that was his problem. I had no interest in living out his bourgeois aspirations for me. In the larger world all hell was breaking loose: the Vietnam War, the secret war in Cambodia, riots on college campuses. I almost flunked out of Milton, and by the end I was so alienated I didn't want to go to my own graduation. My mother and I had a big fight because I didn't want to wear the ridiculous long white dress that was required for the ceremony. Four days after graduation, a friend and I took off for Berkeley. My parents, of course, freaked out. But there was nothing they could do to make me come back.

Audrey never did move back to the East Coast, but in her mid-twenties she reconciled with her parents and went back to college. Beginning in 1974, she made a point of visiting Swann's Way for at least one week every summer. "Oddly enough, I enjoyed it more than I had as a kid," she wrote. "My parents were thrilled to have me back in the fold and acting like a 'normal' person again. Dad would take the week off and we'd play lots of tennis. I didn't spend much time with Stephanie at Swann's Way because we had different circles of friends, but Matt and I would take long bike rides and make ritual stops for lobster rolls." Audrey ultimately earned a BA and a master's degree in social work from UC–Berkeley and built a career working with abused and neglected children. "Mummy often told me how proud she was of me for devoting my career to children in need," her letter continued. Audrey never married or had children but was deeply attached to her nieces and nephews. "For me, the most painful aspect of this horrible fight is that Stephanie no longer allows them to visit me."

Stephanie's life, by her own report, took a more traditional course. She went to Mount Holyoke College, graduated with honors, and married Don Turner, whom she had known since high school. The ceremony was held at Swann's Way. Don became a cardiologist and the couple settled in Wellesley only a few blocks from where Stephanie had grown up. They now had two teenage children, both attending private schools. "Audrey once said that my life was boring and unadventurous," Stephanie wrote, "but I chose that course partly in reaction to seeing how much pain she caused my parents."

Matt graduated from Brown, got a master's in English literature, and began a career teaching English at a New England boarding school. He proved to be a natural leader and soon headed the school's English department. Five years ago, he took the post of headmaster at a day school in Philadelphia. He married Judy Skinner, also a teacher, and they now had three-year-old twins.

All three siblings wrote movingly about their mother's death from ovarian cancer in 1985. "The last year was horrible," Matt wrote. "Mummy was often in pain and Daddy, who had not yet retired, couldn't cope with the situation very well. Stephanie was the only one of us living in the Boston area, so she took responsibility for Mummy's care—doctor's appointments, hospital treatments, and private nurses. I drove down from New Hampshire every weekend and did what I could to help." Stephanie's letter added that Matt was the only member of the family, aside from her mother, who seemed to appreciate the hard work she was doing. "Audrey flew back every six weeks or so for a weekend," Stephanie noted. "Whenever she arrived, my parents acted like it was a national holiday. Mummy would rally, Daddy would laugh at her jokes, and then she'd take off again."

I was beginning to see a pattern in the sisters' relationship.

Five years after his wife's death, Joe Harding married a woman nineteen years his junior. Betsy Taylor, fifty, was the former women's tennis champion at the Wellesley Country Club and recently divorced. Joe was sixty-nine, retired, healthy, and eager to travel. The new couple traveled all over the world but returned every summer to Swann's Way.

When Joe died at the age of eighty-one, he was still a reasonably wealthy man. He left Swann's Way to his children, the Wellesley house to his second wife, and $6 million in investments in trust. Under the terms of the trust, Betsy would receive the income for life. Upon her death, the principal would pass in equal shares to his children. Stephanie wrote of Betsy: "She's a real lady and took wonderful care of Daddy during his last illness, when he required a lot of care." Audrey, who was only ten years younger than her stepmother, wrote, "The way Betsy pampers herself, she'll surely outlive me."

The lawyers sent me copious information on Swann's Way, including photographs that showed it to be a spectacular property. The estate tax appraisal set its value at $4.5 million as of the date of death in 2002. But in the eighteen months since, Cape Cod real estate had experienced a boom. Audrey sent a marketing report from Sotheby's International Realty estimating the fair market value at "no less than $6 million." According to Sotheby's, Swann's Way was a unique property and nothing comparable had come on the local market in fifteen years. Swann's Way had considerably more land than most properties in the area and eight hundred feet of private beach on the bay, a rarity in Truro. The main house, built in 1925, was a large two-story structure with stunning views. Designed in the handsome shingled "summer cottage" style that wealthy families of that era favored, it had been well maintained. The guest cottage, built in 1975, had limited water views but more modern comforts. Stephanie made a point of writing that her parents had built it "to make sure there would be plenty of room for the entire family, including their future grandchildren, if we all wanted to visit at the same time."

Matt and Audrey, however, had foreseen that Swann's Way might cause friction among the siblings after their father's death. Audrey wrote: "Matt talked to Daddy about this several times. With my permission, he strongly suggested that Daddy leave Swann's Way to him and Stephanie, and give me an equivalent amount of cash. My father ignored this advice—probably because he wanted to put all his cash in trust for Betsy."

After their father's death, Audrey wrote, her relationship with Stephanie had deteriorated rapidly. Stephanie seemed depressed and "unable to make decisions." When it became clear that Swann's Way was going to be a point of contention, "it was as though the lid blew off," Audrey's letter went on. "Stephanie started raging at me about past slights, and I retaliated by saying some things I shouldn't have." After several "hideous" telephone conversations between the sisters, Audrey had received a letter from Stephanie, breaking off all contact. Audrey provided me with a copy of that letter, in which Stephanie had written: "You have always treated me badly and been condescending. You have attacked me for my failures and used a derogatory, accusatory tone that I have found very painful. I will no longer allow myself or my family to be subjected to this."

Audrey was distraught over the rupture, which had prevented her from seeing Stephanie and her children for almost a year. "I have sent letters begging [Stephanie] to consider our getting outside professional help. She never replied," Audrey wrote to me. "This is eating away at me. I desperately need closure so I can go on with my life."

Family mediation is so stressful that I try to keep the sessions relatively short and the agendas limited. Our second meeting was scheduled for two hours, and even that, I thought, might be pushing it. This time, the siblings were joined by their lawyers.

I proposed we do two things in the session: (1) create a list of each sibling's interests; and (2) discuss the opportunities and risks presented by Audrey's lawsuit. This would lay a necessary foundation for problem-solving, if we got that far. All three Hardings and their lawyers agreed to this plan.

"Looking to the future," I asked the siblings, "what is important to you? You've all told me what you'd like to see happen with respect to Swann's Way. I'd like to learn more about what's motivating that decision for each of you."

Audrey, as usual, spoke up first. She said her most important interest was to sell her share in Swann's Way at a fair price.

"Why sell?" I asked. "How would you use the money?"

Audrey said she wanted to be able to retire in comfort when she reached age sixty-two and to occasionally travel abroad. She added, "I've always dreamed of having the money to take my nieces and nephews—one at a time—to Europe during a school vacation."

I had set up a flip chart in the room for this discussion. I got up from my chair, chose a green Magic Marker from the array of colors I'd brought, and wrote:

AUDREY'S INTERESTS

- Financial resources for a comfortable retirement
- Financial resources for travel and vacations abroad
- Fair sale price for interest in Swann's Way
- Spend vacation time with nieces and nephews

Seeing me write the words *nieces and nephews* had a visible effect on Audrey. Her eyes welled up with tears. "We had planned that when Jennifer, Stephanie's oldest daughter, turned thirteen she would spend a week with me during her Christmas break. We've talked about it for years. Jen turned thirteen last October and I had all sorts of special activities planned, but Stephanie wouldn't let her come. I was devastated."

"It sounds like sustaining a close relationship with your nephews and nieces is extremely important to you," I said.

"Oh, yes," Audrey said. So I added:

- Sustain close relationship with nieces and nephews

After a pause, Audrey added that she cared about her relationships with Matt and Stephanie. "They and their children *are* my family now." She agreed that I could add three more items to her list:

- Maintain good relationship with Matt
- Repair relationship with Stephanie
- Minimize the emotional and financial costs of resolving this dispute

The last item was one that I suggested that all three of them probably shared.

Next I asked whether Audrey would ever want to spend time at Swann's Way. "I doubt it," she said. "It's a long way from California." I reminded her that her nieces and nephews all spent time there in the summer. Could she imagine spending a week or so there when they were there?

Her eyebrows rose about half an inch. "Fair point," she acknowledged, as if we were conducting a friendly debate. "It *would* be fun to spend time there with Matt and his family. And if Stephanie and I could get past this horror show, I could imagine enjoying time there with her family as well. But surely there's no need for me to own any part of Swann's Way for this to be possible."

Matt said teasingly, "Well, someone in our family would still have to own it!"

This remark coaxed a weak smile from Stephanie. I tore off the sheet headlined AUDREY'S INTERESTS and posted it on the wall with masking tape.

I turned to Matt and asked him a series of similar questions. His goals were so straightforward that it took us only a few minutes to complete a list.

MATT'S INTERESTS

- Maintain close relationships with both sisters

- Minimize the emotional and financial costs of resolving this dispute

- Spend summers at Swann's Way with his wife and children

- Live within his means

The last item was my shorthand for his financial situation. Taxes and maintenance on Swann's Way were about $30,000 a year. Matt could pay half of those costs per year, assuming Audrey was no longer an owner, but he couldn't buy out half her share. Even if he could somehow borrow the necessary $750,000 to $1 million, he said, he couldn't afford to service that much debt—it would be "financially irresponsible" to take on that kind of obligation.

I taped Matt's sheet to the wall and turned to Stephanie. I hadn't purposely left her for last, but she had not seemed eager to talk. She had spent much of the meeting doodling on a pad as if she had no interest in the conversation. But now that I was addressing my questions to her, she was fully prepared to answer them and seemed to enjoy having the floor. Her paramount interest, she said, was keeping Swann's Way in the Harding family so it could be passed on to the next generation. She also wanted to avoid "haggling" over the value of Swann's Way. She insisted on a "rational" process that was "fair." (Terms like *rational* and *fair* can mean radically different things to different people, which in itself can be a source of conflict.[10]) Like her siblings, she wanted to minimize the financial and emotional costs of resolving this dispute. The lawsuit had already forced her to hire a lawyer and spend money on mediation, and she resented it. I asked whether she had any interests with regard to her relationships with her siblings. "I have a good relationship with Matt and his family and I cherish it," she responded. "But frankly, if we have to sell Swann's Way, Audrey will no longer be part of my family. I'll have nothing to do with her."

Such threats are not uncommon in bitter family conflicts, where the disputants may become so fixated on fending off their worst-case scenario that their own conduct makes it more likely. I hoped my next question would help her change course. "Suppose we find a way for Swann's Way to be kept in the family," I suggested to Stephanie. "Might you want to repair your relationship with Audrey then?"

As expected, Stephanie initially tried to dodge the question, but I persisted. "Let's imagine for a moment—even if you think it unlikely— that the three of you come up with not just one way, but a number of ways to keep Swann's Way in the family. Stephanie, what happens to your relationship with Audrey then? What are the possibilities?" Stephanie didn't answer for at least fifteen seconds, which I took as a good sign. Finally she grimaced and said slowly, "Maybe."

So I wrote the following:

STEPHANIE'S INTERESTS

- Keep Swann's Way in the family so it can be used during her lifetime and passed on to the next generation

- Be financially prudent

- Set a fair value on Audrey's interest by a rational process
- Sustain relationship with Matt and his family
- Minimize emotional and financial costs of resolving this conflict
- Perhaps repair relationship with Audrey *if* Swann's Way is kept in the family

I taped Stephanie's sheet to the wall next to her siblings'. Matt surveyed the three colorful sheets covered with my scrawls and remarked, "It looks like the drawings we used to bring home from kindergarten—except that our handwriting then was already far better than yours now." Everyone laughed and I sensed that the siblings were relieved to have gotten through this exercise without suffering any flesh wounds. I told them that they had made a solid start; each of them might want to add to or modify their own list later.

Next we turned to exploring the opportunities and risks of the partition suit.

For this part of the discussion I relied on the lawyers, who appeared to get along well. Because Audrey had filed the suit, I asked her lawyer to begin by describing his understanding of the relevant Massachusetts law.

"Audrey, Matt, and Stephanie own Swann's Way as tenants in common," he said. "They each have a one-third interest in a single piece of property. It's typically very difficult for a one-third owner to sell her interest to an outsider; few buyers would find that an attractive prospect. Normally the entire property can't be sold unless all tenants in common agree. That, of course, creates a risk that one tenant in common will be trapped by the others into remaining a co-owner. Most states, including this one, provide an escape hatch: any tenant in common can file a suit to 'partition' the property."[11]

Audrey's lawyer explained how a partition suit works in Massachusetts. A judge appoints a commissioner to see whether it is feasible to divide the property into parcels of approximately equal value. If so, the property is divvied up and each co-tenant becomes the sole owner of one parcel. If this is not realistic, the court asks the commissioner to arrange for the entire property to be sold, typically at a judicially supervised auction. Proceeds are equally divided.

"What do you think the outcome would be in this case?" I asked.

"For Swann's Way, a physical division into portions of equal value would be next to impossible," he said. "I've told Audrey that if she pursues her partition suit, the court will end up requiring that the property be sold and the proceeds divided."

I asked the other two lawyers whether they agreed. They both nodded.

I sensed that Stephanie's lawyer was in a tough spot. I didn't know how much time he'd had to advise Stephanie before our meeting, and I was even less confident that she had been able to take it all in. "I think that is correct," he said carefully. "However, I've told Stephanie that there are still two ways she can remain an owner of the property. If the property is sold at auction, she can make a bid on it. If she's the high bidder, she'll be the owner—but of course she might be outbid. The second way she can retain the property is if the three siblings agree on some private arrangement that will keep all or part of Swann's Way in the family."

Stephanie appeared not to have heard this second point. She was still focused on the lawsuit. "How can the law be so unfair?" she exclaimed, a note of panic rising in her voice. "Matt and I own two-thirds. Audrey owns one-third. Why should a minority owner be able to force a sale?"

Audrey's lawyer noted that Massachusetts law was clear on this point.[12]

"But Daddy didn't *want* Swann's Way to be sold," Stephanie insisted. "He told me that he wanted it kept in the family. Doesn't that matter?"

"Only if he had made that clear in his will," Audrey's lawyer responded. "But he didn't do that. His will said only that he was leaving it to the three of you in equal shares. An oral statement counts for nothing when it comes to inherited real estate. I think your lawyer would agree."

Stephanie's lawyer nodded. So did Matt's.

At this point I offered a summary: "It sounds like the law is reasonably clear: as a tenant in common, Audrey can force a sale of the entire property, regardless of what Joe Harding may have wanted or what Stephanie and Matt want now. But remember, the three of you have the power to make any number of other arrangements, *if* you agree."

"But Audrey's in the driver's seat!" Stephanie shouted. "Is that what you're saying? We have to make concessions so she'll drop the suit?"

Audrey wheeled around in her chair and shot her sister a look that could have cut glass. "How can we explore other possibilities when you won't even speak to me? I've *had* it with your victim act! I'm not the one making threats here! If anything, you're the one who has been threatening me. How long do you expect me to sit here and take this shit?"

To help them disengage, I leaned forward and addressed each of them in turn, as if the other were not in the room. "Audrey, it sounds like you're angry and hurt by what Stephanie has been saying. You're feeling attacked and you want it to stop. You're wondering whether we will make any progress in this mediation if Stephanie continues to be so angry with you that she chooses not to speak to you. You also know that we can't make Stephanie participate. That's up to her. So you must feel stuck in a very tough position." I waited for Audrey to indicate whether I had gotten it right.

When Audrey nodded, I turned to Stephanie. "Stephanie, I imagine that this meeting has been very hard for you as well. You may have been aware of the legal issues when you walked into this meeting, but today the lawyers have really spelled it out for you: Audrey can unilaterally impose a sale if the three of you don't make some alternative arrangement. For you this must seem profoundly unfair. And I wonder if you're feeling backed into a corner by this news."

Stephanie nodded yes.

"My question to all three of you," I continued, "is quite straightforward: Are you willing to stick with the mediation to see if we can come up with something that *better* serves everyone's interests? We'll take a break so you can talk privately with your lawyers and think it over. Matt and Stephanie, feel free to call your spouses and discuss it with them. I think we've done enough today. Let's reconvene briefly at four P.M. and see where we are."

The suggestion was welcome. The room emptied in seconds.

At four o'clock everyone returned but Stephanie. Her lawyer said she was exhausted and had gone home. She was willing to meet again next week, but "she instructed me to say that under no circumstances will she consider any option based on a valuation other than $4.5 million."

I thanked him for conveying the message and we scheduled the next session for the following Friday. I also scheduled a conference call with the lawyers the next day to discuss the agenda for that session.

As everyone was packing up their belongings, Audrey turned to me and said vehemently, "Stephanie is so dug in—I don't think she'll budge. I just want you to know that I'm not going to accept a $4.5 million valuation just to buy her love."

"Audrey, I appreciate your willingness to hang in there. This isn't easy. And you've made it clear that you will only sell at a price *you* think is fair. I look forward to seeing you next week."

Mediators need to be optimists, but at the end of the second session I was worried. If the property were sold at auction, the bidding was unlikely to stop at $4.5 million. If Stephanie didn't find some way to negotiate with her sister, she was probably going to lose the property. Her inflexibility would lead to a terrible outcome for her. Why, I wondered, was he being so rigid?

Stephanie had given us plenty of hints. This was a very angry woman, and I suspected that the anger was the product of sibling rivalry with roots that went deep into her past. Stephanie seemed to view herself as the loyal, dutiful child who had always done the right thing and never gotten what she deserved in return. In Stephanie's view, Audrey had been the favored child. (And for all I knew, this diagnosis was right.) Even after Audrey had moved three thousand miles away from home, she'd *still* managed to soak up more parental attention. And when Audrey had reconciled with her parents and come back home to visit, she had been celebrated as the prodigal daughter.[13]

The Bible is full of cautionary tales about sibling jealousy and rage.[14] Scholars have written that sibling rivalry, particularly over issues of parental favoritism, often intensifies after a parent has died, in part because the parent is not around to redress the favoritism, mediate the conflict, or at least inhibit the fighting. It was no accident, I mused, that the two sisters were still fighting over the value of their respective "shares." When the parents are gone, there are no more shares of parental love to be divided, but property can serve as a new battleground. Both siblings had framed the dispute as a zero-sum game, and it was one that Stephanie couldn't win. If she paid Audrey top dollar, she would view it as simply the latest in a long line of undeserved special benefits going to Audrey. If she refused to pay more than $1.5 million, Audrey had the legal power to "take away" Swann's Way.

But anger usually doesn't produce the kind of paralysis that seemed to be afflicting Stephanie. Underneath her anger, I sensed, was a fear of losing more than a summer home. Swann's Way seemed to be central to her identity. In her view, she was the child who kept the family together and preserved its legacy—the keeper of the flame. Swann's Way was her most tangible link to her parents and her children, the past and future of her family. If Swann's Way no longer belonged to the Hardings, where would that leave her?

I empathized with Stephanie's dilemma but I disagreed with her strategy. Stephanie was threatening to terminate her relationship with her sister—and cut Audrey off from her nieces and nephews—if Audrey didn't make concessions. This is a common hard-bargaining tactic: to "hold the relationship hostage" when negotiating with a counterpart who places a high value on preserving the relationship. But such a tactic often backfires. While Audrey might make concessions, it was more likely that she would react defensively, fearing that she would be a sucker if she gave in.

Obviously Audrey and Stephanie had a terrible relationship. What I had to decide was what, if anything, I should do about it. Was there any reason to think I could do much to repair it as a mediator? The Hardings had come to me for help resolving a real estate dispute. They hadn't hired me as a therapist. Would it be wise to invite them to address their relationship directly in the mediation?

———

In some family mediations, a conversation about relationships can help pave the way for problem-solving. I was leaning toward raising the subject with the Hardings, but I decided to sound out the lawyers first. During our conference call on Monday, I asked whether they shared my perception that the sisters' relationship was at the heart of the problem. They immediately agreed. Stephanie's lawyer said, "If we didn't have to worry about our clients' hostility toward each other, I'm confident that we could negotiate a reasonable deal and keep this case out of court."

I said, "I'm wondering whether part of our next session should be devoted to a conversation between Audrey and Stephanie about their relationship. I would facilitate, of course. If the sisters were willing, do you think having such a conversation would be advisable?"

"I wouldn't risk it," advised Stephanie's lawyer. He thought there was a good chance Stephanie would walk out of the mediation in reaction to something Audrey said.

Audrey's lawyer was also worried, but to him it was worth the risk because Audrey really wanted to improve her relationship with her sister. Matt's lawyer said that Matt desperately wanted his sisters to repair their relationship and would be supportive.

"I'd like to try," I said. The sisters knew how to push each other's buttons, I acknowledged, but without some sort of improvement in their relationship I doubted there would be a good outcome. It would be harder for them to reach a negotiated deal, and even if they did, it might fall apart before it was fully implemented. "If we could somehow help them learn how to communicate more effectively with each other, they would have a better chance of reaching a deal that met their interests."

I then assigned some homework to both lawyers and clients. I said I had taken the liberty of sending each of them a copy of *Difficult Conversations: How to Discuss What Matters Most*, a book written by three of my colleagues at Harvard's Program on Negotiation.[15] I urged that they all read it before the next session. When we met again, I would ask the Hardings whether they were willing, with my help, to have a "difficult conversation" about their relationship. If any of them objected, I wouldn't push it.

Audrey's lawyer said he liked this plan and was confident Audrey would be motivated. "Is there something constructive that Audrey can do in the meantime to prepare?"

"That's a great question," I said. "After you and Audrey have read the book, you might ask *her* that question in light of the recommendations of the book. After all, she really knows her sister and the history of their relationship."

———

At the appointed hour, the siblings and their lawyers arrived for our third session. I was delighted to find that everyone had read the book. I asked the siblings whether they were willing to explore together whether there were some ideas in the book that might help them communicate more effectively with each other, and they all signaled their willingness.

"What are your reactions to the book? Any ideas you find useful?" I asked.

Audrey spoke right up. "The authors suggest the parties in conflict often have radically different perceptions of what happened in the past and its meaning. They suggest that it's useful to 'disentangle intent from impact.'"

Because Stephanie looked puzzled, I elaborated. Suppose another person has done something that really hurt me. I may too readily infer from my pain, which is real, that the other person must have *intended* to hurt me—that this was a principal motive for their action. But often this is not the case. To make matters worse, when I accuse this other person of having intentionally hurt me, he or she may respond defensively and be unwilling even to acknowledge the impact of their action on me, because they are convinced their motives were pure. The authors of *Difficult Conversations* suggest instead of arguing about whose perception is right (and whose is wrong), it is useful to have a conversation in which each person shares his own perceptions and where both strive to "disentangle intent from impact."

At this point, Audrey broke in and said, "I think we need to do that."

Audrey looked directly at Stephanie. "I've done some thinking," she said. "I now realize the terrible impact my actions have had on you. I've caused you pain by insisting that I be bought out or that Swann's Way be sold. From your perspective, it was selfish and disloyal. You probably think I intended to inflict this pain on you. But I want to assure you that that was never my intention. I love you. My intention was and is simply to find a way to sell my interest in Swann's Way on a reasonable basis."

Stephanie looked down. "Audrey, you are right about one thing— you've hurt me. How could you not have realized how your behavior would affect me and our family?"

"I'm not claiming that I didn't see how angry and distressed you were," Audrey said. "I'm saying something else—that my *motive* was never to hurt you. I guess I wasn't thinking about the impact on you at all. I was just focused on solving my own problem, which is that my savings are pitiful and I'm worried about retirement. Please try to understand my perspective—and my intention. Can you understand why to me it makes no sense to own a summer place I can't afford?"

Stephanie said, "But the way you did it was cold and unfeeling. Surely you must have known how much Swann's Way means to me."

Now Audrey looked annoyed and I sensed she was tempted to go into defense mode. To help her avoid that trap, I suggested that she ask a question of her sister. An honest question, not an attack. Perhaps about Stephanie's intentions in a particular instance that had puzzled Audrey.

Audrey nodded and asked Stephanie, "What was your intention when you cut off communication with me? When you wouldn't let Jennifer come visit me in California last Christmas? You hurt me terribly. And I believe that was your intention."

Stephanie said, "I was furious with you."

Nothing further was said for nearly a minute. Then Audrey said to me, "I feel terrible about what's happened to my relationship with Stephanie. I've asked myself, Why is she so angry with me? Was it that I ran away at eighteen? That I never moved back to the East Coast? That was such a long time ago."

There was another silence, which I did nothing to break.

At length Audrey turned to her sister and asked, "Does some of this go back to Mummy's death?"

The air in my office suddenly became electric. I wondered whether the sisters had ever discussed this subject with each other before. Stephanie looked down and said, "That was a terrible time. Mummy suffered so much."

"And you carried the burden for all of us," Audrey went on. "It must have been incredibly difficult. Stephanie, you were heroic. Daddy couldn't handle it. Matt was busy teaching. I'd breeze in every few weeks and share my latest stories with Mummy and off-color jokes with Daddy. But I didn't do my share. And worse still, I never told you how grateful I was for what you did."

This was not a family that found it easy to express or respond to such emotions. But both sisters looked tearful, and suddenly Stephanie broke down and began to sob. Matt reached out and squeezed her arm. The lawyers and I almost collided with each other as we rushed to offer tissues and handkerchiefs. Our fumbling prompted laughter and eased the tension. At length Stephanie turned to her sister and said, "Thank you." Despite my gentle probing, none of the siblings felt the need to say anything more on the matter.

When everyone had recovered their composure, I suggested that was enough work for the day.

———————

I came to think of that as a breakthrough session. At our next meeting a week later, the atmosphere was noticeably more relaxed. I suggested that the session be devoted to "brainstorming" about options for resolving the conflict over Swann's Way. Brainstorming sounds easy, but most people find it extremely difficult. They fear that if they mention an option, the others will think they are making an offer. I explained that brainstorming was simply a way to think creatively about options, and suggested two ground rules:

No Evaluation: That is, no comments suggesting that an idea is good or bad. We would evaluate the options later.

No Ownership: When an idea was tossed out, no one's name would be associated with it. Just because someone suggested an idea did not mean they *liked* the idea or were making an offer.

I urged everyone to be playful and throw out crazy ideas. "Your crazy idea may provoke someone else to think of a great idea that otherwise would never have occurred to them."

To break the ice, I tossed out two options—both equally unlikely. One was that Audrey would keep her one-third interest. The other was that Stephanie and Matt would each pay Audrey $1 million cash for her interest. I wrote both on the flip chart. Audrey frowned and said she'd never accept the first. Stephanie winced at the second. I smiled and reminded both, "No evaluations—they're out of bounds."

"Okay," Audrey said with a smirk, "how about hiring a hit man to knock off Betsy?" Everyone laughed. It was no secret that Audrey wasn't too fond of her stepmother, and everyone knew that once Betsy was gone, the siblings would have no financial worries: their father's testamentary trust would terminate and the siblings would be loaded. I faithfully wrote, "Hire hit man & terminate trust."

That gave Matt's lawyer an idea: "Audrey needs money for retirement, not now. She won't retire for another seven years. By then, Betsy may have died. Maybe Stephanie could buy Audrey out with a note, which doesn't become due until Betsy dies or Audrey reaches retirement age, whichever comes first."

Audrey's lawyer tossed out the following: "What if we raise cash by selling off a piece of the property—some of the undeveloped land?" Several ideas for doing this were offered. One suggestion was that Swann's Way be subdivided into three separate lots: one containing the main house, one the guest house, and one to be sold. Audrey could get the proceeds of the sale, and there could be side payments among the siblings to equalize the value received by each.

Stephanie reminded us that she didn't want to sell any part of Swann's Way, and Matt worried that it would be difficult to establish the relative value of the various parcels. As the process cop, I reminded them of the ground rules and assured Stephanie that no one was being asked to agree to anything at this point.

The lawyers had experience with valuation methods and suggested a number of ways to value the property, or parts of it. They also had ideas involving charitable gifts and associated tax benefits—for example, conservation easements to the Cape Cod Land Bank that would preserve open space and provide tax deductions.

After we had created a long list of ideas, I asked each Harding to consider the options in light of their own interests and those of their siblings. An "A" meant you would be eager to discuss an option further; a "C" meant you had no interest in discussing it further, and a "B" meant you weren't sure.

Two broad sets of options survived. Audrey and Matt gave an A to the various "subdivision" options (Stephanie gave it a B). Stephanie and Matt gave an "A" to buyout options involving deferred payments to Audrey.

I closed the session by identifying some questions that would need to be explored: How could Swann's Way be subdivided under the local zoning requirements? We would want maps showing various ways of dividing the property and information about how the parcels might be valued. If a new lot was carved out and sold, what safeguards were available to protect the views of the main house and prevent the new owner from building some monstrosity?

Within six weeks of their breakthrough session, the three siblings signed an agreement. The property would be subdivided into only two parcels. One six-acre parcel would include both houses and 650 feet of beachfront. A second parcel—three acres of raw land with 150 feet of beachfront—was carved out for sale, with covenants to protect the two houses.

The big parcel went to Stephanie and Matt. They would remain tenants in common with equal shares, but they entered into a written holding agreement providing that Stephanie would have first call on the main house and in return would pay the lion's share of the maintenance costs, taxes, and insurance. Matt would primarily use the guest house and pay a smaller portion.

The smaller parcel of raw land went to Audrey along with a $100,000 cash payment from Stephanie and a note for $100,000 from Matt. The note provided for annual interest payments at 4 percent, with a balloon payment of the entire principal in ten years.

It was not easy for Stephanie to agree to have the property subdivided, but in the end she decided that it was better to carve off a piece than try to come up with the money necessary to buy Audrey out. I was surprised that the Hardings didn't create three separate parcels, giving Stephanie the main house and Matt the guest house. But Stephanie strongly preferred that she and Matt remain tenants in common because she liked the idea of them remaining "partners" and she thought this might allow them to plan together what might be done for the next generation of Hardings. Matt, as usual, was amenable to this plan.

The story of the Hardings had a happy ending. The conflict over Swann's Way was permanently resolved. Stephanie kept most of the property in the family without financial strain. Matt got a summer place for himself and his family that he could afford. Audrey sold her parcel for $1,550,000 and netted about $1,400,000 after paying commissions and taxes. She also got an improved—but not perfect—relationship with Stephanie. I later learned that Audrey returned to Swann's Way for a week or two every summer when the kids were there. She took Stephanie's fifteen-year-old daughter, Jennifer, to Paris for ten days, and the younger nieces and nephews were looking forward to their turns.

ASSESSMENT

Stephanie and Audrey were not evil people. They inherited a hard problem that overloaded an already fragile relationship. Audrey's desire to liquidate her interest in Swann's Way was rational. Stephanie's senti-mental attachment to Swann's Way struck me as quite genuine and not narrowly selfish. Both were legitimate interests and some sort of con-flict was inevitable. Conflict in itself is not bad—it's an inevitable part of life. But when a conflict over family property leads to demonization, vital relationships risk being permanently damaged or even destroyed.

One lesson of this case is the importance of effective estate plan-ning.[16] Joe Harding could have averted, or at least eased, the conflict over Swann's Way if he had talked with his children about their inter-ests before he died, thought through a variety of plans that would have served everyone better than a simple tenancy in common, and adopted one of those plans in his will.[17] There are also ways to design a process to resolve disputes that may arise after the parent dies.[18]

Because he didn't, the Harding sisters fell quickly into negative traps. They saw the conflict in purely zero-sum terms—a dollar more for one was a dollar less for the other. They fell prey to moralism, converting the property valuation dispute into an issue of principle. In Stephanie's eyes, Audrey was acting as if Swann's Way were an investment property and trying to claim every last dollar. In Audrey's view, her richer sister was trying to get a bargain by sheer obstinacy. Each sister tended to see her own motives as good and pure, and the motives of her sibling as corrupt and selfish.

Stephanie, furthermore, fell into the trap of demonization. And for much of the mediation, I feared that she was stuck in this posture for reasons she did not consciously understand and which could hurt her in the long run.

This case poses a new question about the traps. What should you do when *you* are the one being demonized—that is, when *you* are willing to negotiate but the other side refuses? What can you do to help the other side avoid doing something crazy that will hurt everybody in-volved? As is often true in a negotiation, the other side's problem is your problem, too.

Audrey's behavior made all the difference, and she deserves a lot of credit. She, after all, had a great BATNA in terms of her material inter-ests. But she also understood that she had other interests that wouldn't be served by forcing the sale. So she worked hard to demonstrate that she really did understand what was at stake from Stephanie's perspec-tive. She also demonstrated, perhaps even more remarkably, an understanding of her own contribution, going back many years, to the deterioration of their relationship. And she apologized. I have seen this type of acknowledgment bring about similar improvements in other mediations. It is no miracle cure, but it helps.

Note, however, that Audrey did not sacrifice her own interests. This deal served her interests better than a judicially ordered sale, which *might* have yielded more money but would have left her family relationships in a shambles.

The lawyers also deserve a lot of credit. Lawyers are often demonized, sometimes appropriately, because they can inflame disputes. In this case, however, Stephanie's lawyer helped her see the reality of her situation. He helped her understand that by being inflexible she was creating a much greater risk that the entire property would be sold. Audrey's lawyer was also a big help. He helped Audrey focus on the long run and not worry excessively about capturing the last dollar. All three lawyers helped create the solution that was finally adopted.

I, too, deserve credit for encouraging the parties to have a difficult conversation. This was not an easy call. There is often a good reason for focusing solely on the substantive problem—sometimes a disputant simply won't do more. Moreover, once the immediate dispute is resolved the relationship may improve on its own. Lawyers are often very reluctant to have disputants meet with each other, except to discuss the material elements of a deal, because the risk of a blowup is so great. But in family disputes, I believe there is no separating the relationship issues from the substantive issues.

This case also demonstrates the advantages of mediation in family disputes, especially when the parties and the mediator forgo the use of private caucuses. Admittedly, this approach is much more demanding for everyone, including the mediator. But the turning point in this conflict was when Audrey demonstrated her understanding of Stephanie's feelings directly to her, face-to-face. As I discussed in an earlier chapter, decision-making relies on both logic and emotion. My cool analysis of Stephanie's interests would not have been enough to help her let go of her rage.

Lessons Learned

"Should you bargain with the Devil?" If I were pressed to provide a one-sentence answer to this question, it would be: "Not always, but more often than you feel like it."

"Not always" because I reject categorical claims that you should always be willing to negotiate. "More often than you feel like it" for two different sorts of reasons. First, the negative traps and strong emotions may make you feel like fighting when clearheaded analysis would demonstrate that you should negotiate. The second relates to morality. You may feel that choosing to negotiate would violate a moral principle you hold dear, or be inconsistent with your sense of self. In the very hardest cases, you may feel deeply torn between the "principled" choice and the "pragmatic" one. When one is forced to choose between the two, I lean heavily in favor of pragmatism, but I want to acknowledge how painful that choice can be.

Why is it painful? Because you may feel that justice requires more than just a pragmatic resolution—it requires condemnation. In your eyes, the enemy has committed an act for which they should be *punished*, not rewarded. Your honor and integrity demand that you resist. This impulse can be just as powerful in business and family disputes as in international conflicts—perhaps even more so.

I have empathy for this desire to punish those who have wronged us. I share it. When we are caught between the demands of principle and pragmatism, what we really need to ask ourselves is, To what extent should we look backward and to what extent should we focus on the future? There's often an inescapable tension between achieving justice for *past* wrongs and the need for resolution.[1] It is another aspect of the Faustian bargain. If you want to resolve the conflict and move forward, you may have to give the devil something you feel *he doesn't deserve.* This is a bitter pill to swallow.

Now that our journey is nearly over, I owe you some general advice. We've explored together eight high-stakes conflicts where real people had to decide what to do. We've seen the traps at work. We've applied my framework. Eight stories can't capture the full range of situations in which the Devil may make an appearance; nor can they illustrate all the factors that may be relevant in applying my framework.[2] But drawing on my framework and these stories, I can suggest four general guidelines.

1. SYSTEMATICALLY COMPARE THE EXPECTED COSTS AND BENEFITS.

When we *feel* like fighting, we may jump to the conclusion that negotiating a satisfactory resolution is simply out of the question. The best antidote to that kind of knee-jerk impulse and the negative traps is to go through Spock's five questions carefully.

- Who are the parties and what are their interests?

- What are each side's alternatives to negotiation?

- What are the costs of negotiation for each side?

- Are there any potential negotiated agreements that might better serve the interests of both sides than their best alternatives away from the table?

- If such a deal is reached, what is the likelihood that it will be implemented? (In other words, can you trust the other side to live up to it? If not, can it be enforced anyway?)

I am the first to acknowledge that asking these questions will not necessarily lead to a single right answer. This isn't a mechanical exercise, like balancing your checkbook. This is tedious, it's hard, and it requires you to make predictions about future behavior in a context of uncertainty. It isn't value-free. Judgments about values and priorities— what's "good" and "bad," what counts as a benefit and what counts as a cost—will of course be included in your analysis. For example, when evaluating costs, one might ask, "Will a deal here encourage more evil in the future?" Reasonable people assessing the same alternatives may reach different conclusions.

There are also deeper critiques of cost-benefit analysis, two of which I'll address briefly. They suggest that Spock's sort of analysis is not infallible and should not be your exclusive guide to decision-making.

The first is that it favors analytic over intuitive reasoning. As I said earlier, I believe that rationality encompasses *both* analysis and intuition. (Think of an experienced doctor making a medical diagnosis.) But with cost-benefit reasoning, the analytic side of the brain is in charge. Spock doesn't understand intuition, so he may discount or ignore valuable information.

I am not suggesting you ignore your emotions or your intuitions. Instead I'm advising you to probe them. They may be traps, or they may be valuable insights.[3] Ask yourself, What may have triggered this reaction? Is there evidence to support it? Evidence that would point in the opposite direction?

A second criticism of cost-benefit analysis is that it values pragmatic concerns over moral categorical principles. This goes to one of the most profound issues in philosophy: Is it proper to judge the morality of an act only on an assessment of its consequences? Cost-benefit analysis is consequentialist at its core—one makes choices among alternative courses of action solely by evaluating and comparing the consequences of those actions.[4] Some philosophers would argue that this is an incomplete and inadequate form of moral reasoning, and many ordinary people would intuitively agree. There are well-known philosophical puzzles that expose its limitations.[5] Consequentialism doesn't explicitly leave room for philosophical and religious traditions that emphasize categorical principles for human conduct.[6]

So why do I still insist, at least as a first step, that you assess costs and benefits? To prevent you from relying *solely* on intuition or unarticulated moral claims, and to be suspicious of those who do. Conduct the analysis first. If you are still conflicted, you must make the difficult decision whether your moral principle is so absolute that you cannot negotiate, even under these extenuating circumstances.[7]

2. GET ADVICE FROM OTHERS IN EVALUATING
THE ALTERNATIVES:
DON'T DO THE ANALYSIS ALONE.

Like Churchill, you should be willing to expose your reasoning to rigorous questioning by people you respect. When they ask how you reached your decision about whether to negotiate, "I just know it in my gut, I can't explain it" is not an adequate response.

We saw how Churchill initially floundered under fire from Halifax and Chamberlain. It's hard to reduce a powerful instinct to rational explanation. Churchill huffed and blustered, tossing out one half-baked rationale after another. But finally he managed to build a sound argument: Hitler had shown that he was an unreliable negotiating partner, there were substantial risks that negotiations would fail, and a failed negotiation would have a devastating effect on Churchill's ability to rally the British people for war. This logic persuaded everyone but Halifax.

In our own lives, particularly in conflicts that involve demonization, there are times when we all need a War Cabinet. Talk with at least one person who's less emotionally involved. It may be a lawyer. It may be a trusted friend. It may be a group of advisors whose perspectives are different from yours. It may be a mediator who can help all the disputants understand the trade-offs. The point is, let other people help you weed out the traps.

In assessing the costs and benefits of the alternatives, members of your team may disagree. They may be making different trade-offs and predictions, or different value judgments about what counts as a benefit and what counts as a cost. Exposing these differences is helpful, for it will better ensure a considered decision.

3. HAVE A PRESUMPTION IN FAVOR OF
NEGOTIATION, BUT MAKE IT REBUTTABLE.

Suppose your advisors disagree. Suppose that after thinking it through carefully, your mind is in equipoise—you think the costs and benefits of negotiating are roughly equal to those of not negotiating. In case of such a "tie," I would apply a presumption in favor of negotiation.

Now the obvious question is: Why tip the scales in *favor* of bargaining with the Devil? Why not be neutral, or even have a presumption *against* negotiation? After all, this is the Devil we're talking about!

The reason for the presumption is to provide an additional safeguard against the negative traps: Tribalism, Demonization, Dehumanization, Moralism, Zero-Sum Thinking, the Impulse to Fight or Flee, and the Call to Battle. As we've seen, these traps can distort clear thinking. And their effect can be subtle. You may think you're engaging in pure Spockian analysis, but you may be fooling yourself. The traps may already have sprung. You may be starting with your conclusion—having already intuitively decided what to do—and selectively looking for evidence to justify it. My presumption can mitigate this risk.

Apart from breaking ties, my presumption operates in a second way. It puts the burden of persuasion on those who don't want to negotiate. Think of your pugnacious brother-in-law Fred Kramer from the early chapters, who wants to sue Bikuta. My presumption would require him to stop spouting clichés and explain why a lawsuit makes practical sense. It also puts the burden of persuasion on that part of *yourself* that wants to fight; it will force you to justify that impulse.

Note that my presumption is not a flat rule. It is simply a guideline— and it is rebuttable. If you think the situation through and decide you are better off refusing to negotiate, the presumption is overcome. We've seen several examples in this book.[8]

4. WHEN DECIDING ON BEHALF OF OTHERS, DON'T ALLOW YOUR OWN MORAL INTUITIONS TO OVERRIDE A PRAGMATIC ASSESSMENT.

When it comes to making decisions that involve a perceived "devil," there is a difference between individuals acting solely on their own behalf and those acting in a representative capacity—deciding on behalf of others. For an individual, a decision to override a pragmatic assessment based on moral intuitions may be virtuous, courageous, and even wise—as long as that individual alone bears the risks of carrying on the fight. This is not true for a business executive deciding on behalf of a corporation, a union representative acting on behalf of a union, or a political leader acting on behalf of his nation. Perhaps not even for a parent acting on behalf of a child.

A person acting in a representative capacity not only must carefully and rationally assess the expected consequences of alternative courses of action, but also should be guided by that assessment. If cost-benefit assessment favors negotiation, I think it is improper for the representative to decide nonetheless to go to battle based on his personal moral intuitions.[9]

This last guideline brings to mind the challenges facing our national leaders in deciding whether to negotiate with terrorists or leaders of evil regimes.[10] In the Introduction, I said that my personal journey began shortly after 9/11, when President Bush had to decide whether to accept Mullah Omar's invitation to negotiate with the Taliban, which then controlled Afghanistan. I explained why, after applying my framework, I agreed with Bush's decision not to negotiate with the Taliban. But I must confess that I became increasingly troubled during the remainder of his two terms with his general approach to the questions at the heart of this book. Indeed, there is evidence that the president violated all four of my guidelines. Let me explain.

1. According to Scott McClellan, the former White House press secretary, President Bush disliked and avoided systematic cost-benefit analysis of different policy options, preferring to make decisions based on his instincts. "President Bush has always been an instinctive leader more than an intellectual leader. He is not one to delve deeply into all the possible policy options—including sitting around engaging in extended debate about them—before making a choice. Rather, he chooses based on his gut and his most deeply held convictions. Such was the case with Iraq."[11] In other words, Bush was not a Spockian.

2. President Bush, of course, had any number of foreign policy advisors. But there is evidence that his "War Cabinet" acquiesced without pushing him very hard to think through costs and benefits, opportunities and risks. According to McClellan, "[O]verall, Bush's foreign policy advisors played right into his thinking, doing little to question it or to cause him to pause long enough to fully consider the consequences before moving forward. And once Bush set a course of action, it was rarely questioned. . . . That was certainly the case with Iraq. Bush was ready to bring about regime change, and that in all

likelihood meant war. The question was not whether, but merely when and how." [12]

3. President Bush's administration did not apply a presumption in favor of negotiation. Indeed, its rhetoric suggests quite the opposite. As Vice President Dick Cheney declared shortly after September 11, "I have been charged by the president with making sure that none of the tyrannies of the world are negotiated with. We don't negotiate with evil; we defeat it." [13] This implies a strong presumption—if not an absolute rule—against negotiation with "evil" regimes.

4. In refusing to negotiate with certain regimes, President Bush may have allowed his moral intuitions to override more pragmatic choices that would have better served the interests of the American people. His rhetoric was highly moralistic,[14] often strident, and made frequent references to concepts of good and evil.[15]

Of course, rhetoric and decision-making are not the same thing. The president's decisions may well have been made on the basis of a pragmatic comparison of the costs and benefits of different alternatives, and then only justified publicly on the basis of morality. Without looking behind the veil, it is of course impossible to know. But a number of the administration's decisions and policies are consistent with the rhetoric. Bush did not negotiate with Saddam Hussein but instead invaded Iraq. His administration consistently refused to negotiate directly with Iran. And the administration refused to negotiate bilaterally with North Korea concerning its nuclear program. I am not going to explore here the wisdom of these particular decisions. Instead, my point is that President Bush may have relied on his own moral intuitions rather than a careful, pragmatic assessment of the alternatives.

President Barack Obama's strategy and rhetoric are much more consistent with my approach. He avoids public statements that demonize regimes or their leaders. The following example, regarding relations with Iran, is worth quoting at length because of its sophistication and good sense:

> As odious as I consider some of [Iranian] President Ahmadinejad's statements, as deep as the differences that exist between the United States and Iran on a range of core issues . . . the use of

tough, hard-headed diplomacy, diplomacy with no illusions about Iran and the nature of the differences between our two countries, is critical when it comes to pursuing a core set of our national security interests, specifically, making sure that we are not seeing a nuclear arms race in the Middle East triggered by Iran obtaining a nuclear weapon, making sure that Iran is not exporting terrorist activity.[16]

In other words, President Obama is not only *willing* to negotiate with evil, his rhetoric implies a presumption in *favor* of it.[17] He is focusing on American interests—avoiding nuclear proliferation and not exporting terrorism.

That I like his approach does not mean that in the years to come President Obama's decisions will necessarily be wise. As of this writing in 2009, President Obama is still in the first year of his presidency. It is too soon to tell how his approach will translate into practice.

President Obama faces many of the same foreign policy dilemmas that President Bush did. Should we negotiate with the Taliban, Hamas, or Hezbollah? Even though none of these groups currently controls a national government, they each have the capacity to harm the United States. It is easy to imagine possible deals that might serve U.S. interests but would expose a tension between pragmatism and principle.[18] Should we negotiate with Iran and North Korea, and if so, how? I am eager to see how President Obama manages the tensions we've explored in this book. As he and future presidents grapple with these questions, we as citizens will have to decide for ourselves whether their decisions are wise.

My goal in writing this book was not to offer easy answers. I end my journey with a deep sense of humility. Deciding whether to negotiate with the Devil poses profound questions and this book is hardly the last word. But my approach should allow you to think more clearly about how to navigate this terrain with integrity—and wisdom.

Acknowledgments

It took a village. While I am the sole author of this book and responsible for every word, many people contributed to its development.

My primary focus—both as a scholar and a professional—has been negotiation and dispute resolution. As a student of human conflict, I have always borrowed and adapted insights from academic disciplines outside the law in my work. During the past twenty years it has been my profound good fortune to have been part of interdisciplinary research projects that involved distinguished scholars with disciplinary training in other fields.

In 1988, Kenneth Arrow (an economist), Lee Ross (a social psychologist), Amos Tversky (a cognitive psychologist), Robert Wilson (a game theorist), and I co-founded the Stanford Center on Conflict and Negotiation. For five years, I served as SCCN's director, and the five of us explored together, from different disciplinary perspectives, why negotiations fail. Close readers of this book will find evidence of my enduring intellectual debt to these exceptional scholars. With Lee Ross, I've had a continuing conversation about the ideas I have developed here. Shortly before the book went to press, he graciously reviewed several chapters.

In 1993, I moved to Harvard Law School to become chair of the Program on Negotiation (PON), which has been my intellectual home ever since. At PON I was welcomed by three giants in the field of dispute resolution: Roger Fisher, Frank Sander, and Howard Raiffa. All have served as mentors and inspirations. Many PON colleagues directly contributed to the development of this book. Gabriella Blum deserves special thanks. Shortly after 9/11, when Gabby was a graduate student, I began thinking about the limits of negotiation. The work that Gabby and I did together served as a foundation for many of my core ideas.

Max Bazerman, Iris Bohnet, Joshua Greene, Susan Hackley, Jeswald Salacuse, James Sebenius, Guhan Subramanian, Larry Susskind, and Bill Ury read drafts of particular chapters and offered insightful comments. Alain Verbeke, my dear Belgian friend who as a Harvard visiting professor has spent time with PON, read the entire manuscript.

Others at Harvard helped me along the way. On two occasions, I presented portions of this book to the Law School's Faculty Workshop. A number of my Law School colleagues offered helpful suggestions: Richard Fallon and Detlev Vagts are owed special thanks. Two remarkable deans—Elena Kagan and Martha Minow—offered much encouragement and support while I pursued this project. Financial support from the Law School and the Harvard Negotiation Research Project allowed me to hire gifted student research assistants, who tracked down sources, wrote background memoranda, and checked citations. This book wouldn't exist without the help of Nahi Benor, Devin Cohen, Martin Gelter, Joel Knopf, Nicola Carah Menaldo, Alyssa Saunders, Eli Schlam, Ravi Shankar, Karen Tenenbaum, Michelle Wu, and Boris Yankilovich. Students in my Fall 2009 Law School seminar critically read the penultimate draft of this book and made any number of constructive suggestions. My faculty assistants (first Bonnie Rubrecht and now Caryn May) patiently prepared the manuscript, which went through many drafts.

I decided to write this book during the Spring of 2007, when, thanks to Claude Steele, I was a returning Fellow at the Center for Advanced Study in the Behavioral Sciences. While I was thinking through its themes and how I might shape a book that would reach an audience beyond the academy, many colleagues there helped me. Special thanks go to David Perkins, Erica Goode, and Jack Rakove. At the Center that Spring, I began a conversation about this book with my friend Robert Axelrod that continued through its gestation. Bob graciously read and commented on an early draft of nearly the entire book. Jeffrey Seul and Harvey Saferstein also provided useful comments on a number of chapters.

Many people helped me with specific chapters. My daughter Jennifer Mnookin, a law professor at UCLA, provided me with some useful ideas of how best to organize the Introduction. Richard Goldstone, who played a role in the transformation of South Africa, reviewed the Mandela chapter. Miki Breuer, who as a young man lived through the horror of the Nazi occupation of Budapest, and Professor Pnina Lahav graciously read and reviewed the chapter on Kasztner. A conversation with my son-in-law, Professor Joshua Dienstag, helped me untangle the various moral issues implicated in the Kasztner chapter. Gary Bass and William Forbath graciously read the international chapters. Three leading members of the Boston matrimonial bar—Matthew H. Feinberg, David Hoffman, and David H. Lee—reviewed the divorce chapter.

For the chapter concerning the IBM-Fujitsu dispute, in order to check my own recollections and impressions, I recontacted during the past two years a number of the lawyers and executives involved in the dispute. Many reviewed my draft for accuracy. Thanks go to Anthony Clapes, Joseph Davies, Dan Evangelista, Jonathan Greenberg, Michael Jacobs, Masanobu Katoh, William McFee, Rory Millson, Preston Moore, William Schwartz, Martin Senzel, and the late Michio Naruto.

For the chapter on the San Francisco Symphony, I am grateful to Brent Assink, Robert Couture, Joel Cutcher-Gershenfeld, Gary Friedman, Chris Gilbert, Tom Hemphill, Peter Pastreich, and Doug Stone. Gary also reviewed the chapters on family devils. Gary and I have taught mediation together for years, and much of what I know about the dynamics of conflict I have learned from him.

In my work with the Symphony and with IBM and Fujitsu, the disputants gave me permission to tell the story of their conflicts. Other parts of this book are based on real disputes where for reasons of privacy and confidentiality I have changed identifying characteristics of the people involved. I wish I could thank these people by name, as well as scores of others who have taught me so much over the years in my work as a mediator.

My agent, Jim Levine, understood from the beginning what I hoped to do with this book. He patiently helped me shape the proposal that led to the contract with Simon & Schuster. Jim also carefully read every chapter and offered outstanding editorial advice. My lead editor at Simon & Schuster was Alice Mayhew, who well deserves her reputation as one of the greats. This was my first book aimed at a general audience, and Alice's encouragement as she read draft chapters along the way meant a great deal to me. Roger Labrie, Karen Thompson, Gypsy da Silva and the entire Simon & Schuster team made the publication process a pleasure.

My greatest editorial debt is owed to Kathy Holub, who worked with me during the last eighteen months as an editor and writing coach. This book consists of stories as well as ideas. Kathy helped me create the narrative structure for these stories, using my historical research, recollections, and experiences. Whip in hand, she kept me on the schedule that I had set for myself. As I sent her chapters (and portions of chapters) Kathy went through my prose word by word, line by line and unfailingly improved my writing. She had the guts to challenge my ideas, she pushed me to clarify and simplify my language, and most of all she pushed me to say what I really thought. Each chapter went through an iterative editorial process that involved more redrafting than either of us cares to remember. Because of her help, this book is far livelier and far more personal than it would have been had I simply been left to my own devices.

Alas, much of the time to think and write came out of hours that would otherwise have been spent with my wife, Dale Mnookin, the love of my life, who has put up with me now for forty-six years. Were it not for this book, we both would have spent more time in California with our daughters, Jennifer and Allison, their husbands, Joshua and Cory, and our four glorious grandchildren to whom this book is dedicated. I suspect my golf game would have been better as well. But then again, I love my work and feel I'm just getting warmed up.

Robert Mnookin
Cambridge, MA
November 2009

Notes

INTRODUCTION

1. Omar asked the United States to provide proof that bin Laden was implicated in the attack and allow the Taliban to judge its adequacy. He also suggested that his regime might be willing to try bin Laden before an Islamic court in Afghanistan or elsewhere. Mohammed Omar, Address to Ulema at Kabul, Sept. 19, 2001 (transcript on file with author).

2. In his 2005 Tanner Lectures, Avishai Margalit has written about the "clash between peace and justice," and suggests that there are "indecent compromises" and "rotten" bargains. Avishai Margalit, "Indecent Compromise," in the Tanner Lectures on Human Values (delivered at Stanford University, May 2005). See http://www.tannerlectures.utah.edu/lectures/documents/Margalit_2006.pdf. For a more extended discussion published after this book was in press, see Avishai Margalit, *On Compromise and Rotten Compromises* (Princeton, N.J.: Princeton University Press, 2009).

3. With the benefit of hindsight, it might be easy to say that Bush made the right decision. The United States' quick military victory swept the Taliban from power and eliminated the large terrorist training camps operated by al-Qaeda in Afghanistan. On the other hand, a critic might point out that we failed to capture bin Laden or eliminate al-Qaeda, and the Taliban became a powerfully disruptive influence in Afghanistan and parts of neighboring Pakistan. But as I've said, after-the-fact analysis isn't what this book is about.

4. In the summer of 2000, an official of the State department under the Clinton administration testified before Congress that the United States had let the Taliban "know in no uncertain terms that we will hold [the Taliban government] responsible for any terrorist acts undertaken by Bin Laden." "The Taliban: Engagement or Confrontation?" Hearing Before the Committee on Foreign Relations, United States Senate 106-868, p. 6.

5. Choosing to negotiate would also have posed significant domestic political costs for the Bush administration, although my defense of Bush's decision did not attach significant weight to this factor. The American public was shocked and outraged by the attacks. Many Americans wanted retribution. Few were likely to support the kind of negotiation the Taliban had in mind: a conversation about which Islamic court might try bin Laden if he were found.

6. In 1998 bin Laden had published in an Arab newspaper in London a fatwa calling for jihad. It stated that "to kill Americans and their allies, both civil and military, is an individual duty of every Muslim who can, in any country where this is possible, until the Aqsa Mosque [in Jerusalem] and the Haram Mosque [in Mecca] are freed from their grip, and until their armies, shattered and broken-winged, depart from all the lands of Islam." Bernard Lewis, "Jihad vs. Crusade: A Historian's Guide to the New War," *Wall Street Journal,* September 27, 2001.

7. While based on a real case that I mediated, the names of the people, companies, and product have been changed to protect confidentiality.

1: AVOIDING COMMON TRAPS

1. See Hiroshi Ishida, "Class Structure and Status Hierarchies in Contemporary Japan," *European Sociological Review* 5(1) (1989).

2. In the Introduction I acknowledged that *evil* is a slippery term. That is why I have chosen explicitly to offer a definition. My definition exposes the outlook from which I make my own personal judgments.

   The notion of evil, and the definition of good and evil, raises difficult questions central to moral philosophy. Moral philosophy is an active academic discipline, with a rich history that extends back as far as ancient Greece. It is not my discipline. I am not even tempted to offer an elaborate academic defense of my definition. To do so would probably require a book in itself and would involve the exploration of metaphysical questions well beyond my knowledge or training. Nor do I think an elaborate defense of my definition is necessary to achieve my purposes in writing this book.

3. See Philip G. Zimbardo, *The Lucifer Effect: Understanding How Good People Turn Evil* (New York: Random House, 2007). The abuses and torture in Abu Ghraib prison confirm a critical finding of social psychologist Philip Zimbardo: situational influences such as social role and respect for figures of authority and peer pressure can lead otherwise decent people to dehumanize their enemy. Zimbardo also reviews the famous Milgram experiments.

4. Lee Ross, "The Intuitive Psychologist and His Shortcomings: Distortions in the Attribution Process," *Advances in Experimental Social Psychology* 10 (1977).

5. See Harold Kelley and John Michella, "Attribution Theory and Research," *Annual Review of Psychology* 31 (1980): 477–78.

6. J. St. B. T. Evans, "Dual-Processing Accounts of Reasoning, Judgment, and Social Cognition," *Annual Review of Psychology* 59 (2008); J. St. B. T. Evans, "In Two Minds: Dual-Process Accounts of Reasoning," *Trends in Cognitive Sciences* 7(10) (2003); P. C. Wason and J. St. B. T. Evans, "Dual Processes in Reasoning," *Cognition* 3(2) (1975).

7. Paul Slovic, " 'If I look at the mass, I will never act': Psychic Numbing and Genocide," *Judgment and Decision Making* 2(2) (2007): 79–85.

8. See Malcolm Gladwell, *Blink: The Power of Thinking Without Thinking* (Boston: Little, Brown, 2005).

9. One of the four dimensions of personality type measured by the popular Myers-Briggs Type Indicator (MBTI) is "Thinking versus Feeling," which corresponds roughly to one's tendency toward reasoned versus intuitive judgments. For a description of the MBTI and an evaluation of its effectiveness, see Marcia Carlyn,

"Assessment of Myers-Briggs Type Indicator," *Journal of Personality Assessment* 41(5) (1977): 461–73; Robert McCrae and Paul Costa, "Reinterpreting the Myers-Briggs Type Indicator from the Perspective of the 5-Factor Model of Personality," *Journal of Personality* 57(1) (1989): 17–40.

10. See Evans, "Dual-Processing Accounts of Reasoning, Judgment, and Social Cognition."

11. Steven Erlanger, "In Gaza, Hamas's Insults to Jews Complicate Peace," *New York Times,* April 1, 2008.

2: BARGAINING AND ITS ALTERNATIVES

1. "Sometimes we admire the rational actor for his discipline; sometimes we revile him for his ruthlessness." Don Herzog, *Cunning* (Princeton, N.J.: Princeton University Press, 2006), p. 11.

2. Patricia Pattison and Daniel Herron, "The Mountains Are High and the Emperor Is Far Away: Sanctity of Contract in China," *American Business Law Journal* 40 (2003): 491.

3. Jennifer Fan, "Comment: The Dilemma of China's Intellectual Property Piracy," *UCLA Journal of International Law & Foreign Affairs* 4 (1999).

4. Dan Rosen and Chikako Usui, "Japan: The Social Structure of Japanese Intellectual Property Law," *UCLA Pacific Basin Law Journal* 13 (1994).

5. John Owen Haley, "The Myth of the Reluctant Litigant," *Journal of Japanese Studies* 4(2) (1978): 359–90.

6. I also acknowledge that Spock's character has evolved since his television debut in 1966. He initially struggled between his emotional human side and his logical Vulcan side. But eventually logic won out, and it's this Spock I refer to throughout the book.

7. If Bikuta makes a deal with Pressure-Measure, your odds of winning on the jurisdictional issue will be vastly improved because the corporation will have done two deals in Silicon Valley.

8. In addition to assessing the value of each outcome, one should also assess the expected value, which is the value of the outcome (positive or negative) multiplied by the probability of its occurrence. If one is risk neutral, the expected value of the litigation, not the best outcome, will be the yardstick for litigation.

9. Even when you conclude that it is very unlikely there will be a negotiated resolution that is better than your BATNA, you may still conclude that you would find it beneficial to negotiate for diplomatic reasons: in order to appease constituencies or to prove that all "peaceful" methods have been exhausted prior to using a coercive approach.

10. Robert H. Mnookin, Scott R. Peppet, and Andrew S. Tulumello, *Beyond Winning: Negotiating to Create Value in Deals and Disputes* (Cambridge, Mass.: Harvard University Press, 2000), pp. 104–5.

11. Constance C. R. White, "Patterns," *New York Times,* October 29, 1996.

12. See "Postal Service Said to Beckon to Ex-Air Controllers," *New York Times,* August 20, 1982.

3: RECOGNITION, LEGITIMACY, AND MORALITY

1. For a philosophical argument that the morality of an action depends on its consistency with a person's sense of self or identity, see Christine Korsgaard, *Self-Constitution: Agency, Identity, and Integrity* (New York: Oxford University Press, 2009).

2. See J. D. Greene et al., "The Neural Bases of Cognitive Conflict and Control in Moral Judgment," *Neuron* 44(2) (2004); J. D. Greene et al., "An FMRI Investigation of Emotional Engagement in Moral Judgment," *Science* 293 (2001).

3. Jonathan Haidt, " 'Dialogue Between My Head and Heart': Affective Influences on Moral Judgment," *Psychology Inquiry* 13(1) (2002): 54–56, citing R. B. Zajonc, "Feeling and Thinking: Preferences Need No Inferences," *American Psychologist* 35(2) (1980): 151–75. Haidt, like Hume, is of the view that the foundation of morals is in sentiment or feelings. Other psychologists like Forgas believe that there is an interaction between the head and the heart, and that depending on the context and the stakes, feelings can infuse moral judgments to a greater or lesser extent.

4. My discussion of Sharansky relies primarily on his memoir, and the quotations in the remainder of this chapter, unless otherwise indicated, are from that source. Natan Sharansky, *Fear No Evil: The Classic Memoir of One Man's Triumph Over a Police State*, trans. Stefani Hoffman (New York: Public Affairs, 1998).

5. Regents of the University of California, "Science, Faith and Survival, with Natan Sharansky," *Conversations with History*, Institute of International Studies (Berkeley, Calif.: UCTV, October 25, 2004).

6. At the December 1, 1952, Politburo session, Stalin announced, "Every Jewish nationalist is a potential agent of the American intelligence. Jewish nationalists think that their nation was saved by the USA. . . . Among doctors, there are many Jewish nationalists." The next month, shortly before Stalin's death, TASS announced the "unmasking" of an alleged terrorist group of doctor-prisoners, a majority of whom were members of the Jewish Zionist organization. These doctors were accused of being spies and plotting to murder the Soviet leadership. Initially thirty-seven were arrested, but soon there were hundreds of arrests. Many Soviet Jews were dismissed from their jobs, some were arrested and sent to the Gulag, and a few were executed. There were show trials and there was much anti-Semitic propaganda. Wikipedia contributors, "Stalin's antisemitism," *Wikipedia, The Free Encyclopedia*, http://en.wikipedia.org/w/index.php?title=Stalin%27s _antisemitism&oldid=323284710 (accessed November 1, 2009).

7. Regents of the University of California, "Science, Faith and Survival, with Natan Sharansky."

8. I briefly interviewed Sharansky during his visit to Harvard in the fall of 2008 and he confirmed that his decision to refuse to negotiate was made intuitively, not analytically.

9. Sharansky's decision could, of course, be expected to impose extra burdens on his family, especially his wife, Avital. But Sharansky knew that Avital shared his passionate commitment to the Soviet Zionist cause.

4: RUDOLF KASZTNER

1. Rudolf is the German and English equivalent of Rezsö. Kasztner's last name is sometimes spelled Kastner, which is the Anglicized spelling. After World War II, when Kasztner moved to Israel, he used his Jewish first name, Israel—the name given to Jacob after he defeated the Angel of Darkness in battle.

2. There were seventeen thousand Jews in Cluj in 1941. See Yechiam Weitz, *The Man Who Was Murdered Twice: The Life, Trial, and Death of Dr. Israel Kasztner* (Jerusalem: Keter, 1995) (Hebrew original), p. 13.

3. During his lifetime, the town was repeatedly transferred back and forth between Romania and Hungary. Today it is part of Romania and is called Cluj-Napoca.

4. Anna Porter, *Kasztner's Train: The True Story of an Unknown Hero of the Holocaust* (New York: Walker, 2007), pp. 15–17.

5. Ibid., p. 15.

6. Ibid.

7. Ladislaus Lob, *Dealing with Satan: Rezsö Kasztner's Daring Rescue Mission* (London: Jonathan Cape, 2008), p. 73. Fulop Freudiger, a member of the Budapest Jewish Council, later characterized Kasztner as "idealistic, competent, a man of vision," yet at the same time "dictatorial in nature, jealous of the successes of others and terribly lax vis-à-vis deadlines and compliance with agreements." See Szabolcs Szita, *Trading in Lives? Operations of the Jewish Relief and Rescue Committee in Budapest, 1944–1945* (Budapest: Central European University Press, 2005), p. 147.

8. Porter, *Kasztner's Train*, p. 15.

9. Ibid. Porter also writes of Kasztner: "Much to the consternation of his readers in [Cluj], he interviewed members of the [Romanian fascist] Iron Guard, including dedicated anti-Semites who were keen to share their ideas. Even then, he thought it was wise to know the enemy."

10. Ibid., p. 22.

11. Ibid., p. 16.

12. Nazi Germany earlier supported Hungary in 1938 and 1940 in re-annexing Hungarian territory lost after World War I. Hungary entered a formal military alliance with Nazi Germany in November 1940, and its army joined with that of Germany in attacking the Soviet Union in 1941.

13. Ladislaus Lob, *Dealing with Satan*, p. 52.

14. Ibid. The full Hebrew name of the organization was "Vaadat Ezra Ve'Hazalah."

15. Ibid., p. 53.

16. Ibid., pp. 37–38.

17. Ibid., p. 37.

18. Ibid., pp. 36–37.

19. Yehuda Bauer, *Jews for Sale? Nazi-Jewish Negotiations, 1933–1945* (New Haven, Conn.: Yale University Press, 1994), p. 156.

20. Lob, *Dealing with Satan*, pp. 33–34.

21. Through a source in the German army's intelligence unit, Kasztner and Brand learned about the Nazis' plan to invade and occupy Hungary several days before the invasion. See Alex Weissberg, *Desperate Mission—Joel Brand's Story* (New York: Criterion, 1958), pp. 62–66.

22. As it turned out, however, the bribe probably played little to no role. In the sum-

mer of 1942, the Reich stopped the transports from Slovakia under intense pressure from the Slovak government, which needed the Jews to keep its economy running. Lob, *Dealing with Satan*, p. 56. Also see generally Yehuda Bauer, *Jews for Sale?* pp. 91–101.

23. This grand scheme was sometimes called the "Europa Plan," in which the coordinated forces of "World Jewry" would pay the Nazis $2 million to stop deportations of Jews in all of occupied Europe, with the exception of Poland. For a detailed scholarly discussion of these negotiations, see Bauer, *Jews for Sale?* pp. 79–90.

24. Just days before, Stern had played poker with Admiral Horthy, the regent of Hungary, whom he viewed as a personal friend. Porter, *Kasztner's Train*, p. 88.

25. Porter, *Kasztner's Train*, p. 98, relying on Ernö Szilágyi and Attila Novák, Ismeretlen Memoár a Magyar Vészkorszakról (Budapest: Akadémiai, 2005).

26. Immediately after the war, in 1946, Kasztner wrote a report on behalf of the Relief and Rescue Committee of his wartime activities. Fifteen years later it was published in German as *Der Kasztner-Bericht über Eichmanns Menschenhandel in Ungarn* (Munich: Kinder, 1961). I have an unpublished English translation entitled "The Report of the Jewish Rescue Committee from Budapest 1942–1945" (on file with author). The "Kasztner Bericht" is summarized in English in Szita, *Trading in Lives*, pp. 204–7, where it is described as an "authoritative" description of Kasztner's remarkable activities, notwithstanding his "proclivity for exaggeration and self-vindicating analysis"; "partiality for conclusions that justify his own actions"; and "propensity for self-aggrandizement."

In his postwar report Kasztner wrote that Stern found it difficult to quickly adapt to the new situation caused by the Nazi occupation and that his tragedy, and that of the Hungarian Jewry, was that the German occupation disconnected him from the aristocratic-conservative element of the Hungarian leading class and he was thus left isolated. See Kasztner, "The Report of the Jewish Rescue Committee," pp. 38–39. Joel Brand noted that Stern, who had completely assimilated himself with his Hungarian compatriots, later regretted not having supported the Zionists from "the very beginning." See Weissberg, *Desperate Mission*, p. 77. See also Porter, *Kasztner's Train*, pp. 98–99.

27. Porter, *Kasztner's Train*, p. 107.

28. Weissberg, *Desperate Mission*, p. 69; Kasztner, "The Report of the Jewish Rescue Committee," p. 84.

29. Weissberg, *Desperate Mission*, p. 73.

30. Kasztner noted later that "one had to play for time," bearing in mind that the Allies' invasion was approaching. Kasztner, "The Report of the Jewish Rescue Committee," p. 85.

31. The Jewish Agency was inured to Nazi extortions and had previously bribed German officials in Poland, Bulgaria, and France. Porter, *Kasztner's Train*, p. 143.

32. In addition to or in lieu of negotiating with the Nazis, it was of course possible to try to negotiate with the Hungarian authorities to see that no Jews were deported. In fact, throughout the German occupation various Jewish leaders tried to persuade the Hungarian government to take steps to protect Hungarian Jews.

33. Weissberg, *Desperate Mission*, p. 73. See also Porter, *Kasztner's Train*, pp. 108–9; and Kasztner, "The Report of the Jewish Rescue Committee," p. 86.

34. Porter, *Kasztner's Train*, p. 108.

35. Weissberg, *Desperate Mission*, p. 75.

36. "These privileges were not always respected by German or Hungarian gangs, but on the whole they enabled Kasztner and his associates to do their undercover work without constant threat of arrest and deportation." Lob, *Dealing with Satan*, p. 58. Other sources suggest that the Relief and Rescue Committee leaders got these immunity passes at the next meeting, which took place a week later. Weissberg, *Desperate Mission*, p. 82.

37. Ibid., p. 75.

38. Ibid.

39. Ibid., p. 76.

40. This train is more commonly referred to as the "Bergen-Belsen Train," named after the German concentration camp that was its initial stop.

41. Weissberg, *Desperate Mission*, p. 77; Kasztner, "The Report of the Jewish Rescue Committee," p. 89.

42. Randolph L. Braham, "What Did They Know and When?" in *The Holocaust as Historical Experience*, eds. Yehuda Bauer and Nathan Rotenstreich (New York: Holmes & Meier, 1981), p. 117, quoting the following Kasztner testimony: "Toward the end of April 1944, the German military agents informed me that they had finally decided on the total deportation of Hungarian Jews. . . . An agreement was made between Hungary and Slovakia for the transfer of deportation trains from Hungary to Auschwitz. I also received information from Auschwitz that they were preparing there to receive the Hungarian Jews."

43. Porter, *Kasztner's Train*, pp. 116–17.

44. Ibid.

45. When Kasztner complained to Hansi Brand, Joel Brand's wife, that Wisliceny was breaking his word, she responded that an SS officer couldn't be expected to keep his word. Porter, *Kasztner's Train*, p. 117.

46. Porter, *Kasztner's Train*, p. 120, relying also on Brand's testimony at the Eichmann trial.

47. Weissberg, *Desperate Mission*, pp. 93–94.

48. Kasztner, "The Report of the Jewish Rescue Committee," p. 113.

49. Szita, *Trading in Lives?* p. 65.

50. Kasztner, "The Report of the Jewish Rescue Committee," pp. 102–3.

51. Apparently, a few days later Wisliceny explicitly confirmed to Kasztner that all the Jews in Hungary would be deported and this plan could not be stopped. See Braham, "What Did They Know and When?" p. 117, quoting the following Kasztner testimony: "I was allowed . . . to go to [Cluj] and contact . . . Wisliceny. This was approximately May 3, 1944. . . . A few days later I visited Wisliceny at his home in Budapest. He told me that it had finally been decided—total deportation."

52. Porter, *Kasztner's Train*, p. 117.

53. This is an excerpt from Kasztner's July 12 letter to Joseph Schwartz of the American Joint Distribution Committee cited at Porter, *Kasztner's Train*, p. 219.

54. On April 7, 1944, two prisoners escaped from Auschwitz and arrived in Bratislava, Slovakia. They dictated to a Polish Jewish activist there (Oskar Krasniansky) a detailed firsthand account of the extermination camp process at Auschwitz. The report was labeled "The Auschwitz Protocols." It provided an eyewitness-authenticated "account of what was happening in Auschwitz." Yehuda Bauer, *Rethinking the Holocaust* (New Haven, Conn.: Yale University Press, 2001),

p. 229. The document was promptly translated into German and English. Porter, *Kasztner's Train*, pp. 126–29. The record is unclear as to the exact date when the Protocols were forwarded and became known to Kasztner and other Hungarian Jewish leaders. By some accounts Kasztner read the German text during a visit to Slovakia in April as the translations were being prepared and requested that a Hungarian version be prepared as well. Braham, "What Did They Know and When?" pp. 118–21. The text of the Auschwitz Protocols is found in Rudolf Vrba, *I Escaped from Auschwitz* (London: Robson, 2002).

55. The issue of what Kasztner told the leaders in Cluj was at the core of the court trial more than a decade later in Israel. As Braham suggests, this visit "has emerged as a major focus of the controversies surrounding the behavior of Jewish leaders." Braham, "What Did They Know and When?" p. 17. Some of Kasztner's friends later denied being warned in their trial testimony. Hansi Brand said Kasztner did warn others. She also claimed that the leaders were well aware of the threat.

56. When the matter was discussed with the full Relief and Rescue Committee's leadership, Kasztner argued that he or his father-in-law should be the one to go to Istanbul. But Brand insisted on going, and the other committee members supported Brand. Weissberg, *Desperate Mission*, p. 95.

57. See Kasztner's description of the meeting, Kasztner, "The Report of the Jewish Rescue Committee," pp. 116–18.

58. Porter, *Kasztner's Train*, p. 146.

59. Kasztner, "The Report of the Jewish Rescue Committee," p. 118.

60. Lob, *Dealing with Satan*, pp. 80–90.

61. Kasztner later learned, through Wisliceny, that Eichmann had never wanted the deal to succeed. It had been Heinrich Himmler's idea, so Eichmann had been forced to give it lip service, but he sabotaged it as much as he could. Himmler was the Reichsführer SS and was in charge of all police and security forces, including the Gestapo. The quote in the text is from Lob, *Dealing with Satan*, pp. 80–81.

62. Theresienstadt was a Nazi camp in what is now the Czech Republic. According to Nazi propaganda, it was a model ghetto for laborers and a retirement "resort" for elderly Jews. In reality, it was both a forced labor camp where many Jews died of disease and malnutrition, and a collection point for Jews destined for Auschwitz and other extermination camps.

63. Kasztner, "The Report of the Jewish Rescue Committee," pp. 126–29; Lob, *Dealing with Satan*, p. 82.

64. Lob, *Dealing with Satan*, pp. 82–83.

65. Eichmann also insisted that the exodus would have to look like a deportation so that Hungarian officials would not realize what was happening. Lob, *Dealing with Satan*, p. 86. Therefore, the train would have to go to a detention camp in Germany before reaching a neutral country.

66. Porter, *Kasztner's Train*, p. 148, citing interview with Hansi Brand.

67. Adolf Eichmann, "To Sum It All Up I Regret Nothing," Part 2, *Life*, December 5, 1960. Eichmann had a clear incentive to depict himself and Kasztner as equals, but his comparison of Kasztner with Gestapo officers is absurd. Interestingly, Hannah Arendt, who covered the Eichmann trial for *The New Yorker*, went out of her way to accuse Kasztner and other Jewish leaders of complicity in the destruction of their own communities. See Hannah Arendt, *Eichmann in Jerusa-*

lem: A Report on the Banality of Evil (New York: Penguin, 1994), pp. 117–18. I disagree with Arendt's merciless accusation.

68. Kasztner, "The Report of the Jewish Rescue Committee," p. 165; Lob, *Dealing with Satan,* p. 89, translates the phrase as "merciless task."

69. Lob, *Dealing with Satan,* pp. 83–84. See also Kasztner, "The Report of the Jewish Rescue Committee," p. 132.

70. Bauer, *Jews for Sale?* p. 156.

71. In late August, some three hundred people from the Kasztner train reached the Swiss border, as a Nazi goodwill gesture. On that day Becher, two other Nazi representatives, and Kasztner met on the Swiss border with Saly Mayer, the representative of "World Jewry" who was in contact with the American government. On December 6, after Kasztner had persuaded Saly Mayer to wire Becher in Germany 5 million Swiss Francs that was available, the remaining Jews on Kasztner's train (about 1,400) arrived in Switzerland. Becher wired back that if the balance of the 15 million Swiss Francs that had been discussed was promptly paid, Budapest's Jews would be protected. Bauer, *Jews for Sale?* pp. 220–29.

72. Hitler had issued an unambiguous order that the concentration camps should be emptied of all living inmates before the Allied armies were able to liberate them. Mark Mazower, *Hitler's Empire: How the Nazis Ruled Europe* (New York: Penguin, 2008), pp. 406–7.

73. For a general assessment see Szita, *Trading in Lives,* pp. 219–23, describing the "human trade" practice as "complex and contradictory," "involving ruthless, fanatical executioners as well as desperate men and women fighting to save the lives of others." Szita concludes that, notwithstanding any criticism that may be directed toward Kasztner and other Committee members, their "self-sacrificing efforts had a great part in helping a large number of Hungarian Jewish children and occasionally entire families."

74. A much higher proportion of the Jews in Budapest survived the war for a number of reasons. First, and most important, the Nazis directed their attention to Budapest last. Second, it was much easier to hide in Budapest. Third, the Jews were not put into a single ghetto but instead ordered into "Jewish Houses," which were scattered among many neighborhoods. Finally, by the end of the summer, the Hungarian government, under international pressure, required the Nazis to suspend deportations.

75. Lob, *Dealing with Satan,* p. 223.

76. In the summer of 1945, one of Kasztner's old rivals from Budapest claimed that Kasztner had stolen money earmarked for rescue efforts and had missed opportunities to save Jews by focusing solely on the train. The next year, at the World Zionist Congress in Basel, Switzerland, rumors suggested that Kasztner had collaborated with the Nazis and enriched himself in the process. Lob, *Dealing with Satan,* pp. 225–26.

77. Ibid.

78. Kasztner, "The Report of the Jewish Rescue Committee."

79. Lob, *Dealing with Satan,* pp. 225–26.

80. Ibid., pp. 242–43. He was the director of public relations to several cabinet-level ministries.

81. Ibid., p. 244.

82. Ibid., p. 245.

83. Hansi Brand and some in Kasztner's family opposed his participation in the lawsuit. See Porter, *Kasztner's Train*, p. 327; Weitz, *The Man Who Was Murdered Twice*, p. 104. The attorney general, Haim Cohen, later reported that the decision to sue was not up to Kasztner. Cohen, influenced by David Ben-Gurion, thought that no one should be allowed to accuse a senior government official of collaboration with the Nazis "without there being a response." Tom Segev, *The Seventh Million: The Israelis and the Holocaust*, trans. Haim Waltzman (New York: Henry Holt, 2000), pp. 263–64. Elizabeth Kasztner later claimed that Kasztner would not have taken action had not the Israeli attorney general given him this ultimatum.

84. Segev, *The Seventh Million*, p. 282.

85. The judge upheld the libel claim only with respect to Grunwald's suggestion that Kasztner had financially profited from his dealings with the Nazis.

86. There is no English text of the entire opinion, which is, of course, in Hebrew. Any quotes are the translations from Lob, *Dealing with Satan*.

87. For an analysis of the contractual framing and its possible implications see Leora Bilsky, "Judging Evil in the Trial of Kasztner," *Law & History Review* 19 (2001): 117.

88. The judge, some years later, expressed regret about using this expression, but the harm had been done. I will explore later the notion that as the quid pro quo for accepting Eichmann's "gift" of rescuing some sixteen hundred of Hungarian elite, Kasztner had implicitly promised Eichmann that he would not alert the masses of Hungarian Jews about their fate.

89. Notably, most of the participants in the trial—the judge, the prosecutor, the defense attorney, and the defendant—had spent the war in Palestine. Professor David Luban alluded to the idea of Kasztner as the "old European" as opposed to the "New Israeli," stating: "Kasztner and the Judenräte had exhibited the typical sniveling mentality of the exile, the very opposite of the tough and combative mentality of Israelis." David Luban, "A Man Lost in the Gray Zone," *Law & History Review* 19 (2001): 172.

90. Lob, *Dealing with Satan*, p. 243.

91. Porter, *Kasztner's Train*, pp. 330–31.

92. One Israeli scholar argues that at the time the Jewish Agency was aware of Kasztner's efforts on Becher's behalf and may have even supported his actions. She claims that Kasztner might have been acting on behalf of the state to promote secret interests. Consequently, she suggests the possibility that Kasztner might have lied in court to protect the government of Israel. See Shoshana Barri (Ishoni), "The Question of Kasztner's Testimonies on Behalf of Nazi War Criminals," *Journal of Israeli History* 18(2) (1997): 139. I find credible the possibility that Israeli officials knew, long before the trial, that Kasztner had helped Becher, but I don't find persuasive that Kasztner's motive for lying on the stand was to protect others. I believe his primary motive was to preserve his own reputation. Barri offers no direct evidence that anyone asked Kasztner to lie.

93. Kasztner's standing was also damaged by testimony at the trial suggesting that he had failed to save, and perhaps even betrayed, three young Jewish parachutists who arrived in Hungary in the late spring of 1944 to organize Jewish resistance against the Nazis. Hanna Szenes, poet, was one of the trio. She was captured, tortured, and killed by the Nazis but never gave the Nazis any information. Her mother testified at the trial that after her daughter's capture, she went to ask for

Kasztner's help in securing her release but that he refused to see her. There was also testimony at the trial that Kasztner persuaded the other two parachutists to give themselves up when they were being hidden in the same location as those who were to later be allowed to go on the Kasztner train. At the time of the trial, and to this day, all three parachutists are celebrated in Israel and are part of the heroic narrative of the "fighting Jews." For an account of this affair, see Porter, *Kasztner's Train*, pp. 185–89, 338. For the impact at the trial, see Lob, *Dealing with Satan*, pp. 247–51.

94. Lob, *Dealing with Satan*, p. 264.

95. Ibid., p. 264; Weitz, *The Man Who Was Murdered Twice*, pp. 273–74.

96. Criminal Appeal 232/55 *Attorney General v. Grunwald*, PD 12, 2017. Technically of course, Kasztner was not a party to the proceeding and the reversal of the district court's ruling meant that Grunwald was convicted of libel. All five justices, however, agreed that historical claims of this sort should never have been tried by a court of law but should instead have been evaluated by a commission of inquiry. For an outstanding discussion of this case and of Chief Justice Agranat's role and reasoning, see Pnina Lahav, *Judgment in Jerusalem: Chief Justice Shimon Agranat and the Zionist Century* (Berkeley: University of California Press, 1997).

97. Primo Levi, *The Drowned and the Saved*, trans. Raymond Rosenthal (New York: Summit, 1988).

98. Kasztner's postwar report does not include specific information on what he did on May 3. Professor Weitz cites Kasztner's court testimony, in which Kasztner claimed he had issued a warning, telling Jewish leaders that because of the danger of deportation to extermination camps, anyone who was able to should flee and hide. Weitz, *The Man Who Was Murdered Twice*, p. 210, cites the court transcript from August 19, 1954. I believe the date given by Weitz for the testimony is incorrect, as Kasztner did not testify on that date. However, in his testimony on September 16, 1954, he did indeed claim that he had issued a warning in Cluj.

99. One of these witnesses was a Cluj local leader who met with Kasztner on May 3. The District Court refers to Yechiel Shmueli, David Rosner, Eliezer Rosental, and others who testified that had they been warned, they would have sought alternatives, including fleeing to Romania or going into hiding.

100. This is perhaps explained because appellate courts are supposed to defer to trial court findings based on the credibility of witnesses unless there is plain error. In his concurring opinion, Deputy Chief Justice Cheshin of the Supreme Court did not accept the District Court's holding that Kasztner gave no warning because he found the facts ambiguous. He went on to argue that even if Kasztner knew about the risks and failed to warn, this did not prove that his motive was to help the Nazis. Criminal Appeal 232/55 *Attorney General v. Grunwald*, PD 12, 2017 at 2292.

101. David Luban, "A Man Lost in the Gray Zone," *Law & History Review* 19 (2001): 171, suggests that "everyone" knew the ultimate plan was extermination, but there was no place to hide or to which to escape. See also Bauer, *Jews for Sale?* pp. 150–61.

102. Eichmann proceeded with such speed that by early summer of 1944, there were no Jews left in the provinces to warn.

103. See Daniel Kahneman and Amos Tversky, "Conflict Resolution: A Cognitive Per-

spective," in *Barriers to Conflict Resolution*, ed. Kenneth Arrow et al. (New York: Norton, 1995), p. 45, suggesting that in framing things under conditions of uncertainty, people will try to avoid losses.

104. R. F. Moore, "Caring for identified versus statistical lives: An evolutionary view of medical distributive justice," *Ethology and Sociobiology* 17(6) (1996): 379–401.

105. On "optimistic overconfidence," see Kahneman and Tversky, "Conflict Resolution: A Cognitive Perspective," pp. 46–50.

106. Mark Mazower, *Hitler's Empire*, p. 406.

107. The evidence is somewhat ambiguous. Some commentators suggest Kasztner never thought it was really possible. Others conclude that Kasztner came to believe his own arguments to Eichmann and others that World Jewry could really pull it off.

108. Porter, *Kasztner's Train*, p. 170.

109. Bauer, *Jews for Sale?* p. 196. (Emphasis added.)

110. Szita, *Trading in Lives*, pp. 87–88. "An examination of the history of the four months following the German occupation of Hungary suggests that *the tactics* of the occupational apparatus, of Eichmann and his staff, *actually worked out.*" (Emphasis in original.)

111. After Kasztner's death, when Kasztner couldn't contradict him, Eichmann claimed that Kasztner had made such a deal.

112. When the train left Hungary, some called it a "Noah's Ark" because it included a remarkable mixture of Jews. There were Zionists and anti-Zionists; Orthodox and secular Jews; Hungarians as well as Poles and Slovaks; children and elderly people; rich and poor; city sophisticates and rural farmers. In addition, "[s]ome people who did not belong to any of these categories jumped on the train or sneaked onto it and became part of the ark." Bauer, *Jews for Sale?* p. 199. See also Lob, *Dealing with Satan*, pp. 269–71.

113. Kasztner might have had another motive to include members of his own family— to persuade others, many of whom thought this was a Nazi trick, that he, Kasztner, sincerely believed the train offered a better chance of survival than remaining in Cluj.

114. William Styron, *Sophie's Choice* (New York: Vintage, 1979). Sophie committed suicide because she could not live with the psychological burden of having made this choice. Kasztner afterward wrote about the awful burden of having to make such decisions.

115. The philosopher Claudia Card writes that "knowingly to enlist others . . . in the betrayal, oppression or murder of those they love is as diabolical an evil as I can imagine." Claudia Card, *The Atrocity Paradigm: A Theory of Evil* (New York: Oxford University Press, 2002), p. 216.

116. Sissela Bok, *Lying: Moral Choice in Public and Private Life* (New York: Vintage, 1999). Bok acknowledges that it would be appropriate for someone hiding a Jew in the basement to lie to the Nazi who knocks on the door and asks whether there are any Jews inside.

117. See Porter, *Kasztner's Train*, Lob, *Dealing with Satan*, and Luban, "A Man Lost in the Gray Zone." Gaylen Ross's fascinating documentary film, *Killing Kasztner* (2008), which received widespread publicity in Israel, is very sympathetic. Yad Vashem, the Israeli museum devoted to memorializing the Holocaust, only recently began exhibiting a display on Kasztner. In July 2007, the museum invited—

for the first time—train survivors to participate in a ceremony marking their rescue.

118. Professor Ladislaus Lob, one of those rescued on Kasztner's train, has written: "Kasztner was ambitious, overbearing and devious, but also . . . had a sharp mind, remarkable diplomatic skills, enormous courage, the ability to make difficult decisions and the determination to perform his task without regard to his own comfort and safety. Many of his traits may seem less than admirable in our relatively normal circumstances, but in those chaotic times they were precisely what was needed to carry on a relationship with the Germans." Lob, *Dealing with Satan*, p. 75.

5: WINSTON CHURCHILL

1. Hugh Dalton, *The Fateful Years: Memoirs, 1939–1945* (London: Muller, 1957), p. 335, quoted in John Lukacs's outstanding history, *Five Days in London: May 1940* (New Haven, Conn.: Yale University Press, 1999), p. 4.

2. Churchill's exact words were not officially recorded but are reported in Hugh Dalton's diary entry in slightly different language, see *The Second World War Diary of Hugh Dalton, 1940–1945*, Benjamin Pimlott, ed. (London: Cape in association with the London School of Economics and Political Science, 1986), pp. 27–29. The language quoted in my text is found in the margin of that entry. Lukacs suggests that it is possible that Churchill himself offered the correction to Dalton later. See John Lukacs, *Five Days*, pp. 4–5.

3. See, e.g., Martin Gilbert, *Winston S. Churchill: Finest Hour, 1939–1941* (Boston: Houghton Mifflin Harcourt, 1983). Note that a few revisionist historians dissent. See John Charmley, "Rethinking Negotiating With Hitler," *New York Times*, November 25, 2000.

4. Neither Churchill nor Halifax would later acknowledge their debate in the War Cabinet. Churchill wrote: "[T]he supreme question of whether we should fight on alone never found a place upon the War Cabinet agenda." Winston S. Churchill and John Keegan, *The Second World War, Volume II: Their Finest Hour* (New York: Houghton Mifflin, 1986), p. 157. In 1942, Halifax falsely claimed to someone involved in writing the official history of the war that there had never been consideration of the "idea" of "asking Mussolini to mediate peace terms between [Great Britain] and Germany." Andrew Roberts, *The Holy Fox: The Life of Lord Halifax* (London: Weidenfeld & Nicolson, 1991), p. 227. It was as if they both wanted to reinforce the heroic narrative that they had never seriously considered negotiation.

5. Only in January 1990 were the secret minutes of the War Cabinet released. See CAB 65 War Cabinet Conclusions and Confidential Annexes, Public Records Office, London.

6. See generally Lukacs, *Five Days*. See also G. N. Esnouf, "British War Aims and Attitudes Towards Negotiated Peace, September 1939 to July 1940," Ph.D. dissertation, King's College, London, 1988.

7. They were members of the War Cabinet because Churchill's new "National Government" included Labor.

8. Paul Kennedy, *Strategy and Diplomacy 1870–1945* (New York: HarperCollins, 1983), p. 16.

9. Roberts, *The Holy Fox*, p. 49.
10. Ibid.
11. Lukacs, *Five Days*, p. 50.
12. German war documents indicate that Hitler would have immediately backed down if there had been resistance. At the time, France and Belgium had wanted to call Hitler's bluff by responding with force and asked Britain to join them. But Prime Minister Stanley Baldwin refused to do anything concrete. With tears in his eyes, he argued that Great Britain lacked both the public will and the military resources to enforce her treaty guarantees. Roberts, *The Holy Fox*, pp. 58–60.
13. Roberts, *The Holy Fox*, p. 58.
14. Ibid., pp. 70–71.
15. Ibid., p. 75.
16. Martin Gilbert, *Churchill: A Life* (New York: Henry Holt, 1992), p. 599.
17. Winston S. Churchill, *Blood, Sweat, and Tears* (New York: G. P. Putnam's Sons, 1941), p. 66.
18. Its remaining territory was carved up among Germany, Hungary, Poland, and a newly independent Slovakia.
19. The summer before the outbreak of the war, Halifax delivered a speech that clearly warned Germany that Britain "was neither bluffing, nor willing to put up with further blackmail." He said in the speech, "The threat of military force is holding the world to ransom, and our immediate task is to resist aggression. I would emphasize that tonight with all the strength at my command, so that nobody may misunderstand it ... Hitler has said that deeds, not words, are necessary. That is also our view." In response, Churchill toasted Halifax and said that "in principle there are no differences between us. We have all, from various standpoints, accepted the policy which you and the Prime Minister have now proclaimed. If differences remain, they will only be upon emphasis and method, upon timing and degree." Roberts, *The Holy Fox*, p. 164.
20. Churchill was both ambivalent and skeptical about the wisdom of this treaty. On the one hand, he applauded a change in British policy that suggested Britain would resist further German aggression. On the other hand, he doubted that, without the Soviet Union's help, the British and the French could prevent German military moves in Eastern Europe. See Roy Jenkins, *Churchill: A Biography* (New York: Farrar, Straus & Giroux, 2002), pp. 543–44.
21. In a secret appendix to the Molotov-Ribbentrop Pact, the German government and the Soviet Union had agreed to divide Eastern Europe. For further reading on the Molotov-Ribbentrop Pact, see I. J. Vizulis, *The Molotov-Ribbentrop Pact of 1939: The Baltic Case* (Westport, Conn.: Greenwood, 1990). Germany would later declare war on the Soviet Union and occupy the remainder of Poland.
22. Roy Jenkins, *Churchill: A Biography*, p. 22.
23. Ibid., p. 10.
24. Ibid., p. 22.
25. Ibid., p. 116.
26. Kay Halle, *Irrepressible Churchill* (New York: Facts on File, 1985), pp. 52–53, cited at http://quotationsbook.com/quote/44624/.
27. Roberts, *The Holy Fox*, p. 187.
28. Jenkins, *Churchill*, p. 464.

29. Roberts, *The Holy Fox,* p. 187.

30. Ibid., p. 209.

31. "[O]n 23 May the majority of the British people did not know how catastrophic the situation of their army was." Lukacs, *Five Days,* p. 38.

32. Hugh Dalton on Churchill, quoted at ibid., p. 4.

33. Roberts, *The Holy Fox,* pp. 4, 6. Halifax inherited his father's title and became a viscount in 1935 (p. 47). Halifax had earlier become the Baron of Irwin in 1926. Ibid., (p. 18).

34. Ibid., p. 6.

35. Ibid., p. 9.

36. Ibid., p. 303.

37. Ibid.

38. Ibid., quoting Halifax Diary, September 22, 1940.

39. Roberts, *The Holy Fox,* p. 212.

40. Jenkins, *Churchill,* pp. 599–600.

41. Lukacs, *Five Days,* p. 94. In Halifax's report of the meeting, Germany's name is not explicitly mentioned. But the contemporaneous report of the Italian ambassador was much more direct about the need for German involvement in such discussions. As Bastianini wrote, Halifax had been told that, given the "special German-Italian relationship," any problems between the Italians and the British could only be considered within the "greater and more enduring framework of a just and enduring European settlement."

42. King Leopold II of Belgium surrendered to the Germans two days later, on May 28.

43. Lukacs, *Five Days,* p. 106.

44. War Cabinet Conclusions and Confidential Annexes, CAB. 65/13 WM 139.

45. War Cabinet Conclusions and Confidential Annexes, CAB. 65/13 WM 140.

46. Lukacs, *Five Days,* p. 113.

47. War Cabinet Conclusions and Confidential Annexes, CAB. 65/13 WM 140.

48. Ibid.; Lukacs, *Five Days,* p. 114.

49. Roberts, *The Holy Fox,* p. 214.

50. War Cabinet Conclusions and Confidential Annexes, CAB. 65/13 WM 140.

51. Lukacs, *Five Days,* p. 115.

52. Roberts, *The Holy Fox,* p. 217.

53. War Cabinet Conclusions and Confidential Annexes, CAB. 65/13 WM 140.

54. Ibid.

55. Esnouf, "British War Aims," p. 223, quoted in Lukacs, *Five Days,* p. 119, n. 16. Roberts makes the same point in *The Holy Fox,* p. 95.

56. John Lukacs, *The Duel: The Eighty-Day Struggle Between Churchill and Hitler* (New Haven, Conn.: Yale University Press, 2001), p. 97.

57. Ian Kershaw, *Ten Decisions That Changed the World: 1940–41* (New York: Penguin, 2007), p. 38.

58. Lukacs, *Five Days,* pp. 137–39.

59. Lukacs, *Five Days,* p. 143. Since becoming prime minister, Churchill had written to Roosevelt several times pleading for help. But "during the dramatic last days of May there was no direct communication between Churchill and Roosevelt." Lukacs, *Five Days,* p. 145.

60. Lukacs, *Five Days,* p. 145, quoting Cadogan Diaries, p. 290.

61. War Cabinet Conclusions and Confidential Annexes, CAB. 65/13 WM 142.
62. Ibid.
63. Ibid. The quotations that follow are drawn from this source. See also Lukacs, *Five Days*, pp. 147–51. Note that Churchill's rebuttal at this point speaks only to the goal of keeping Italy out of the war. It didn't address Halifax's other purpose: to use discussions with Italy as an opportunity to explore the possibility of ending the war altogether.
64. Chamberlain indicated that he thought it likely that Hitler might make a definite offer to France, and if France indicated that it could only consider Hitler's terms with the consent of Great Britain, he thought Hitler would say, "I am here, let them send a delegate to Paris." Would Great Britain send a delegate to discuss the terms offered to France? Churchill thought the answer "could only be no," and it appears that a majority of the War Cabinet agreed.
65. Roberts, *The Holy Fox*, pp. 220–21, quoting Halifax Diary, May 27, 1940 (emphasis added).
66. Roberts, *The Holy Fox*, p. 222; compare Lukacs, *Five Days*, p. 153. There was a third War Cabinet later that evening that began at 10 P.M. and dealt with the consequences of the Belgian surrender.
67. Roberts, *The Holy Fox*, p. 222.
68. Gilbert, *Winston S. Churchill*, p. 417.
69. War Cabinet Conclusions and Confidential Annexes, CAB. 65/13 WM 145.
70. As indicated above, there is no transcript of Churchill's precise words. This quote is from Hugh Dalton's contemporary diary entry, which reported what Churchill had said. See Lukacs, *Five Days*, p. 5.
71. The passage, which was of course written much later, continues, "There was no doubt that had I at this juncture faltered at all in leading the nation, I should have been hurled out of office. I was sure that every minister was ready to be killed quite soon, and have all his family and possessions destroyed, rather than give in. . . . It fell to me in those coming days and months to express their sentiments on suitable occasions. This I was able to do because they were mine also. There was a white glow, overpowering, sublime, which ran through our island from end to end." Churchill and Keegan, *The Second World War: Their Finest Hour*, pp. 99–100.
72. War Cabinet Conclusions and Confidential Annexes, CAB. 65/13 WM 145.
73. Roberts, *The Holy Fox*, p. 221.
74. But, as Churchill would wryly note, wars are not won by evacuations.
75. Hugh Sebag-Montefiore, *Dunkirk: Fight to the Last Man* (Cambridge, Mass.: Harvard University Press, 2006), p. 541.
76. Lukacs, *Five Days*, p. 128.

6: NELSON MANDELA

This chapter draws extensively on Nelson Mandela's autobiography, and all quotations not otherwise footnoted with a reference come from this source. Nelson Mandela, *Long Walk to Freedom* (New York: Little, Brown, 1995).

1. On January 31, 1985, President P. W. Botha publicly announced to the South African Parliament that he was offering Mandela his freedom if he "unconditionally rejected violence as a political instrument." Nelson Mandela, *Long Walk*

to Freedom (New York: Little, Brown, 1996), p. 521. President Botha thought that this was a "brilliant solution" to the international pressure the government was receiving for keeping Mandela behind bars. He thought that "if Mandela refused, then the whole world would understand why the South African government could not release him." Allister Sparks, *Tomorrow Is Another Country* (Chicago: University of Chicago Press, 1996), p. 49.

2. Sisulu had been Tambo's predecessor as secretary-general of the ANC.

3. Tom Lodge, *Mandela: A Critical Life* (Oxford, U.K.: Oxford University Press, 2006), p. 2; Mandela, *Long Walk to Freedom*, p. 5.

4. His teacher gave him the name "Nelson"; his given name, *Rolihlahla*, means "pulling the branch of a tree," or "troublemaker." Mandela, *Long Walk to Freedom*, p. 3.

5. In 1949, Sisulu would eventually become the secretary-general of the ANC, Oliver Tambo's predecessor as the head of the organization. Like Mandela, Sisulu would pay a high price for his fight against apartheid. He too would be arrested many times, eventually convicted of treason, and serve more than twenty-three years in South Africa's prisons, many of them alongside Mandela.

6. Lodge, *Mandela*, p. 28.

7. The relationship with Great Britain was loosened in the early 1930s when the Union of South Africa became an independent country that was a member of the British Commonwealth with its own monarch. In 1961, South Africa became a republic.

8. In all but the Cape Province no blacks and few "coloreds" had the franchise. The Cape Province required property ownership as the qualification for voting, but even there blacks were barred from being members of Parliament. Graham Leach, *South Africa: No Easy Path to Peace* (London: Routledge & Kegan Paul, 1986), p. 41.

9. Ibid. For a limited period of time, in the Cape Province the tiny minority of black property owners were allowed to vote.

10. In 1952, when Mandela was thirty-four, he became one of four deputy presidents of the ANC.

11. Patti Waldmeir, *Anatomy of a Miracle: The End of Apartheid and the Birth of the New South Africa* (New York: W. W. Norton & Company, Inc., 1997), p. 17. See also Daniel Lieberfeld, *Talking with the Enemy: Negotiation and Threat Perception in South Africa* (Westport, Conn.: Praeger, 1999).

12. Allister Sparks, *Tomorrow Is Another Country*, p. 23.

13. In 1985, 859 people died in political violence. See Adrian Guelke, *Rethinking the Rise and Fall of Apartheid* (New York: Palgrave Macmillan, 2005), p. 148.

14. Sparks, *Tomorrow Is Another Country*, p. 26.

15. Ibid.

16. Ibid., p. 27.

17. Waldmeir, *Anatomy of a Miracle*, p. 100.

18. Sparks, *Tomorrow Is Another Country*, p. 35.

19. Ibid.

20. Ibid., p. 36.

21. Waldmeir, *Anatomy of a Miracle*, p. 100.

22. The responses of his prison mates were varied. Walter Sisulu thought the talks were a good idea but "wished that the government initiated talks with us rather

than us initiating talks with them." Two wholeheartedly supported the idea, one of them exclaiming, "What have you been waiting for? We should have started this years ago." The fourth colleague summarily rejected the talks on the grounds that they would be perceived as capitulation. But he told Mandela, he would not stand in his way. Mandela, *Long Walk to Freedom*, p. 535.

23. Waldmeir, *Anatomy of a Miracle*, p. 101.
24. Ibid., p. 102.
25. Sparks, *Tomorrow Is Another Country*, p. 61.
26. Waldmeir, *Anatomy of a Miracle*, p. 104.
27. Ibid., p. 106.
28. Ibid., p. 109.
29. When the ANC leaders returned to their homes and began speaking publicly on behalf of the ANC, they were not arrested, signifying an effective lift of the ban on the ANC. De Klerk also began to erase the social restrictions of apartheid, opening up beaches, public parks, theaters, and other public facilities to citizens regardless of color. Mandela, *Long Walk to Freedom*, p. 553.
30. Lodge, *Mandela*, p. 166.
31. Ibid., pp. 169–82.
32. On March 2, 1990, the ANC leadership re-affirmed that Mandela was Deputy President, and the next year he would become its President. Lodge, *Mandela: A Critical Life*, p. 260. Tambo would die in 1993.
33. Sparks, *Tomorrow Is Another Country*, p. 128.
34. Belgium is an example of a "democratic" country that does not have simple majority rule. The French-speaking minority have veto rights over some actions that might be taken by the Flemish speaking majority. For a full discussion of "consociational democracies," see Arend Lijphart, *Democracy in Plural Societies: A Comparative Exploration* (New Haven: Yale University Press, 1977).
35. Sparks, *Tomorrow Is Another Country*, p. 127.
36. In his memoir, de Klerk emphasizes the importance of the fall of the Berlin Wall in the timing of his decisions relating to Mandela's release. See F. W. de Klerk, *The Last Trek: A New Beginning* (London: Macmillan, 2000).
37. While Mandela was in prison, the Zulu community had become split between the ANC and Inkatha. After Mandela's triumphal release from prison, the Inkatha chief, Mangosuthu Buthelezi, became angry when some of his younger followers switched allegiance to the ANC. This led to violence between the two groups. See Mandela, *Long Walk to Freedom*, pp. 575–76.
38. Mandela investigated and was told that Operation Vula, as it was called, was a "moribund operation." Mandela, *Long Walk to Freedom*, p. 585.
39. Sparks, *Tomorrow Is Another Country*, p. 123.
40. The MK had not carried out any violent acts against the government since 1989 and had simply maintained its recruiting activities. Lodge, *Mandela*, p. 172.
41. Sparks, *Tomorrow Is Another Country*, p. 124.
42. Lodge, *Mandela: A Critical Life*, p. 172.
43. In July 1990, the ANC was tipped off that an attack was planned against ANC members in the Sebokeng Township. The ANC notified the police and asked them to prevent armed Inkatha from entering the township the following day. Instead, the police escorted the armed Inkatha into the township by bus. When the rally ended, the Inkatha engaged in a grisly attack, killing more than thirty

people in broad daylight. Mandela was incensed and demanded an explanation from de Klerk. De Klerk did not respond or even acknowledge publicly that the event had occurred. Mandela was outraged. "[I]n any other nation," he told de Klerk, "where there was a tragedy of this magnitude, when more than thirty people were slain, the head of state would make some statement of condolence." De Klerk never did so and never provided an explanation. Mandela, *Long Walk to Freedom*, pp. 587–88.

44. Mandela, *Long Walk to Freedom*, p. 589. This explosive disclosure by the *Guardian*, based on top secret documents, caused a public uproar. De Klerk appointed Judge Richard Goldstone to head a new commission to investigate the facts, and Goldstone turned up even more damaging evidence of state involvement in fomenting black-on-black violence.

45. In April 1991, Mandela apologized to the ANC leadership for having previously vouched for de Klerk, saying that he had "misjudged" the president's character. But as furious as he was, Mandela avoided demonizing de Klerk in public. He understood that such tactics, however temporarily satisfying, might result in a complete breakdown of the negotiations. Sparks, *Tomorrow Is Another Country*, p. 139.

46. In a positive development, the ANC and the National Party did manage to agree on a process for negotiation. There were some nine parties involved by this time, and the task of negotiating a new constitution promised to be Herculean. Therefore, they agreed that the process would consist of two stages. First, an "all-party congress," composed of delegates from all of South Africa's political parties, would negotiate the basic ground rules for electing a constituent assembly and the terms of an "interim constitution," some terms of which would not be subject to change. In the second stage, a constituent assembly would be elected and form an interim government, which would then negotiate a permanent constitution, pursuant to the basic rules of the first congress. Sparks, p. 129. Stage One, christened the Convention for a Democratic South Africa (CODESA), progressed in fits and starts for about six months and ended in deadlock over the core political issue: majority rule versus "group rights."

47. Even moves that might have promoted progress across the table ended up hampering it. In March 1992, de Klerk unexpectedly called for a snap referendum, asking white voters whether they supported his decision to enter into negotiations to create a new South Africa. Although the referendum question did not specify what kind of political structure the new nation would have, de Klerk promised to ensure that the white minority would be protected from the black majority through some sort of constitutional provision. It was a promise that he would not be able to keep, but he won by a two-thirds majority, with more than 80 percent of all whites participating in the referendum. Such solid backing behind the table did not help move the negotiations forward, however. Instead, de Klerk became more inflexible. He had a strong mandate for negotiations, but not for a concession on a key issue: one man, one vote. See Sparks, *Tomorrow Is Another Country*, p. 134.

48. The strike immobilized the industrial centers and powerfully showcased the party's strength in numbers. Sparks, *Tomorrow Is Another Country*, p. 140.

49. On June 17, an Inkatha posse raided the township of Boitapong. Mandela, *Long Walk to Freedom*, p. 603.

50. Martin Meredith, *Nelson Mandela: A Biography* (New York: St. Martin's, 1998), p. 495.
51. Sparks, *Tomorrow Is Another Country*, p. 151.
52. Lodge, *Mandela*, p. 179.
53. Sparks, *Tomorrow Is Another Country*, p. 152.
54. Waldmeir, *Anatomy of a Miracle*, p. 231.
55. Martin Meredith, *Nelson Mandela: A Biography* (New York: St. Martin's, 1998), p. 493.
56. See Robert D. Putnam, "Diplomacy and Domestic Politics: The Logic of Two-Level Games," *International Organization* 42:3 (1988): 427.
57. Waldmeir, *Anatomy of a Miracle*, p. 252.
58. Ibid., p. 232.
59. My colleague Roger Fisher first coined this phrase. See Roger Fisher and William Ury, *Getting to Yes* (New York: Penguin, 1991).
60. http://nobelprize.org/nobel_prizes/peace/laureates/1993/press.html
61. "Nelson Mandela & F. W. De Klerk," *Time*, January 3, 1994.
62. Waldmeir, *Anatomy of a Miracle*, p. 231.

7: GIANT SOFTWARE WARS

1. Some of the IBM programs that IBM claimed Fujitsu copied were not, strictly speaking, operating system software programs but "middleware" programs that are closely related and worked in conjunction with the operating system. For various definitions of the terms, see p. 149.
2. Dan Evangelista, telephone interview by author, March 4, 2009.
3. Confidential interview by author, January 30, 2009.
4. Robert Mnookin, "Spreading the Word about Spreadsheet Software," *California Lawyer* 4(4) (1984):5. The first spreadsheet software program, VisiCalc, was introduced in 1979 and ran on the Apple II computer. Lotus 1-2-3 and Excel were successor spreadsheet programs that were aimed at the IBM PC market.
5. Takuma Yamamoto, *Fujitsu: What Mankind Can Dream, Technology Can Achieve*, trans. Dick Belcher (Tokyo: Toyo Keizai, 1992), p. 18.
6. This is usually done by the agreement of the parties or of the arbitrators they have designated. If they can't agree, the forum institution—here, the American Arbitration Association—is empowered to select.
7. For anecdotes about IBM's willingness to bear staggering legal costs, see James B. Stewart, *The Partners: Inside America's Most Powerful Law Firms* (New York: Simon & Schuster, 1983), pp. 97–98.
8. The government surrendered in 1982. As the Justice Department explained, the computer world was changing and the government no longer believed it could prove that IBM was an illegal monopoly.
9. Stewart, *The Partners*, p. 54.
10. "A Celebration of the Life of Thomas D. Barr," Cravath, Swaine & Moore LLP, April 4, 2008, p. 1.
11. Under the American Arbitration Association rules at the time, a three-person panel could decide to proceed in one of two ways. One way, which I call the "partisan model," allowed each party-appointed arbitrator to meet privately for discussions with the party (and counsel) that appointed him. Under this model, the

party-appointed arbitrator is simply an advocate for that party and tries to win over the chairman. This process might eventually lead to a coalition between the chair and one of the party arbitrators, or the chair might end up mediating a compromise between the two arbitrator-advocates, but either way the chair essentially decides the outcome. There is very little room for mutual problem-solving or value creation. The other approach is for all three arbitrators to act as independent neutrals and impartially evaluate the case on the merits. See Opinion of Panel at n.3, *International Business Machines Corporation v. Fujitsu, Ltd.,* Case No. 13T-117-0636-85, September 15, 1987 (American Arbitration Association Commercial Arbitration Tribunal) (Unpublished Opinion). Under contemporary AAA rules the "partisan model" applies only if the "parties have specifically agreed . . . that the party appointed arbitrators are to be non-neutral." See AAA Commercial Arbitration Rules, Rule R-12 (b). See http://www.adr.org/sp.asp?id=22440.

12. At that time there were seven other major computer companies, but people would joke about "IBM and the Seven Dwarfs." Fujitsu was in the data processing business but not even a dwarf. See Paul E. Ceruzzi, *A History of Modern Computing* (Cambridge, Mass.: MIT Press, 2003), p. 248; Emerson Pugh, *Building IBM: Shaping an Industry and Its Technology* (Cambridge, Mass.: MIT Press, 1995), p. 296.

13. Two developments in the 1960s led to the realization that IBM's mainframe operating system software was of enormous economic importance. IBM's dominance in the mainframe world was substantially enhanced after the introduction in 1964 of a new family of computers—the IBM System\360—all of which used the *same* operating system. This allowed a business customer to start small and build up without a total reinvestment in software applications and peripherals each time the computer needed to be replaced by a newer and more powerful one. For example, a customer's application program designed to run on a particular central processing unit (such as an IBM model 30) could, for the first time, run equally well on a more powerful processor (such as an IBM model 40).

   The second change was IBM's decision to "unbundle" some of its software from its hardware and impose a separate charge or license fee. This was done for some programs in 1969 and for operating system software in the late 1970s. Although IBM had invested hundreds of millions of dollars in software development, the IBM software had previously been included as part of the hardware package. Unbundling allowed IBM to better match software development costs with revenues. Over time, it also made it abundantly apparent to IBM executives that software licensing fees were a potential gold mine.

14. MITI assigned to Fujitsu the task of developing large and small computers and to Hitachi those that were midsized.

15. This was the strategy of Gene Amdahl, who left IBM to start his own company to develop IBM compatible mainframe computers. Fujitsu would later acquire Amdahl. See Yamamoto, *Fujitsu,* pp. 86–89.

16. Programmers write software in "source code," which another programmer can read and understand, but which a computer cannot read until it is "compiled" or translated into "object code" consisting only of 0's and 1's—bits and bytes. Programmers cannot "read" or modify object code unless it is somehow "decompiled" or reverse-engineered back into source code. In the early 1980s, IBM

generally stopped distributing source code of new programs or significant additions.

17. Yamamoto, *Fujitsu*, p. 52. He also suggested that the desire to "add our own unique 'Fujitsu functions' [created] a veritable mountain of difficulties for our engineers to scale." Ibid., p. 89.

18. Ibid.

19. Eventually Hitachi pleaded guilty in California to criminal espionage relating to hardware. An individual defendant confessed that he had been copying software as well as hardware. For a discussion of the Hitachi criminal case, see James B. Stewart, *The Prosecutors* (New York: Simon & Schuster, 1987), pp. 87–133. Hitachi later settled IBM's civil claim and signed a settlement agreement that was very similar in form to the one that Fujitsu signed with IBM in 1983. (See pp. 151–53 for a description of the IBM-Fujitsu Settlement Agreement.) I surmise from this that Hitachi also had improperly made use of IBM system software in its efforts to be compatible.

20. Stewart, *The Prosecutors*, p. 111.

21. Ibid., pp. 121–22. Because the quote was anonymous, we will never know whether it was accurate. My point is that it was published and highly inflammatory.

22. *Apple Computer v. Franklin Computer Corporation*, 714 F.2d 1240 (3rd Circuit 1983), was the first appellate court decision holding that United States copyright law applied to operating system software. This decision was issued on August 30, 1983, about two months after the parties' Settlement Agreement. Moreover, as discussed later, this holding would not necessarily be recognized in Japan.

23. To turn up the heat on Fujitsu, IBM also went to MITI, the Japanese government agency, and suggested that Fujitsu might be encouraged to agree to adequate corrective measures to avoid another embarrassing public disclosure.

24. A one-page "Protective Procedure" prohibited Fujitsu software programmers from having access to IBM materials, with certain exceptions that were not adequately defined. For example, there were exceptions for "research" and "high-level architectural design" but those terms were not defined.

25. In order to write an application program that works with a particular operating system, a programmer must have certain interface information about the operating system so that the application can obtain services from the operating system. This interface information defines the form in which requests and deliveries for services must be made.

26. Joseph W. S. Davis, counsel for IBM Japan, interview by author, February 24, 2009. Davis later wrote an insightful book about conflict resolution in Japan. See Joseph W. S. Davis, *Dispute Resolution In Japan* (Den Haag: Kluwer Law International, 1996).

27. Philip J. McConnaughay, formerly a Morrison & Foerster partner who now is dean of Penn State Dickinson Law School, makes this point in his interesting article, "The Risks and Virtues of Lawlessness: A 'Second Look' at International Commercial Arbitration," *Northwestern University Law Review* 453 (1998–99): 458. Phil cites and quotes my now-deceased Harvard Law colleague Professor Arthur T. von Mehren, who some fifty years ago, after a visit to Japan, wrote that "a potential source of misunderstanding in international transactions [with the Japanese is that] the parties may hold different conceptions of 'contract' even though both understand clearly the terms of agreement." Arthur T. von

Mehren, "Some Reflections on Japanese Law," *Harvard Law Review* (1958): 1494 n. 25.

28. Under the 1983 Settlement Agreement, a "Final Report" detailing alleged violations was a prerequisite to initiating arbitration.

29. Masanobu Katoh, interview by author, January 26, 2009.

30. I recognized Nicholas Katzenbach, sitting at the back of the room. By that time IBM's general counsel, he was a revered figure to many in my generation. When I was an undergraduate in the 1960s, Katzenbach played an instrumental role in one of the most famous incidents of the civil rights era. As deputy attorney general in the Kennedy administration, he confronted Governor George Wallace, who was trying to prevent two black students from enrolling at the University of Alabama. This incident was later dubbed the "Stand in the Schoolhouse Door." Katzenbach also served as attorney general and deputy secretary of state in the Johnson administration.

31. Fujitsu maintained that all of its uses of IBM material were permissible because they: (1) dated to uncopyrighted versions of IBM programs and were therefore in the public domain; (2) did not constitute protected expression under the copyright laws of the United States or Japan; (3) constituted use of "External Information" within the intent of the 1983 Settlement Agreement and Externals Agreement; (4) were subject to immunity under the 1983 Settlement Agreement; (5) constituted research or high level architectural design authorized under the 1983 Settlement Protective Procedure; or (6) constituted standard programming techniques of a sort that were not subject to copyright. In other words, Fujitsu was arguing, "Between the DP list and the Externals Agreement, we can do anything we want."

32. The panel granted Fujitsu's motion for summary judgment on two issues. We ruled that the provision of the Settlement Agreement relating to triple license fees was unenforceable because it was punitive. We also rejected IBM's claim that, because Fujitsu had violated the Settlement Agreement, IBM had no further obligations to Fujitsu under the Externals Agreement.

33. Deciding each individual claim would set a very narrow precedent that would be of little help in evaluating what "substantial similarity" meant in the context of another set of facts.

34. For further reading on a model of mediation that favors the parties meeting together, see Gary Friedman and Jack Himmelstein, *Challenging Conflict: Mediation Through Understanding* (Chicago: ABA, 2008). I followed this approach as a mediator in chapter 10 herein.

35. Macdonald, a Canadian, might have thought of himself as a North American rather than an American.

36. Over the years, Fujitsu would develop deep ties to Morrison & Foerster. In appreciation of Raven's contribution to the company, Mr. Yamamoto, Fujitsu's president, would plant a tree in the special plot at Fujitsu's Namazu facility to honor him. Today, Mr. Katoh is president of Fujitsu America.

37. What would happen if Jones and Mnookin disagreed? We never did, but the Agreement for Further Arbitration provided for the appointment of a third arbitrator if necessary.

38. Jack and I decided rather easily that Fujitsu was entitled to try to maintain application program compatibility—that is, that application programs written for

IBM's operating system should be able to run on top of Fujitsu's operating system. A much more complicated and demanding form of compatibility involved "multi-vendor interoperability." This mouthful related to the degree to which an operating system allowed customers to connect IBM and Fujitsu mainframe hardware. We decided to give Fujitsu only a limited opportunity in this regard.

39. The process was an interesting one. When the technical team got stuck, we would offer informal "guidance," or sometimes issue a ruling. Occasionally our rulings on these highly technical matters would make little sense to either side. The technical team would negotiate a revision we would gladly accept. Indeed, I suspect the *in terrorem* effect of having the two of us rule on highly technical questions created a powerful incentive for the technical teams to agree.

40. We ended up promulgating literally hundreds of pages of rules and procedures in order to ensure that Fujitsu programmers writing the Fujitsu programs had access only to the information on the Survey Sheets, not to restricted IBM programming materials. As noted earlier, the 1983 Agreement contained a "protective procedure" that was about a page long and totally inadequate. It allowed Fujitsu programmers to have access to IBM materials only for "research and high level design," but those terms were left undefined.

41. We announced that IBM would be entitled to the lump-sum equivalent of the present value of its expected semiannual license fees under the 1983 Settlement Agreement for all of Fujitsu's DPs, old and new. In making this calculation, we would take into account the fact that the programs would not remain on the DP list forever; Fujitsu had the ability over time to rewrite them to remove the taint. So there were lots of variables. What interest rate should be used to compute present value? How many Fujitsu customers would use each DP? How tainted was each DP and how long would it take Fujitsu to clean it up?

42. We required each party to submit the testimony of its experts in written, affidavit form. The only live testimony was the cross-examination of these experts.

43. As part of each party's submissions we asked for spreadsheets into which we could plug our own estimates for each variable. Jack and I were comforted by the fact that when we plugged our estimates into each side's spreadsheet, the IBM spreadsheet produced a *lower* dollar amount than the Fujitsu spreadsheet. Moreover, the two spreadsheets produced numbers in the same neighborhood. Then we created our own spreadsheet and plugged in our estimates for different variables.

44. I later learned that on each side some of the lawyers had a pool going. The social scientist in me would love to know what those estimates were.

45. Michael Miller, "Fujitsu Payments to IBM to End Software Fight to Be $833.2 Million," *Wall Street Journal*, November 30, 1988.

46. Many years later, after the Secured Facility Regime was up and running, Barr offhandedly told me that he had never thought it likely that an arbitration panel would force Fujitsu to remove the offending software from its customers.

47. When the Externals Agreement was signed in 1983, I suspect that no one within IBM thought it might be used to create the sort of affirmative obligation that the panel ultimately (and in my mind reasonably) imposed. Even if Spock had pointed out this risk, I suspect such a reading of the Externals Agreement was so far from IBM's original intention that nothing similar to the Instructions— with its standards and rules—could have been negotiated. IBM might well have

rejected a Secured Facility solution for strategic reasons as well. I could imagine someone within IBM thinking, "While the regime provides some safeguards for us, it lets Fujitsu know in advance what it can use. Why should we give them that kind of certainty and security? Aren't we better off tormenting them after the fact?"

48. The idea of "reactive devaluation" has been developed by Lee Ross and his students. See Ross, "Reactive Devaluation and Negotiation in Conflict Resolution," in *Barriers to Conflict Resolution*, ed. Kenneth Arrow et al. (New York: Norton, 1995).

49. For a general discussion of the issue, with a comparison of practices in various countries, see Gabrielle Kaufmann-Kohler, "When Arbitrators Facilitate Settlement: Towards a Transnational Standard," *Arbitration International* 25(2) (2009): 187–206.

8: DISHARMONY IN THE SYMPHONY

1. My mistake. I later learned that bassists come in all sizes.

2. Although my initial meeting was with five musicians, the Players' Committee also included a sixth member.

3. It is exceedingly difficult to remove a tenured musician. To do so, the director of the orchestra must persuade a majority of a "non-renewal committee"— consisting only of musicians—that the player in question has demonstrated a "[m]aterial deficiency in musical performance and material failure to perform at the artistic level of the Orchestra."

4. The contract provides for a minimum salary with a pay scale that is based on seniority. In 1997, the first step on the scale provided for a minimum annual salary of $80,340, with an increase for each year of service. In addition, individual musicians can negotiate for pay above the scale. Although this is not discussed publicly, about half the musicians earn overscale.

5. String players work in pairs, sharing a single folio of sheet music that sits on a stand. The inside player (the one farther from the audience) turns the pages.

6. Established in 1909, the Wiffenpoofs are the oldest collegiate a cappella group in the country. Each spring, scores of Yale college juniors compete for fourteen spots with the all-male group.

7. Peter Pastreich, "Response: Orchestra Planners and Players: Harmony or Dissonance?" *Symphony Magazine* (1981): Vol. 32, no. 6, p. 62.

8. Among other things, the musicians' flyers said, "Through our music, we are bringing you food for your soul. We worry that when we return to our families, we may not be able to provide food for our table."

9. In late November, just before the contract expired, the orchestra voted not to strike while they were still on tour—out of respect, they said, for MTT and "our audiences." Pastreich privately harrumphed at that. He thought, "Respect has nothing to do with it! If they go on strike we'll stop paying for their meals and hotel rooms—not to mention their airfare back to San Francisco. [A strike] made no sense at all. How were they going to get home? They could hitchhike as far as we were concerned."

10. Jascha Heifetz (1901–87) is regarded as one of the greatest violinists in history. Heifetz once said, "You know, child prodigism—if I may coin a word—is a dis-

ease which is generally fatal. I was among the few to have the good fortune to survive."

11. Sol Babitz, "The Good Orchestra Violinist," in *The Professional Symphony Orchestra in the United States*, ed. George Seltzer (Metuchen, N.J.: Scarecrow, 1975), pp. 193–94.

12. Tom Hemphill, "Meet the Musicians: Tom Hemphill Biography," San Francisco Orchestra, http://www.sfsymphony.org/music/MeetTheMusicians/MembersOf Orchestra.aspx.

13. Carl Flesch, "The Orchestra Violinist," in *The Professional Symphony Orchestra in the United States*, ed. George Seltzer (Metuchen, N.J.: Scarecrow, 1975), pp. 190–92.

14. Sipser was counsel to the International Conference of Symphony and Opera Musicians (ICSOM), part of the American Federation of Musicians, and had organized and represented symphony musicians in contract negotiations throughout the country.

15. As Hemphill later recalled: "[A]sking the orchestra to explore ways to develop a collaborative relationship with management seemed a nearly impossible stretch. It would probably have been easier to sell the orchestra on the idea of building up a huge strike fund for use in three years."

16. Joel Cutcher-Gershenfeld had used this exercise frequently in his labor-management training programs.

17. Joel Cutcher-Gershenfeld, "How Process Matters: A Five-Phase Model for Examining Interest-Based Bargaining," in *Negotiations and Change: From the Workplace to Society*, eds. Thomas A. Kochan and David B. Lipsky (Ithaca, N.Y.: Cornell University Press, 2003), pp. 141–60.

18. Gary Friedman helped the musicians find an attorney who would represent them on this basis. He later reported that it was not easy to find a labor law specialist who would play that nontraditional role.

19. From the musicians' perspective, the name "San Francisco Symphony" meant the orchestra. From management's perspective, it meant the organization. This had been a sore point with the musicians in the past. The parties agreed that the new contract would contain language that resolved the issue. In the final contract, the preamble read, in part: "It is recognized and acknowledged that the 'San Francisco Symphony' encompasses the Musicians of the San Francisco Symphony, Administrative Staff, and the Board of Governors."

20. Late in the process, when the parties wanted to know whether there was a bargaining range of deals acceptable to both sides, I suggested that each side write on a piece of paper the furthest they thought their side could go on these money issues. I promised not to disclose the amounts. Their offers "crossed"—that is, management's maximum number was higher than the minimum the committee was willing to accept. I reported this fact to both sides. Soon thereafter a deal was made on a number in between.

21. Joshua Kosman, "S.F. Symphony Contract OK'd Early, Amicably: Two Sides Learned How to Negotiate," *San Francisco Chronicle*, January 14, 1999.

22. Chris Gilbert and Steve Braunstein were the only members of the committee who had been part of the old negotiation team or who had received training. Disappointed by the others' attitude, Gilbert subsequently resigned from the commit-

tee. Three years later, Tom Hemphill was elected to the Negotiating Committee but resigned for the same reason.

23. "Interest-Based Bargaining: In Whose 'Interest'?" *Senza Sordino* Newsletter, June 2001, p. 5. As it turns out, attorney Leibowitz may not be representing any musicians' unions in the future because of his own legal problems. On July 14, 2009, he was arrested in New York City and accused of embezzling $150,000 from a union client he had represented. See Simon Akam, "Dance Union's Lawyer Accused of Embezzling," *New York Times,* July 15, 2009. I must confess some schadenfreude.

24. Peter Pastreich to Leonard Leibowitz, August 6, 2001.

25. See "Advisory on Interest-Based Bargaining," American Federation of Musicians, Symphonic Services Division (2008).

26. Perhaps if the musicians had stuck with a three-year contract, they would have felt a stronger impetus to maintain conflict resolution skills in the face of more imminent negotiations. At the very least, they would have had an opportunity to at least try to address the disparity in scale wages sooner, which might have defused some of the anger that built up by the end of the five-year contract.

9: A DEVILISH DIVORCE

1. This chapter is based on an actual case, but names and identifying details have been changed to protect confidentiality.

2. Eleanor Maccoby and Robert Mnookin, *Dividing the Child: Social and Legal Dilemmas of Custody* (Cambridge, Mass.: Harvard University Press, 1992).

3. For a discussion of the four divorces, see ibid., pp. 19–57. For a similar discussion, see also P. Bohannan, "Six stations of divorce," in *Divorce and After,* ed. P. Bohannan (Garden City, N.Y.: Doubleday, 1970), pp. 29–55.

4. Every divorce poses four distributional questions, each governed by a different body of legal doctrine:
   - How should the couple's property—the stock of existing wealth owned together or separately—be divided? (Marital property law)
   - What ongoing claims will each spouse have on the future earnings of the other? (Alimony law)
   - What ongoing claims should a parent have for support of a child? (Child support law)
   - How should the responsibilities and opportunities for child-rearing be divided in the future? (Child custody and visitation law)

   See Mnookin and Kornhauser, "Bargaining in the Shadow of the Law: The Case of Divorce," *Yale Law Journal* 88 (1979): 950–97; Maccoby and Mnookin, *Dividing the Child,* pp. 39–57.

5. In Massachusetts, someone with Thomas's annual income—$225,000 a year in salary plus $25,000 in dividends from the inherited stock—would be required to pay $4,758 a month in child support alone. See Administrative Office of the Trial Court, Commonwealth of Massachusetts, Child Support Guidelines (2009). Under federal tax laws, child support would not be tax-deductible for Thomas, but unallocated family support would be. In such cases, both parties can often benefit by labeling support in terms of "family" rather than "child," thus mini-

mizing the couple's combined tax burden. See IRS Publication 504, "Divorced or Separated Individuals" (2008): 12–15.

6. Diana's countermotion requested an interim order awarding Brenda sole custody, $4,758 for monthly child support, and $2,700 a month for alimony.

7. The judge ordered Thomas to pay Brenda the scheduled child support amount and to continue making the monthly mortgage payments of $1,900.

8. Massachusetts law explicitly states that there is "no presumption either in favor of or against shared . . . physical custody" unless there is evidence of abuse. Mass. General Laws, Chapter 208, Section 31.

9. Although Diana had asked that Thomas be ordered to pay Brenda's legal fees, the judge had declined, saying that for the time being, "I want each party to bear his or her own legal costs."

10. Before the final hearing, the parents would be asked again to submit a "parenting plan" spelling out in detail the custodial arrangements: one parenting plan if they agreed on the terms, or separate parenting plans if they disagreed. Massachusetts Probate and Family Court Guide, "Planning for Shared Parenting: A Guide for Parents Living Apart."

11. In the California study I conducted with Eleanor Maccoby, 933 families had obtained a divorce decree by the time we finished. I love to ask people to guess how many of these cases went all the way to a judge for a custody ruling. Many people guess half, perhaps because the media pays a lot of attention to courtroom battles. But in our sample, the figure was only 1.5 percent (fourteen cases). All the rest were settled through negotiations.

This is not to say that there wasn't conflict in the cases that settled. The spouses reported either substantial or intense conflict in about a quarter of those cases. Still, nearly all of them settled, sometimes through hard bargaining between lawyers and sometimes only after mediation or custody evaluation. California requires court-annexed mediation and a custody evaluation as preconditions of going to court. Both of these procedural requirements caused many of the high-conflict cases to settle. Only a trivial number of high-conflict cases required formal adjudication.

In one respect, Brenda and Thomas's case was somewhat characteristic of our high-conflict cases. Two factors turned out to have a high correlation: cases in which the father expressed a high degree of hostility toward the mother and cases in which either parent expressed misgivings about whether the child would be adequately cared for in the other household.

For three-quarters of the families we studied, the parents told us they experienced little to no conflict over the terms of the divorce.

12. Diana had explained the risks associated with the stock in Thomas's company. If the judge awarded Brenda the actual certificates instead of their cash equivalent, the shares couldn't be easily sold. If the judge converted the value to cash, he was unlikely to give Brenda more than $150,000 for her share. At trial, she would also have to pay an expert to value the stock.

13. In setting the financial terms (other than child support), the statute requires consideration of each parent's "conduct," a term that is left undefined.

14. Before a case goes to trial, Massachusetts's rules require a "four-way meeting" with both lawyers and divorcing spouses to see if any issues can be resolved.

Diana reported that in this case the meeting lasted less than two minutes. Brenda told Thomas, "We have nothing to discuss."

15. The parents shared legal custody and Thomas got substantial visitation rights.

16. If the parties had been able to agree on the amount of support, it could have been characterized as "unallocated" or "family" support. This would have made it tax-deductible to Thomas and taxable income to Brenda. Because her tax rate was much lower, this would mean Thomas could have paid Diana a greater combined amount at lower net cost than what the court ordered. See note 5 above.

17. In view of Thomas's greater wealth, the judge ordered him to pay Brenda's legal fees.

18. This is exactly what the American Law Institute has suggested. It also appears to be the arrangement in New Hampshire. See *Principles on the Law of Family Dissolution: Analysis and Recommendations* (Philadelphia: American Law Institute, 2002).

10: SIBLING WARFARE

1. This chapter is based on an actual case, but names and identifying details have been changed to protect confidentiality.

2. Not all inherited property is difficult to divide. If the Hardings had jointly inherited nine hundred shares of Apple stock, for example, they wouldn't have needed a mediator. The market value would be easy to determine; one share would be no different than any other; and after the division each heir could decide whether to sell or hold.

3. For further readings on the difficulties associated with dividing family property, see Sandra Titus, Paul Rosenblatt, and Roxanne Anderson, "Family Conflict Over Inheritance of Property," *Family Coordinator* 28(3) (1979): 337–46; Janet Taylor and Joan Norris, "Sibling Relationships, Fairness, and Conflict Over Transfer of the Farm," *Family Relations* 49(3) (2000): 277–83; Norah Keating and Brenda Munro, "Transferring the Family Farm: Process and Implications," *Family Relations* 38(2) (1989): 215–18; Olivia Boyce-Abel, "When to Use Facilitation or Mediation in Estate and Wealth Transfer Planning," *Family Office Exchange* 9(35) (1998); and Robert Solomon, "Helping Clients Deal With Some of the Emotional and Psychological Issues of Estate Planning," *Probate & Property* 18 (2004): 56. For readings dealing specifically with family vacation property, see Judith Huggins Balfe, *Passing It On: The Inheritance and Use of Summer Houses* (Chapel Hill, N.C.: Professional Press, 1999); Ken Huggins, "Passing It On: The Inheritance, Ownership, and Use of Summer Houses," *Marquette Elder's Advisor* 5 (2003): 85.

4. The four common types of auctions are: (1) ascending bid, or English auctions; (2) descending bid, or Dutch auctions; (3) first price sealed bid auctions; and (4) second price sealed bid, also known as Vickrey auctions. There is a vast economic literature on the subject of auctions, and the impact of auction structure on price. See generally Paul Klemperer, *Auctions: Theory and Practice* (Princeton, N.J.: Princeton University Press, 2004).

5. For more readings on the effects of a parent's death on sibling rivalry, see Kathren Brabender, "The Effects of Sibling Rivalry Across the Lifespan: Positive or

Negative?" Ph.D. diss., Widener University Institute for Graduate Clinical Psychology, 2006; Esme Fuller-Thomson, "Loss of the Kin-Keeper? Sibling Conflict Following Parental Death," *Omega: Journal of Death & Dying* 40(4) (1999): 547–59.

6. A number of studies have shown that parental favoritism greatly increases sibling rivalry between the favored and disfavored child. For further readings on the effects of parental favoritism on the sibling relationship, see M. Stein, "Sibling Rivalry and the Problem of Envy," *Journal of Analytical Psychology* 35(2) (1990): 161–74; Leslie Brody et al., "Mommy and Daddy Like You Best: Perceived Family Favouritism in Relation to Affect, Adjustment, and Family Process," *Journal of Family Therapy* 20(3) (1998): 269–91; Irving D. Harris and Kenneth Howard, "Correlates of Perceived Parental Favoritism," *Journal of Genetic Psychology* 146(1) (1985): 45–56; Linda Zervas and Martin Sherman, "The Relationship Between Perceived Parental Favoritism and Self-Esteem," *Journal of Genetic Psychology* 155(1) (1994): 25–33.

7. Over the years I have collaborated with Gary Friedman and Jack Himmelstein, whose book describes this model of mediation. See G. Friedman and J. Himmelstein, *Challenging Conflict: Mediation Through Understanding* (Chicago: American Bar Association, 2008). In my preface to that book, I describe the challenges of this model. Ibid., pp. xi–xiv.

8. Together with their lawyers, we would develop some ground rules relating to confidentiality, how my fees would be paid, and how the lawyers might participate in the mediation.

9. In order to educate myself, I normally meet with the lawyers before an initial session with the parties to establish a schedule and request four memoranda from each party and his or her lawyer. The first memorandum should give me each party's "story": their view of the history of the relationships and the dispute. The second should look to the future and describe each party's underlying needs and interests—as well as their perceptions of the *other* parties' interests. The third memorandum, presumably prepared by the lawyers, should describe each party's legal arguments and their assessment of the litigation opportunities and risks. The fourth should provide the history of any settlement negotiations so far. In the Hardings' case, the fourth memorandum would be very short: each sister had essentially made one offer. But in more complex cases there is often a long history of offers and counteroffers, some in writing and others oral, and there is often a big discrepancy among the parties' reports of these offers.

10. Siblings often develop different definitions of "fairness" in childhood. For further readings on the effect of this divergence on sibling conflict, see Titus, Rosenblatt, and Anderson, "Family Conflict over Inheritance of Property"; Norris and Taylor, "Sibling Relationships, Fairness, and Conflict over Transfer of the Farm."

11. See Mass. General Laws, Chapter 241, Section 1.

12. In a leading case, Massachusetts's Supreme Judicial Court said, "One cannot be required to hold a tenancy in common against his consent." *Roberts v. Jones*, 307 Mass. 504, 30 N.E.2d 392, 132 A.L.R. 663 (1940).

13. In the New Testament parable of the prodigal son, when the older brother complained about his sibling's favored treatment, the father said: "Son, thou art ever with me, and all that I have is thine . . . we should make merry, and be glad: for

this thy brother was dead, and is alive again; and was lost, and is found" (Luke 15:32, King James Version).

14. See the Old Testament story of Cain and Abel (Genesis 4:1–16). When Cain saw the Lord preferring Abel's gift, sibling jealousy led to fratricide.

15. Douglas Stone, Bruce Patton, and Sheila Heen, *Difficult Conversations: How to Discuss What Matters Most* (New York: Viking Penguin, 1999).

16. For further reading on estate planning for vacation homes, see Wendy Goffe, "Planning Strategies for Keeping the Vacation Home in the Family," *Journal of Practical Estate Planning* 32 (2005): 3; Wendy Goffe, "Keeping Vacation Property in the Family," Heckerling Institute on Estate Planning (2007); Balfe, *Passing It On*; Huggins, "Passing It On."

17. In two other cases I have mediated, I have told the adult siblings that, in my view, the conflict was not their fault but the result of poor planning by their parents. In one instance a father left three siblings a number of pieces of valuable real estate as tenants in common. All the liquid assets in the estate were left to a foundation. This meant none of the siblings had the liquid assets to buy one another out. They were faced with a number of difficult decisions as co-owners. Which properties should be kept? Which should be sold? Which should be subdivided? How should the properties be valued? One sibling wanted to keep a particular property for sentimental reasons. The conflicts led to litigation. Although the disputes were ultimately resolved through mediation, the relations among the siblings were permanently damaged.

18. I love thinking about these kinds of problems. A parent may often simply leave "all personal property" such as jewelry, furniture, pictures, and the like to "my children in equal shares" with no specific allocation. There are lots of methods to divide things up: (1) "you divide, I choose"; (2) rotating choice; (3) flip a coin; (4) an internal auction, where each heir is given the same number of points to allocate among items; or (5) a sealed bid auction, where each sibling makes a dollar bid for the item in question; the high bidder gets the item, and the other heirs divide his payment. There are fascinating strategic implications of different process designs, and it is essential to think these through carefully. No single method is perfect. Depending on the context, an otherwise reasonable method may result in a very one-sided outcome. Rotating choice, for example, works badly if there is one item that is much more valuable than the others. "You divide, I choose" can be risky for those whose preferences are obvious. If I know your preferences and I get to divide, I can guarantee for myself a greater portion of the surplus. See Mnookin, "Divorce Bargaining: The Limits on Private Ordering," *University of Michigan Journal of Law Reform* 18 (Summer 1985): 1015–37. See also Howard Raiffa with John Richardson and David Metcalfe, *Negotiation Analysis: The Science and Art of Collaborative Decision Making* (Cambridge, Mass.: Harvard University Press, 2002), pp. 232–33 (alternative process solutions to division problems) and 338–40 (division of art collection between brothers).

CONCLUSION

1. See generally Avishai Margalit's Tanner lecture and recent book cited in the Introduction, n. 2. Avishai Margalit, "Indecent Compromise," in the Tanner Lectures on Human Values (delivered at Stanford University, May 2005). See http://

www.tannerlectures.utah.edu/lectures/documents/Margalit_2006.pdf.; Avishai Margalit, *On Compromise and Rotten Compromises* (Princeton, N.J.: Princeton University Press, 2009).

2. In my seminar on this topic at Harvard Law School, my students have come up with literally scores of other examples in which a disputant faces a difficult decision of whether negotiation makes sense. Should a district attorney offer immunity to a mob hit man in exchange for testimony that might help convict his boss? Should Israel negotiate with Hamas over an exchange of prisoners? Context matters. My framework requires the careful assessment of the facts and circumstances of a particular dispute at a particular time.

3. Psychologists still have much to learn about the intricacies of human judgment and decision-making. A number of journals, including *Judgment and Decision Making* and the *Journal of Behavioral Decision Making*, are devoted to the subject. For a review of current psychological research on decision-making, see Elke U. Weber and Eric J. Johnson, "Mindful Judgment and Decision Making," *Annual Review of Psychology* 60 (2009): 53–85.

4. One can translate virtually any moral principle into cost/benefit terms, by attaching "weight" to it and then including it in the balance when comparing consequences.

5. Suppose, for example, you have the opportunity to save twenty lives if you are willing to kill one innocent child. Would you be prepared to shoot the child? If you are a strict consequentialist, you might pull the trigger. After all, that action would save nineteen more lives. On the other hand, many of us would find that sort of reasoning abhorrent and would *not* pull the trigger on the moral principle that it is *always* wrong to intentionally cause the death of an innocent person.

This example is analogous to the famous streetcar paradox. Suppose a streetcar is out of control, heading for five people who are tied to the track ahead. You have the opportunity to pull a switch and divert the car onto a different track, where only one person is tied to the track. Most people would opt for pulling the switch. Suppose now that you are standing on a footbridge above the streetcar, which is still headed for the five people. You have the opportunity to push a person off the footbridge so that he will land in front of the streetcar, stopping it before it reaches the five people tied to the track. Do you still choose to sacrifice one person to save five others? See Philippa Foot, "The Problem of Abortion and the Doctrine of the Double Effect," in *Virtues and Vices: And Other Essays in Moral Philosophy* (Oxford U.K.: Oxford University Press, 2002); Judith Jarvis Thomson, "The Trolley Problem," *Yale Law Journal* 94(6) (1985).

For a discussion of the philosophical issues, and the fascinating psychological experiments suggesting that different parts of the brain are involved in different kinds of moral reasoning, see Joshua Greene and Jonathan Haidt, "How (and Where) Does Moral Judgment Work?" *Trends in Cognitive Sciences* 6(12): 517–23.

6. Religious traditions that emphasize categorical moral rules (e.g., the Ten Commandments) are in tension with a consequentialist approach, as are some philosophical approaches to morality. For example, deontological approaches to morality suggest that the morality of an act depends not on the act's consequences but on the character of the act itself and whether it is consistent with

certain immutable principles. See, e.g., Immanuel Kant, *Groundwork of the Meta-physics of Morals,* trans. Mary J. Gregor (New York: Cambridge University Press, 1998). For an example of a neo-Kantian argument, see Christine Korsgaard, *Self-Constitution: Agency, Identity, and Integrity* (New York: Oxford University Press, 2009). Another approach to morality, that of "aretology," emphasizes the character of the moral agent and the cultivation of virtue. See, e.g., Alasdair MacIntyre, *After Virtue: A Study in Moral Theory,* 3rd ed. (Notre Dame, Ind.: University of Notre Dame Press, 2007).

7. For an interesting philosophical argument that to be "too moral" in a categorical sense may not be wise because it can foreclose other important human considerations, see Susan Wolf, "Moral Saints," *The Journal of Philosophy,* Vol. 79, No. 8 (Aug. 1982), pp. 419–39.

8. The two examples are President Bush's decision not to negotiate with the Taliban in 2001 and Churchill's decision not to pursue negotiation with Nazi Germany in May 1940.

9. I am not suggesting, of course, that a representative must always do what his client or constituent wants, even if it is illegal or unethical. Nor am I suggesting that the representative should not try to persuade his client or constituent that negotiation would be wrong.

10. Political scientists have long debated how extensive a role moral values should and do play in the formulation of a nation's foreign policy. "Realists" suggest that power and national interests are what count, not morality. Others see values playing an important role. See generally, Richard M. Price, *Moral Limit and Possibility in World Politics,* Cambridge Studies in International Relations 107 (New York: Cambridge University Press, 2008); Cathal J. Nolan, *Ethics and Statecraft: The Moral Dimension of International Affairs,* 2nd ed., Humanistic Perspectives on International Relations (Westport, Conn.: Praeger, 2004); Andrew Valls, *Ethics in International Affairs: Theories and Cases* (Lanham, Md.: Rowman & Littlefield, 2000); Gordon Graham, *Ethics and International Relations,* 2nd ed. (Malden, Mass.: Blackwell, 2008).

11. Scott McClellan, *What Happened: Inside the Bush White House and Washington's Culture of Deception* (New York: PublicAffairs, 2008), p. 127.

12. Ibid., p. 128.

13. Leslie H. Gelb, "In the End, Every President Talks to the Bad Guys," *Washington Post,* April 27, 2008.

14. President Bush once said: "There is a value system that cannot be compromised— God-given values." Bob Woodward, *Bush at War* (New York: Simon & Schuster, 2002), p. 131. These values Bush said included "freedom and the human condition and mothers loving their children." His frequent references to God made me think, Whose God? U.S. citizens hold many different views of God and spirituality. If Bush based his foreign policy decisions on his personal moral and religious views, that in my view would not be a responsible basis for decision-making.

15. His characterization of Iran, North Korea, and Saddam Hussein's Iraq as an "axis of evil" was unwise on pragmatic grounds, even if it did not influence his subsequent decisions. See President George W. Bush, "State of the Union Address of the President to the Joint Session of Congress," http://www.c-span.org/executive/transcript.asp?cat=current_event&code=bush_admin&year=2002. My objection is not based on any disagreement that these were evil regimes. I believe that

this blatant demonization served no useful diplomatic purpose and only made it more difficult for Iran to explore secretly with the United States the possibility of a "grand bargain." See Jahangir Amuzegar, "Iran's Crumbling Revolution," *Foreign Affairs* 82(1) (2003): 46.

16. Barack Obama, "Remarks Following a Meeting with Prime Minister Silvio Berlusconi of Italy and an Exchange with Reporters," in June 15, 2009, *Daily Compilation of Presidential Documents* (Superintendent of Documents, 2009), 3. DCPD 20090046 at p. 3.

17. He supports the "clear principle that where we can resolve issues through negotiations and diplomacy, we should." Barack H. Obama, "Remarks Following a Meeting with Prime Minister Benjamin Netanyahu of Israel and an Exchange with Reporters," in May 18, 2009, *Daily Compilation of Presidential Documents*, 4. DCPD 200900375 at p. 4.

18. It is easy to imagine a deal with the Taliban that offers substantial pragmatic benefits for the United States but may seriously harm others for whom we should feel some responsibility. For example, suppose a large group of Taliban "nonstate actors" agrees to stop harboring terrorists in exchange for complete autonomy over a region of Afghanistan and Pakistan. The Taliban further guarantees that no terrorist acts against the United States will originate from within their borders. Assuming you think this deal can be enforced, it would serve the United States' immediate interests quite well. However, this bargain would allow the Taliban to impose its version of Islamic law on the entire region, which in turn would lead to the closure of all schools for girls. Would this be, in Avishai Margolit's terms, a "rotten compromise," which he defines as "an agreement to establish or maintain an inhuman regime, a regime of cruelty and humiliation"?

Index

About the Author

Robert Mnookin is a leading scholar in the field of negotiation and conflict resolution. He is the Samuel Williston Professor of Law at Harvard Law School, the Chair of the Steering Committee of the Program on Negotiation at Harvard Law School, and the Director of the Harvard Negotiation Research Project. He has written or edited nine books and numerous scholarly articles.

Mnookin is an experienced arbitrator and mediator who has resolved many complex commercial disputes. He is a teacher, lecturer, and consultant who has applied an interdisciplinary approach to a broad range of conflicts. He has trained thousands of executives and professionals in negotiation and mediation skills and has served as a consultant to governments, international agencies, major corporations, and law firms.

Before joining the Harvard faculty and leading its Program on Negotiation, Professor Mnookin was a professor at Stanford Law School, where he co-founded and directed the Stanford Center on Conflict and Negotiation, an interdisciplinary group concerned with overcoming barriers to the negotiated resolution of conflict. He is a Fellow of the American Academy of Arts and Sciences.

For additional information relating to this book or Professor Mnookin see www.bargainingwiththedevil.com or www.mnookin.com.